GUIDE TO CONTEMPORARY
NEW YORK CITY ARCHITECTURE

GUIDE TO CONTEMPORARY
NEW YORK CITY ARCHITECTURE

JOHN HILL

W. W. NORTON & COMPANY
NEW YORK • LONDON

Copyright © by John Hill

Unless otherwise noted, photos are by the author.
Photo on this page by David Plakke, courtesy of the Austrian
Cultural Forum, New York.

For information about permission to reproduce selections from
this book, write to Permissions, W. W. Norton & Company, Inc.,
500 Fifth Avenue, New York, NY 10110

For information about special discounts for bulk purchases, please
contact W. W. Norton Special Sales at specialsales@wwnorton.com
or 800-233-4830.

Digital production by Joe Lops
Composition and book design by Matt Bouloutian
    & Vivian Ghazarian, Modern Good
Manufacturing by Four Colour Print Group
Production Manager: Leeann Graham

Library of Congress Cataloging-in-Publication Data

Hill, John, 1973–
Guide to contemporary New York City architecture / John Hill. – 1st ed.
    p. cm.
Includes bibliographical references and index.
ISBN 978-0-393-73326-6 (pbk.)
1. Architecture–New York (State)–New York–History–21st century–
Guidebooks. 2. New York (N.Y.)–Buildings, structures, etc.–Guidebooks.
3. New York (N.Y.)–Guidebooks. I. Title.

NA735.N5H55 2011
720.9747'109051–dc22

                                         2011000433

ISBN 13: 978-0-393-73326-6 (pbk.)

W. W. Norton & Company, Inc., 500 Fifth Avenue, New York, N.Y. 10110
www.wwnorton.com
W. W. Norton & Company Ltd., Castle House, 75/76 Wells St., London
W1T 3QT

0 9 8 7 6 5 4 3 2 1

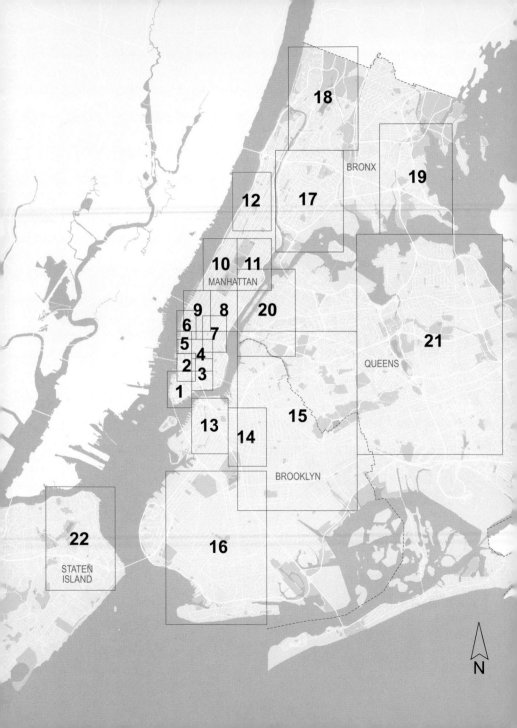

CONTENTS

Acknowledgments 8
Introduction 10

MANHATTAN 16
1. Lower Manhattan 18
2. Tribeca, SoHo 30
3. Chinatown, Lower East Side, Nolita 38
4. NoHo, East Village, Greenwich Village 50
5. West Village, Meatpacking District 62
6. Chelsea 79
7. Flatiron District, Gramercy Park, Murray Hill 90
8. Midtown East 100
9. Midtown West 118
10. Upper West Side 128
11. Upper East Side 140
12. Harlem, Morningside Heights, Hamilton Heights, Washington Heights 150

BROOKLYN 162
13. Downtown Brooklyn, Brooklyn Heights, Carroll Gardens, Gowanus, Park Slope 164
14. Prospect Heights, Crown Heights, Bedford-Stuyvesant, Clinton Hill, Fort Greene 176
15. Greenpoint, Williamsburg, Brownsville, East New York 188
16. Flatbush, Homecrest, Coney Island, Borough Park, Sunset Park 198

BRONX 208
17. Mott Haven, Highbridge, Hunts Point 210
18. Bronx Park, Fordham, North Riverdale 218
19. Castle Hill, Throgs Neck, Morris Park, Baychester 226

QUEENS 234
20. Long Island City, Astoria 236
21. Flushing, Bayside, Jamaica, Ozone Park 244

STATEN ISLAND 256
22. St. George, Snug Harbor, Clove Hill, Grymes Hill 258

NEW YORK CITY 2020 266

Notes 290
Glossary 291
Selected Bibliography & Resources 295
Credits 297
Architect/Building Index 299
Index by Building Type 304

ACKNOWLEDGMENTS

Thanks to my family, my friends, and the people who have encouraged me over the years, contributing in one way or another to my efforts to write this book. You know who you are. Below I'd like to thank the people that directly helped in making this book.

Thanks to the architects who responded to my queries, supplied me with photographs and renderings under unrealistic deadlines, and, of course, created the architecture that is found in these pages. As an architect I understand all too well the difficulty in realizing a building while retaining the vision throughout the process.

Thanks to the institutions that helped me with photos and other bits of information. I would especially like to thank the Austrian Cultural Forum New York for their generosity with the cover photo.

Thanks to the photographers whose images bring out the best in the projects and make this book so much more handsome than my personal photos alone; they inadvertently pushed me to elevate the quality of my images, interspersed with theirs (I hope it worked). I'd especially like to thank the photographers who generously shot original photos for the book, to whom I'm indebted: Amy Barkow, Jackie Caradonio, Aaron Dougherty, and Albert Vecerka and his students at City College. Thanks to Francis Dzikowski for sharing photos from the book he made with Jean Phifer, *Public Art New York*. Thanks to other photographers who supplied me with numerous photos: Scott Norsworthy, Adam Friedberg, Michael Moran, Marc Lins, Erik Freeland, David Joseph, Jonathan Wallen, Paul Warchol, Elizabeth Felicella, Dean Kaufman, and John Bartelstone. Thanks to Erica Stoller at Esto for being so patient and understanding with my sometimes unreasonable requests.

Thanks to Andrea Costella Dawson at W. W. Norton for believing this book would be a good one to make and then helping this first-time author actually get it done. Thanks to Amanda Heller for her thorough edits and coordination of the text. Thanks to Matt Bouloutian and Vivian Ghazarian at Modern Good for shaping the words, photos, and maps into a book both easy to use and beautiful to look at and hold.

Thanks to my friend Eric Bohn for letting me borrow his car, usually at the last minute, as I zipped to and fro to check out buildings and photograph them, sometimes with his camera. Thanks to Walton Chan for supplying me with the backgrounds for the maps; it made my additions that much easier.

Manhattan's changing skyline, as seen from the top of Rockefeller Center.

And thanks to Karen, for not only putting up with a project that devoured so much time, but for also being the ideal partner to bounce ideas off of, for keeping me focused on the important things, and for joining me on trips around the city. The last frequently happened with our daughter, Clare, to whom this book is dedicated.

Architecture in New York City

in the first decade of the twenty-first century was a roller-coaster of highs and lows bracketed by two generation-defining events: the terrorist attacks of September 11, 2001, and the economic collapse marked by the September 2008 bankruptcy of Lehman Brothers. Among many, perhaps more significant impacts, these events affected the design and construction of buildings. A major change driven by the first was heightened and overt security measures in both public and private buildings and spaces, and the second led to a dramatic slowdown in new construction in New York City, and the country as whole. But in between, a building boom gripped the city. It saw a renewed embrace of big plans—new mixed-use developments centered on aging infrastructure (e.g., Hudson Yards) and the resurrection of major projects long on hold (e.g., the Second Avenue Subway)—and also an increased attention to the small-budget things such as infill projects and public spaces that nevertheless affect one's on-the-ground experience in the city. These seemingly contradictory movements reflect an effort to come to terms with the conflicting legacies of Robert Moses, who saw the city as a canvas for large infrastructure projects, and Jane Jacobs, embracer of the city's fine-grain qualities. Increasingly it is becoming apparent that a synthesis of the two extremes is the city's preferred course of action.

The building boom between September 11 and the Lehman Brothers collapse was an exceptional one—really a continuation of the late-1990s boom—in which architects (including many imported "starchitects") and clients alike got carried away with projects of formal exuberance. Many were crushed by the recession, but others came to life and can be found in the following pages. Two factors that contributed to this desire for standout iconic structures were the 1997 completion of the Frank Gehry–designed Guggenheim Museum in Bilbao, Spain—heralding a desire in many cities to replicate the "Bilbao effect," in which a piece of architecture contributes to a city's revitalization and recognition—and advances in computer technology that enabled the design and construction of ever more complex forms. While it's close to impossible to realize such a sprawling and complicated display of form in the dense, predominantly late-nineteenth- and early-twentieth-century urban fabric of New York City, the projects collected here illustrate myriad attempts to infuse the city with its own brand of attention-getting architecture.

Looking at 7 WTC (10) before the redevelopment of the World Trade Center site.
Photo by Ruggero Vanni.

But architecture's response to the September 11 tragedy and the financial collapse is not the only theme explored in this book. Architecture responds to numerous conditions, be they economic, political, social, or environmental. Increasingly the last is being pushed to the fore, as concerns for the effects of climate change and energy depletion dictate public policy and the way architects practice. Building "green" has been aided by the U.S. Green Building Council's LEED rating system, the most popular of many gauges of sustainability in buildings. In New York City this trend was basically mandated by the 2005 Local Law 86, which requires LEED Silver certification for most publicly funded projects, and encouraged by Mayor Michael Bloomberg's later PlaNYC, which outlines ten goals for making the city more sustainable in the coming decades. Building green is also embraced by developers who utilize LEED as a marketing tool, and by architects increasingly skilled in designing sustainable architecture that need not cost more than the norm. Not limited to buildings, the city's sustainability efforts have also taken the form of added parkland, much of it on former industrial land and infrastructure.

Any architect worth his or her salt will tell you the key to a great building is a great client, and in this regard the City of New York has become one of the best clients for contemporary architecture. This is happening primarily through the efforts of the Department of Design and Construction (DDC) and its Design and Construction Excellence (D+CE) program beginning in 2004. Under the program, the city partners with some of the best local architects for the design of its museums, libraries, fire and police stations, parks, and streetscapes. A number of these projects, many found in this guidebook, also incorporate sustainable features, stemming from DDC's own High Performance Building Guidelines and the adoption of Local Law 86. Interspersed in this guide among the larger and more high-profile residential developments, office buildings, and other private commissions, these municipal projects have the potential to transform the city, especially for its residents, as much as or more so than the grand developments that steal the front-page headlines.

Yet beyond these important events and other influences on the buildings and spaces that shape New York City, this book is first and foremost a guide, a means of getting out and exploring the city, ideally on foot.

SELECTION CRITERIA

The more than two hundred buildings and spaces found in this guide are hardly an objective list of the best architecture in New York City since 2000. If such a list were possible, it would have to include buildings and interiors not visible by or accessible to the public—the offices, penthouses, and residential loft conversions that pepper the city and provide work for some of its best architects and designers. This list would include as well buildings and interiors that are fleeting, such as the shops, bars, and restaurants that come and go as quickly as the clothing styles worn by their patrons. (That said, a couple of the sidebars, described below, do briefly present some retail and dining spaces.) By way of indicating what this book does *not* include, I should make clear the first two criteria I've set for selecting the entries. First, the projects are accessible in one form or another to *all* people, whether viewable only from the street or from the building's interior. Second, the buildings and spaces are long-term additions to the cityscape, part of its evolving transformation, not just temporary interiors and installations that, albeit influential in many ways, will not be around in a year, much less five or ten years.

Given these general criteria, most of the projects in the pages that follow are buildings that prominently occupy the public realm. They are not hidden, even though a fair number are not open to the public. (Every effort has been made to explain accessing the buildings presented, but readers should use tact and common sense in regard to private buildings—offices, schools, private residences—whose occupants do not want or allow the public to saunter in off the street.) These criteria also apply to the inclusion of parks and other open spaces, acknowledging the importance of public space in our daily lives and the role of landscape architects in shaping our experiences.

Design quality is ultimately a subjective judgment. I did not let awards, publications, or other more or less objective criteria dictate what is considered good or what should be in this book, even though many of the projects have won their fair share of awards. Instead, I fell back on my experience as an architect with over ten years of practice under my belt and the same amount of time writing about architectural design both on-line and in print. In matters of taste, disagreements abound. Arguments over style and what is appropriate are many times heated and even nasty; as will be seen, they sometimes involve the courts. Readers may quibble about projects left out of the book, as will architects, even if they find themselves noted in these pages.

Admittedly, my most glaring bias may involve tall buildings. While this book is not completely lacking in them, other guides do include more. Perhaps the slight is unthinkable in a city with a skyline dominated by skyscrapers, and some of the most recognizable ones at that. But I find myself siding with architectural historian Kenneth Frampton's contention (I'm paraphrasing his comments from a lecture) that the majority of tall buildings are not architecture, because after a certain height, concerns about money outweigh concerns about design. In respect not just to tall buildings but to all the projects I've included in this book, the reader's experience of the city and its architecture is paramount; where a building meets the ground determines how we interact with it, regardless of how tall it is. This sort of thinking determined what projects found their way into this guide.

HOW TO USE THIS GUIDE

THIS GUIDE CONSISTS OF FOUR SECTIONS:
• Two hundred projects, or main entries, make up the bulk of the book. Clearly numbered 1–200 and keyed to the maps, they are organized regionally by borough (Manhattan, Brooklyn, the Bronx, Queens, and Staten Island).
• Sidebars that mention additional buildings (often "themed") or other projects of interest.
• A final chapter, "New York City 2020," which takes a look ahead at some projects that will shape the city in the coming decade.
• Supplemental material: a glossary, selected bibliography, and indexes by architect/building name and building type.

1 Looking east at the hard-to-miss signage from below the long canopy.　2 A winter view from the ferry terminal shortly before the plaza's completion.

1 WHITEHALL FERRY TERMINAL
FREDERIC SCHWARTZ ARCHITECTS, 2005

4 South Street, at Whitehall Street
to South Ferry; to Whitehall Street–South Ferry

In 1992 Pop architecture forefather Robert Venturi won a competition to design the Manhattan terminus for the Staten Island Ferry, a design marked by an oversized (old-timey clock facing Upper New York Bay. A pared-down design with expansive windows overlooking Lower Manhattan and an LED billboard followed, sans clock. Budget cuts led Venturi to withdraw from the project, and co-architect Frederic Schwartz took over. As executed ten years later, the design retains the 75-foot-high glass wall on the north side, but the LED display is reduced to just a ticker inside the bright white and open space. In front of the terminal, extending from large-scale letters spelling STATEN ISLAND FERRY, is a sinuous canopy that cradles the newly created Peter Minuit Plaza. The terminal handles about seventy thousand ferry passengers a day, provides connections to train and bus transit, and saves energy through solar panels on the roof.

2 NEW AMSTERDAM PLEIN AND PAVILION
UNSTUDIO with Handel Architects, 2011

Peter Minuit Plaza, at Whitehall and Water Streets
to South Ferry; to Whitehall Street–South Ferry

The year 2009 marked the four hundredth anniversary of Henry Hudson's arrival in New York Harbor after he was hired by the Dutch East India Company to find a northwest passage to Asia. That expedition failed, but Hudson's exploration laid the groundwork for the Dutch colonization of the region. As they say, the rest is history, and now four centuries of friendship is expressed in this gift from the Netherlands to New York, a 5,000-square-foot flower-shaped pavilion atop a paved and landscaped platform (the Dutch plein) in Peter Minuit Plaza, named for the Dutch director-general who "purchased" the island of Manhattan from local Indians in 1626. Dutch architects Ben van Berkel and Caroline Bos created a curving, sensual design that raises the question, "What is it?" Four radiating bars equipped with electronic LED façades are programmed as a visitor center and café, a twenty-four-hour hub in the stone plaza. The last features seating and tables designed by the architects, walkways engraved with passages from Russell Shorto's narrative of Manhattan's founding, The Island at the Center of the World and a carved stone map of the 1660 Castello Plan of New Amsterdam.

20

THE MAIN AND SIDEBAR PROJECTS INCLUDE THE FOLLOWING INFORMATION:
• Photographs, at least one for each project.
• Project name, or the name given by the architect; official address.
• Design architect; particularly the firm's name, sometimes accompanied by the name of the associate architect or some other important contributor.
• Project address; the nearest subway stop or other transit information is included for the main entries.
• Project description, with occasional cross-references to other projects (bolded entry numbers in parentheses) in the guide.

The two hundred projects are broken down into twenty-two chapters focusing on one or more neighborhoods within the city's five boroughs. I begin with the borough containing the most buildings (Manhattan) and end at the one with the least (Staten Island). The neighborhoods in the chapters are organized from south to north in Manhattan and from most concentrated to least concentrated areas of building in the other boroughs. Most of the neighborhoods can be comfortably traversed on foot; a quarter-mile-radius scale is provided in the center of each map to help gauge distance. Projects in less concentrated areas may require numerous subway rides to get there, or better yet a bicycle; those maps show a one-mile-radius scale.

While separated into tourable sections, this book is not meant to be a strict turn-left-here-and-look-at-this-building walking guide. The order of the numbered projects, aided by the accompanying maps, offers an implied route, but veering from a connect-the-dots path is encouraged. The maps highlight the sidebar projects as well as nearby buildings and spaces: well-known landmarks and open areas, other projects mentioned in the book, and projects from the New York City 2020 chapter. In addition to the names of streets and bodies of water, the maps show the subway lines and stops.

———

Commuters give the city its tidal restlessness;
natives give it solidity and continuity;
but the settlers give it passion.
   —E. B. White, *Here Is New York* (1949)

My wife and I settled in New York City in 2006. Before that we traveled here at least once a year, visiting museums, going out to restaurants and bars, visiting with friends. A lot of the time I was schlepping my wife around the city to look at architecture. This new building, that new building. Now living here, and with toddler in tow, we continue our explorations, even though I'll admit how easy it is—for all residents—to put off seeing this building or that building, knowing it can be seen just as easily tomorrow or the next day. So this guide is directed not only to visitors to New York City but also to the people who call it home. Consider it an invitation to get out and experience parts of the city you may have put off visiting in the past; you will see some great architecture in the process.

"Starchitecture" in Chelsea: Jean Nouvel's 100 Eleventh Avenue **(58)** visible beyond Frank Gehry's IAC Building **(59)**. Photo by Scott Norsworthy.

MANHATTAN

LOWER MANHATTAN **1**

TRIBECA, SOHO **2**

CHINATOWN, LOWER EAST SIDE, NOLITA **3**

NOHO, EAST VILLAGE, GREENWICH VILLAGE **4**

WEST VILLAGE, MEATPACKING DISTRICT **5**

CHELSEA **6**

FLATIRON DISTRICT, GRAMERCY PARK, MURRAY HILL **7**

MIDTOWN EAST **8**

MIDTOWN WEST **9**

UPPER WEST SIDE **10**

UPPER EAST SIDE **11**

HARLEM, MORNINGSIDE HEIGHTS, **12**
HAMILTON HEIGHTS, WASHINGTON HEIGHTS

Hudson
River

See Map
2
Tribeca

See Map
3
Lower East Side

Tribeca Bridge •
Teardrop Park •
The Solaire •
Verdesian •
• BPC Community Center

Riverhouse **12**•
• NYPL BPC Branch
• Irish Hunger Memorial
•**11** **200 West Street**

• Jacob Javits Plaza

• PANYNJ
Ferry Terminal

•**13** **101 Warren Street**

• African Burial Ground
National Monument

Fiterman Hall •   • Park51
1 WTC •

•**10** **7 WTC**

World Financial Center •

• Kowsky Plaza
National September 11 •
Memorial & Museum

2 WTC •
• WTC Transportation Hub

City Hall Park

•**9** **8 Spruce Street**

3 WTC •
4 WTC •   Fulton Street •
Transit Center

W New York Downtown •

Rector Street Bridge •

•**5** **Zuccotti Park**

1/4-mile
radius

Seamen's Institute •

3LD Art & Tech. Center •

•**4** **The Visionaire**
• P.S./I.S. 276
• Museum of Jewish Heritage

Historic Front Street 8•

• One Chase
Manhattan Plaza

• NYSE/Financial District Streetscapes

•**3** **Skscraper Museum**

• Imagination Playground

South Street Seaport •

• Robert F. Wagner, Jr. Park

•**6** **William Beaver House**

• East River Waterfront

Battery
Park

• Wall Street Ferry Terminal

•**7** **Elevated Acre**
at 55 Water Street

East
River

•**2** **New Amsterdam Plein and Pavilion**

• Battery Maritime Building
•**1** **Whitehall Ferry Terminal**

Upper New
York Bay

This guide to twenty-first-century New York City architecture starts where most guidebooks to the city begin: at the southern tip of Manhattan, site of the original seventeenth-century Dutch settlement. Here the layering of centuries is most evident, found in the winding network of narrow streets between wide modern thoroughfares, the sharp juxtapositions between old masonry buildings and glassy high-rises, and the waterfront's mix of recreation with signs of its industrial past. Lower Manhattan commonly encompasses a number of neighborhoods below 14th Street, but for this guide that northern edge is defined by Chambers Street and the Brooklyn Bridge. This area includes the Financial District, City Hall, the Civic Center, Battery Park City, and the area around the World Trade Center site.

This last, of course, involves the rebuilding under way after two planes flew into and destroyed the Twin Towers on September 11, 2001, killing 2,752 people. In the aftermath of the event, the Lower Manhattan Development Corporation (LMDC) was created by then-Governor George Pataki and then-Mayor Rudolph Giuliani to oversee the area's rebuilding. The ongoing revitalization includes the rebuilding of the roughly 10 million square feet of office space destroyed that day, the creation of a memorial to the lives lost in the attacks, and the addition of related cultural components; it also includes the rebuilding of other nearby buildings and spaces damaged or destroyed by the collapse of the Twin Towers, the creation of thousands of housing units in new and renovated buildings, and the reconstruction and expansion of transportation infrastructure.

Yet just as the tragedy occurring below Chambers Street had wide-ranging effects on all five boroughs, the rebuilding effort spread to a much larger area, in essence ripening the conditions for developments throughout the city, many championed by the New York City Economic Development Corporation (NYCEDC). The World Trade Center redevelopment sparked a return to the big plans reminiscent of the Robert Moses era, before the influence of Jane Jacobs, his occasional antagonist, drove development toward a smaller scale. Today, such big plans include Atlantic Yards in Brooklyn, Hudson Yards on Manhattan's West Side, and the redevelopment of Willets Point in Queens. As these projects trail behind the admittedly lethargic pace of the World Trade Center redevelopment, Lower Manhattan will continue to be the center for the experiment in urbanism that it has been since the Dutch settlement of New Amsterdam.

1 Looking east at the hard-to-miss signage from below the long canopy.

2 A winter view from the ferry terminal shortly before the plaza's completion.

1 WHITEHALL FERRY TERMINAL
FREDERIC SCHWARTZ ARCHITECTS, 2005

4 South Street, at Whitehall Street
1 to South Ferry; **R** to Whitehall Street–South Ferry

In 1993 Pop architecture forefather Robert Venturi won a competition to design the Manhattan terminus for the Staten Island Ferry, a design marked by an oversized old-timey clock facing Upper New York Bay. A pared-down design with expansive windows overlooking Lower Manhattan and an LED billboard followed, *sans* clock. Budget cuts led Venturi to withdraw from the project, and co-architect Frederic Schwartz took over. As executed ten years later, the design retains the 75-foot-high glass wall on the north side, but the LED display is reduced to just a ticker inside the bright white and open space. In front of the terminal, extending from large-scale letters spelling STATEN ISLAND FERRY, is a sinuous canopy that cradles the newly created Peter Minuit Plaza. The terminal handles about seventy thousand ferry passengers a day, provides connections to train and bus transit, and saves energy through solar panels on the roof.

2 NEW AMSTERDAM PLEIN AND PAVILION
UNSTUDIO with Handel Architects, 2011

Peter Minuit Plaza, at Whitehall and Water Streets
1 to South Ferry; **R** to Whitehall Street–South Ferry

The year 2009 marked the four hundredth anniversary of Henry Hudson's arrival in New York Harbor after he was hired by the Dutch East India Company to find a northwest passage to Asia. That expedition failed, but Hudson's exploration laid the groundwork for the Dutch colonization of the region. As they say, the rest is history, and now four centuries of friendship is expressed in this gift from the Netherlands to New York, a 5,000-square-foot flower-shaped pavilion atop a paved and landscaped platform (the Dutch *plein*) in Peter Minuit Plaza, named for the Dutch director-general who "purchased" the island of Manhattan from local Indians in 1626. Dutch architects Ben van Berkel and Caroline Bos created a curving, sensual design that raises the question, "What is it?" Four radiating bars equipped with electronic LED façades are programmed as a visitor center and café, a twenty-four-hour hub in the stone plaza. The last features benches designed by WXY Architecture + Urban Design, walkways engraved with passages from Russell Shorto's narrative of Manhattan's founding, *The Island at the Center of the World*, and a carved stone map of the 1660 Castello Plan of New Amsterdam.

39 Battery Park Place, near 1st Place
④ ⑤ to Bowling Green

The Skyscraper Museum was founded in 1996 by historian Carol Willis, author of *Form Follows Finance*, an award-winning and highly recommended book on the evolution of tall buildings in Chicago and New York City. According to the museum's website, it celebrates New York City's "rich architectural heritage and examines the historical forces and individuals that have shaped its successive skylines." For the museum's first seven years, this "celebration" occurred in four temporary spaces in Lower Manhattan, until the opening of its permanent home in Battery Park City. Fittingly, it was the first museum to open downtown since the tragedy of September 11, 2001.

The 5,800-square-foot ground-floor space—donated by the developer of the mixed-use tower above—was a challenging canvas for the private, nonprofit educational corporation focused on buildings big and tall. In addition to the slab of the second floor above, a high water table and basement facilities further reduced the museum's vertical space. Roger Duffy of Skidmore, Owings & Merrill (SOM) dealt with these constraints using a strategy of amplification. Polished stainless steel covers the floors and ceilings, giving the effect of an infinite vertical space even though it is not much more than 10 feet high. The museum includes two galleries for permanent and temporary exhibits, a bookstore, and an office mezzanine. The galleries and bookstore are reached by a ramp that rises above the encroaching basement facilities; the offices are tucked above the bookstore to give the galleries more precious vertical room. It is a gem of a space that expresses as much about the desire to build taller as do the buildings that surround the museum.

3 From the entrance the narrow ramp ascends to the galleries (left). Reflected display cases become skyscrapers in miniature (right). Photos by Robert Polidori.

4 THE VISIONAIRE

PELLI CLARKE PELLI ARCHITECTS with SLCE Architects, 2009

70 Little West Street, at 3rd Place

④ ⑤ to Bowling Green; ❶ ⓡ to Rector Street

Since the early days of Battery Park City's (BPC) rise on landfill, produced in part by the construction of the World Trade Center, architect Cesar Pelli's office has played a large role in the evolution of the nearly one hundred–acre site. Following aesthetic guidelines developed by Cooper, Eckstut Associates in 1979, the four-building World Financial Center designed by Pelli was completed in 1988. Atop the stepped towers are geometric caps, superficial abstractions of historical references. A more popular feature of the complex was the Winter Garden, so much so that it was immediately rebuilt after the destruction of September 11, 2001; it is a space appreciated even more now for its views of the rebuilding of Ground Zero. Pelli's contributions continued after the BPC Authority developed sustainability guidelines in the late 1990s, with his son Rafael designing three residential towers. The Solaire in 2003 (the first BPC project to follow the green guidelines) was followed by The Verdesian three years later and most recently The Visionaire, making up a trilogy of sorts.

For The Visionaire, the architects contend that advances in sustainable building technology, combined with a desire to surpass the achievements of the Solaire and Verdesian, pushed them to incorporate innovations in energy use, indoor air quality, and water use, earning the thirty-three-story condominium tower a LEED Platinum certification, the highest rating. The tower is articulated toward the Hudson River as a curving glass wall, but it is orthogonal to the east and the skyscrapers of the Financial District beyond. A ten-story base on Battery Place houses a maintenance facility for the BPC Parks Conservancy, designed with Dattner Architects, which also designed a new school across the street. Exterior materials of terracotta rain screen and energy-efficient glass predominate, striping the tower and giving the project a strong presence at street level.

4 Looking north with the new BPC School by Dattner Architects in the foreground (left). From Battery Place looking up, the tower curves to the south (below).

ZUCCOTTI PARK 5

COOPER, ROBERTSON & PARTNERS, 2006

Broadway and Liberty Streets
4 5 to Bowling Green; **1 R** to Rector Street

Liberty Plaza Park, an unremarkable but popular 1960s-era concrete oasis southeast of the World Trade Center (WTC), was a casualty of the destruction of the Twin Towers on September 11, 2001. Five years later the renovation of the 33,000-square-foot park by Cooper, Robertson & Partners reopened and was renamed for the chairman of Brookfield Properties, the owner of the park. The design emphasizes a diagonal connection between the WTC site and the Financial District, a northwest-southeast vector defined by the direction of granite benches, the placement of honey locust trees, a diagonal stone paving pattern, and the siting of Mark di Suvero's *Joie de Vivre* at the corner of Broadway and Cedar. The last is a 70-foot-high bright red steel sculpture that echoes Isamu Noguchi's famous tottering *Red Cube* across Broadway. At night the space is illuminated by white glass pavers lit from below, a striking design feature that ties the elements of the park together even in the darkest hours.

WILLIAM BEAVER HOUSE 6

TSAO & MCKOWN ARCHITECTS with SLCE Architects, 2009

15 William Street, at Beaver Street
2 3 to Wall St; **J Z** to Broad Street

Not surprisingly, residential occupancy in Lower Manhattan decreased after the September 11 attacks, spurring incentives targeted at renters and developers alike to counter this effect. With the digitization of Wall Street, many new residential developments are conversions of commercial space, but William Beaver House is the only ground-up residential development in the winding canyons of the Financial District south of Wall Street. Located on a previously vacant lot at William and Beaver Streets, the forty-seven-story tower designed for hotelier Andre Balázs by Calvin Tsao and Zack McKown is a pixelated composition of black and gold brick. This gives the impression of a glittering mass exuberantly rising from the narrow, winding, densely built streets around Wall Street like an obelisk drizzled in gold flakes. In an effort to capture the chaos of the surrounding buildings, the base of the tower is a composition of broken charcoal "street walls" that run counter to the supposed luxuriousness of the more than three hundred apartments within.

5 Looking towards *Joie de Vivre* from Liberty Street (far left). Photo © Francis Dzikowski/Esto.

6 Looking across William Street towards the broken street wall (left). Photo by Richard Bryant.

7 The walkway flows upwards towards the beacon and views towards Brooklyn (left). Photo by Nathan Sayers. The glowing beacon seen from the rectangle of grass (right). Photo © Francis Dzikowski/Esto.

7 ELEVATED ACRE AT 55 WATER STREET

KEN SMITH LANDSCAPE ARCHITECT and ROGERS MARVEL ARCHITECTS, 2005

55 Water Street, near Old Slip
2 **3** to Wall St; **R** to Whitehall Street–South Ferry

This one-acre plaza overlooking the East River is one of three Privately Owned Public Spaces (POPS) at 55 Water Street, a 1972 Emery Roth & Sons design that still boasts the largest floor area of any office building in New York City. These open spaces—the other two are an arcade and the Vietnam Veterans Plaza—allowed the developer to achieve this top ranking by swapping open space for additional floor area. Thirty years after the initial completion, the Municipal Art Society held a competition for the redesign of the raised plaza, considered a barren and underused space. Given its location 40 feet above sidewalk level and its physical remove from the pedestrian flow of Water Street, a strong design was needed to draw people up into the space.

The winning team of landscape architect Ken Smith and architects Rob Rogers and Jonathan Marvel achieves this goal with a design that melds architecture and landscape—two often diverging disciplines that find synergy here—and brings the park down to street level. Tucked beneath the glass link between the two buildings of 55 Water, new escalators and an elevator bracket stairs interspersed with planters, a hint at the fauna above. The Elevated Acre is basically split into three zones: an abstracted dunescape with native plantings and seating along a concrete plank walkway, tiered seating next to a carpet of grass used for outdoor events (this open area frames the upper portion of the 1911 New York City Police Museum building to the north), and a boardwalk ending at a glass beacon overlooking the East River and the Brooklyn Bridge. At night the beacon is illuminated, effectively extending the visual impact of the design beyond its one-acre confines.

HISTORIC FRONT STREET 8

COOK + FOX ARCHITECTS, 2005

Front Street, between
Peck Slip and Beekman Street
② ③ ④ ⑤ Ⓐ Ⓒ Ⓙ Ⓩ to
Fulton Street, Broadway-Nassau

What is now called the South Street Seaport can be seen as a remnant of Manhattan's centuries-old shoreline, a once ubiquitous scene of working piers and warehouses ending with the 2005 shuttering of the Fulton Fish Market, relocated to Hunts Point in the Bronx. In 1968 an eleven-block area bound by Dover, John, and Water Streets and the East River was designated a historic district, embalming it in a reconstructed nineteenth-century state centered on the South Street Seaport Museum, an outdoor "living" museum. The institution partnered with the Rouse Company in the late 1970s to develop the area as a "festival marketplace," a recipe the developer had already implemented successfully in Boston and Philadelphia. An infusion of shops and restaurants— initially local but increasingly national chains—turned the area into one of the most popular tourist destinations in New York City.

This is the context—a mix of history, interpretation, and commerce—into which the architects inserted three new residential buildings with retail space on Front Street at the north end of the historic district; they also renovated eleven buildings for apartments. Their designs meld a contextual approach to massing and materials with a deep commitment to sustainability, in most cases not visible (ten geothermal wells extend a quarter mile into bedrock). Brick predominates, but the corner building at Front and Peck Slip features a fully glazed wall that clearly expresses a contemporary aesthetic, layered with wood louvers, a green vernacular of sorts in line with the historic neighbors.

8 The corner building at Front and Peck Streets (right).
Photo by Seong Kwon. **Detail of the corner building (above).**

9 8 SPRUCE STREET
GEHRY PARTNERS, 2011

8 Spruce Street, between Gold and Nassau Streets

❷ ❸ ④ ⑤ Ⓐ Ⓒ Ⓙ Ⓩ to Fulton Street, Broadway-Nassau

Frank Gehry's second ground-up building in New York City—after the IAC Building (**59**) in Chelsea—is a seventy-six-story residential tower steps from City Hall and the Brooklyn Bridge. About ten years before its realization, the most famous architect at the turn of the century tried to build a second New York Guggenheim (forty years after Frank Lloyd Wright's famous design overlooking Central Park), proposed for a spot in the East River below the nearby South Street Seaport. Shelved in 2002, it would have been a follow-up to the enormously successful Guggenheim branch in Bilbao, Spain, which catapulted the architect into the public spotlight and inspired the phrase "Bilbao effect," referring to the impact of the cultural venue on the industrial town. So Gehry's first building downtown is not a billowing, curling manifestation of metal ribbons containing art but undulating stainless steel panels rising up the efficiently planned 1 million–plus-square-foot condo tower.

Forest City Ratner Companies—Gehry's old client on the high-profile Atlantic Yards project in Brooklyn—is the developer of the project, initially called the Beekman Tower. Through an agreement with the Department of Education, a new school is part of the development, housed in the plain-looking six-story brick base, which also includes space for the New York Downtown Hospital and the requisite ground-floor retail. Two through-block plazas bracketing the building on the east and west were designed by Field Operations with Dutch planting designer Piet Oudolf, but the project's raison d'être is its presence on the skyline, not these open spaces or the way the building meets the ground (a weak point in many of Gehry's designs, the IAC Building included). Gehry has taken the shallow zone afforded to architectural expression on tall buildings, the exterior envelope, and exploited it for effect, sending ripples up the building to give residents bay windows, a unique amenity in high-rise living. Combined with the reflectivity of the stainless steel, the effect is that of a shimmering jewel rising from Lower Manhattan's stone canyons.

9 From the north Gehry's building has a classical symmetry not visible from other sides (left). Photo by Jackie Caradonio. **The ripples are like wind patterns solidified in stainless steel (right).** Photo © Aaron Dougherty.

10 The stainless steel base subtly identifies the building number (left). Photo © David Sundberg/Esto. **Looking towards Holzer's scrolling words from Koons's balloon-like sculpture (right).** Photo © Francis Dzikowski/Esto.

7 WTC **10**

SKIDMORE, OWINGS & MERRILL with James Carpenter Design Associates, 2006

250 Greenwich Street, at Vesey Street
E to World Trade Center; **2** **3** to Park Place

When the North Tower of the World Trade Center collapsed at 10:28 a.m. on September 11, 2001, debris ignited fires inside Building 7, leading to its collapse nearly seven hours later. That building was one of five smaller WTC buildings ringing the Twin Towers, but the only one removed from the massive multi-block plinth bound by Vesey, Church, Liberty, and West Streets. Building 7 occupied its own block north of Vesey Street, linked to the rest of the WTC by two pedestrian bridges. Among other tenants, the building housed the Office of Emergency Management, since relocated to Brooklyn (**128**).

Not long after its destruction, Larry Silverstein—who famously signed a lease for the World Trade Center months before the attacks and received over $4 billion in insurance money in 2004—hired Skidmore, Owings & Merrill for the replacement on the same site, forty-two floors of office space situated above a ten-story power substation. This last piece was part of the original building, and its importance enabled the new design by SOM's David Childs to be realized relatively quickly, with construction commencing in 2002 and its completion four years later.

The replacement cuts the trapezoidal plan of its predecessor into a parallelogram and triangle, rising from the southward extension of Greenwich Street to the WTC site. The tower sits on the parallelogram to the west, opposite a triangular park designed by landscape architect Ken Smith with a sculpture by Jeff Koons, *Balloon Flower (Red)*. Commissioned art extends across the street and into the lobby, where poetry scrolls across a wall of LEDs, an installation by Jenny Holzer. In between is a highly transparent cable-net glass wall that gives a clear view of the installation while providing blast resistance at the entrance. (The cable structure allows the wall to flex under enormous stress.) These lobby elements and the building's two types of exterior envelope—the taut clear glass wall of the office tower and the variegated stainless steel wire screen wrapping the substation—owe a great deal to the contributions of James Carpenter Design Associates. Their expertise in the effects of glass and natural light helped create a cohesive and crystalline expression of rebuilding before the rest of the WTC reconstruction effort could even get under way.

11 200 WEST STREET

PEI COBB FREED & PARTNERS with Adamson Associates Architects, 2010

200 West Street, between Murray and Vesey Streets

❶ ❷ ❸ Ⓐ Ⓒ to Chambers Street

Called by its address instead of the name of its sole tenant, the new headquarters for Goldman Sachs is the only office building in Battery Park City north of the World Financial Center. In Henry Cobb's design the west-facing curve of the forty-three-story tower captures the sun's rays, like The Visionaire (**4**) in the neighborhood to the south, but it also appears to be gesturing at its kin, the Cesar Pelli–designed Goldman Sachs Tower across the Hudson River in Jersey City. The plan of Cobb's $2.5 billion tower is a quarter ellipse engaging below it a rectangular mass facing east and north. A podium containing six huge trading floors for the investment banking and securities firm is rendered with the same stainless steel horizontals as the tower, crisp and flat, the antithesis of the brick and stone that predominate in BPC's north residential area.

Between 200 West Street and the hotel to the west is a pedestrian walkway capped by a dynamic canopy that seems to bow under the pressure of its neighbors. Architect Preston Scott Cohen describes his design of the canopy as a "tectonic surface"[1] comprising three triangular surfaces that follow a hyperbolic parabola. The complex geometry is created by steel beams that bend along lines extending the length of the arcade; the beams are sandwiched between glass surfaces whose reflectivity further animates the narrow space. A walk under the canopy is enlivened by glimpses of a Franz Ackerman mural in the lobby of 200 West Street.

11 The covered public arcade, with Goldman Sachs on the right (left). The curved tower seen from the Irish Hunger Memorial (right). Photos by Jackie Caradonio.

RIVERHOUSE 12
ENNEAD ARCHITECTS, 2009

1 River Terrace, at Vesey Street
1 2 3 A C to Chambers Street

The contributions of Ennead Architects (formerly Polshek Partnership) to Battery Park City are numerous; starting with Liberty House in 1986, followed by the Cove Club four years later, and the 2001 Ritz Carlton Downtown, which also houses the Skyscraper Museum (**3**). The firm's 2009 design, by partner Todd Schliemann, is its first in the north residential area and its first project designed to—and

12 The west side overlooks Rockefeller Park (left).

surpassing—the BPC Authority's sustainability guidelines. Riverhouse appropriately overlooks the Hudson River and extends a curving street wall with its neighbor to the north, the Solaire, the first building to follow the same guidelines. Riverhouse also extends Teardrop Park, an intimate design by Michael Van Valkenburgh with distinctive rocky outcroppings, a children's play area, and heliostats mounted on adjacent buildings to bring natural light into the shadowy space surrounded by towers. In addition to luxury condos, the U-shaped building also houses the BPC Branch of the New York Public Library, designed by 1100: Architect (see page 138), and Poets House, designed by architect Louise Braverman.

101 WARREN STREET 13
SKIDMORE, OWINGS & MERRILL, 2009

101 Warren Street, at Greenwich Street
1 2 3 A C to Chambers Street

With the pre-2008 boom in condominium towers consisting mainly of buildings in glass and metal, it's refreshing to see how SOM's Mustafa Abadan wraps the glass boxes of this two-acre development in a "lace screen" of stone. Originally slated for commercial development, the project shifted to residential use after September 11, 2001. A total of 1 million square feet is spread across 220 condo units, 163 rental apartments, and a retail base; the first are located in the thirty-three-story tower to the west, the second fit in eight- and twelve-story segments toward Greenwich Street, and both are both propped up by a grocery store and a bookstore. Tying it all together is the lace screen of sand-colored granite in front of a glass and metal curtain wall. The stone is articulated in alternating two-story sections, giving the tower a distinctive presence even from a distance. Through its massing and façades, Abedan's design aims to synthesize Tribeca's low-scale masonry buildings to the north and the glass office towers to the south, including the nearby 7 WTC (**10**), also designed by SOM.

13 The lace screen continues in front of the terraces (right). The west tower seen from Battery Park City (far right). Photos © Aaron Dougherty.

See Map
5
West Village

See Map
4
Greenwich Village

Hudson
River

Houston St

King St

Charlton St • Studio-X

Vandam St

Sixth Av

MacDougal St

Sullivan St

Thompson St

West Broadway

Houston St

Wooster St

Spring St

Urban Glass House •

Prince St

• Alessi Store

B **D**

F **M**

497 Greenwich Street 17• •**16** **C** **E**
Trump SoHo Hotel

Apple Store SoHo •

Dominick St

Taschen Bookstore •

• **Prada**

Broome St

Scholastic Building 18•

N **R**

Longchamps • • Donald Judd Studio Museum

Renwick St

Watts St

Canal St

Desbrosses St

Vestry St

Laight St

Hudson River Park

• V33

1

Spring St

Bar 89

1/4-mile
radius

• Grand Street Hotel

Broadway

6

Crosby St

Lafayette St

Hubert St

• 408 Greenwich Street

A **C** **E**

•**15** One York

• SoHo Mews

One Kenmare Square 20•

• Petrosino Sq

• Storefront

Beach St

Hudson St

Varick St

Greene St

Mercer St

Grand St

Broome St

•**19** **40 Mercer
Residences**

Kenmare St

N Moore St

• tribecalSSEYMIYAKE

Canal St

Lispenard St

• Derek Lam

Harrison St

West Street

1

Sixth Av

Walker St

N **Q** **R**

Howard St

Grand St

White St

• Projected Image

6

New York Law School 14•

Leonard St

Franklin St

J **Z**

See Map
3
Chinatown

Greenwich St

• 172 Duane Street

West Broadway

Worth St

• P.S. 234

Church St

Thomas St

Duane St

Lafayette St

Centre St

Broadway

Canal St

Chambers St

Reade St

See Map
1
Lower Manhattan

2

If any two neighborhoods illustrate New York City's shift from

blue-collar industry to white-collar global business, they are Tribeca and SoHo. Ironically, despite this transition, these areas have substantially retained their old industrial architecture. This is due in part to the efforts of the Landmarks Preservation Commission (LPC), in terms of both designating historic districts (sections of Tribeca as early as 1991 and SoHo's Cast Iron District in 1973) and adopting a fairly liberal stance toward what can be built in historic districts. The prevailing position is that contemporary or modern architecture best respects historical architecture by letting old and new represent their respective time periods. The historical architecture has been kept intact, too, because of the flexibility of predominantly open floor plans of buildings used in the past as warehouses and factories and now as apartments and offices; in between, both neighborhoods were home to artists, drawn by this same feature. Nevertheless, the building boom of the early 2000s saw a number of high-profile projects inserted into these historic areas.

Tribeca (*Tri*angle *be*low *Ca*nal) is bound by Canal Street on the north, Broadway on the east, Chambers Street on the south, and the Hudson River on the west. Two different street grids split this area roughly in two, east and west of Hudson Street, a division arising from the way two separate owners laid out plots for development in the late eighteenth century. In this historical fabric, the converted loft buildings that make up much of the neighborhood are some of the most expensive real estate in the city. This fact, along with the eminently walkable short blocks traversed by pretty people, was not lost on developers intent on bringing condo high-rises to Tribeca, most notably Five Franklin Place by UNStudio and 56 Leonard Street by Herzog & de Meuron; each project fizzled during the 2008 financial crisis.

SoHo (*So*uth of *Ho*uston, pronounced "Howston") is bounded by Houston Street on the north, Lafayette Street on the east, Canal Street on the south, and anywhere from West Broadway to the Hudson River on the west, depending on whom one talks to. (Alternatively the area from West Broadway to Sixth Avenue is referred to as South Village, and farther west is increasingly called Hudson Square; this book takes the SoHo moniker literally and extends it to the river.) Like Tribeca, SoHo contains some of the most expensive real estate in the city, be it the open-plan residential lofts in old warehouses or the retail spaces in the outdoor mall that is the Cast Iron Historical District. More than Tribeca, SoHo is credited with pioneering gentrification through artistic intervention, a process in which artists move into cheap industrial relics (illegally at first, in this case) and infuse the area with a cultural vibrancy that eventually attracts more affluent people. It is a phenomenon that was repeated in Chelsea after artists and the galleries that serve them were priced out of SoHo, and it continues in Williamsburg, Brooklyn, and, to a lesser extent, parts of the Bronx and Queens.

14 NEW YORK LAW SCHOOL
SMITHGROUP with BKSK Architects, 2009

185 West Broadway, at Leonard Street
❶ to Franklin Street

New York Law School was established in 1891 in a revolt against the Columbia College School of Law and its traditional teaching methods. Housed in a number of buildings during its early years, the young institution had become the largest law school in the country less than fifteen years after its founding, acquiring a building of its own on Fulton Street four years later. A number of moves occurred in the decades that followed before the law school settled in its current location in 1962. Its facilities doubled with this 200,000-square-foot expansion by SmithGroup's Washington, D.C., office, working with the local firm BKSK Architects.

   A number of disconnected nineteenth-century cast iron buildings were linked by the new building. Five stories above grade and four stories below

contain classrooms, lounges, study rooms, dining facilities, and a library. A 200-foot-long five-story glass façade gives contemporary expression to the law school's motto, "Learn Law and Take Action." This north-facing elevation—corporate but befitting an institution such as this one—contains corridors and stairs that, as in other institutions of higher education in the city and around the country, foster informal interaction. This façade also puts the activities of the school on display in the hopes of "creating a civic landmark for Tribeca,"[1] according to the architects.

14 The view east down Leonard Street; the long north elevation is visible.

ONE YORK 15
TEN ARQUITECTOS, 2008

1 York Street, at Sixth Avenue
1 A C E to Canal Street

Seen from the west across Sixth Avenue, One York appears to be a glass tower that has landed on a six-story brick building and split it in two. In essence this is what has happened, as one of two existing buildings on the site was demolished to make way for forty-three loft dwellings; the remaining building on the site was enlarged in the process. This fractured effect is fostered by the dynamic plan of the upper floors, angled differently from the masonry bases that follow the surrounding streets, and kinked where the glass splits the brick below. While Enrique Norten's design can be seen as a commentary on the transformation of Manhattan from an island of manufacturing to one of global capital, the various angles capture the convergence of Canal Street and Sixth Avenue in front of the site. The latter street bends as it crosses Canal, and its course is visually terminated by this project as seen from the north, visible as far as Houston Street.

15 The small tower is like a glass and stone fissure.
Photo by Eduard Hueber/Archphoto.

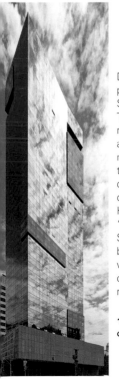

TRUMP SOHO HOTEL 16
HANDEL ARCHITECTS with Rockwell Group, 2010

246 Spring Street, at Varick Street
C E to Spring Street

Donald Trump's first foray into downtown Manhattan, like his properties that litter Midtown and the Upper East and West Sides, is notable more for its moniker than its architecture. The Trump SoHo Hotel is also notorious for the way zoning restrictions were skirted to bring a forty-six-story tower to an area of five- to fifteen-story buildings. Client and developers managed to do this by opting to build a condo-hotel—meaning that privately owned units are occupied for a restricted amount of time during the year and rented as hotel suites the remainder of the time—a building type allowed in manufacturing districts. Handel Architects' exterior design articulates the tall mass with "skybox windows" that relate to distant vistas, including the Statue of Liberty. To passersby the building hides its amenities behind glass fritted in a vertical pattern across a podium that wraps around all four sides. To the east is a small plaza, a public concession unique in a project clearly focused on its upscale residents—make that guests.

16 Looking east down Spring Street, the skybox windows stand out from the reflected façade. Photo © Aaron Dougherty.

17 Seen from the north, the wave-like façade abuts a glass box by Handel Architects (left). The concrete balconies project from the gap between brick and glass (right).

17 497 GREENWICH STREET

ARCHI-TECTONICS with David Hotson Architect, 2004

497 Greenwich Street, between Canal and Spring Streets
C E to Spring Street

Glass walls atop and beside existing masonry buildings are a repeated contemporary tactic in Manhattan, found in SHoP Architects' Porter House Condo (**51**) and TEN Arquitectos' One York (**15**), among other residences replacing manufacturing uses. One of the first twenty-first-century forays into new wrappings for old buildings is this eleven-story addition to an old six-story warehouse on Greenwich Street in an area sometimes called Hudson Square. In the design by the Dutch-born Winka Dubbeldam, a blue-green glass wall cascades water-like down the L-shaped façade to the street-level entry and gallery space; between new and old jut narrow balconies in folding concrete. The undulating glass wall follows the city's zoning envelope, a tapering invisible line mandated to allow sunlight to reach the spaces between buildings. Usually this envelope is managed with setbacks, thereby creating towers on bases or terraced masses. Here Dubbeldam finds inspiration in the restrictions and allows the façade to be not only spatially rich but also unique—using combinations of flat and curving glass panes—for most of the twenty-two lofts within, including a few designed by the architect herself.

    Dubbeldam's project is also the first major piece in a small section of SoHo–Hudson Square northeast of Canal and Hudson Streets. Popular with residential developers before the 2008 bust, this triangular area is home to a glut of condo projects—no fewer than six others—some completed but others stalled by the economic collapse. Most notable is Urban Glass House, Philip Johnson's last project, carried out with Annabelle Selldorf.

18 Looking north up Broadway, with the Singer Building on the right (left).
A close-up of the Mercer Street façade (right).

SCHOLASTIC BUILDING **18**
ALDO ROSSI and MORRIS ADJMI ARCHITECTS with Gensler Associates, 2001

557 Broadway, between Prince and Spring Streets
Ⓝ Ⓡ to Prince Street

Italian architect Aldo Rossi died in a car accident four years before his only building in New York City was completed, and only weeks after the project was approved by the city's Landmarks Preservation Commission. Rossi's design is said to have been an easy one for the Milan-based architect, who espoused "that the city itself is the collective memory of its people"[2] and therefore relished the opportunity to build in SoHo's Cast Iron Historic District. The ten-story headquarters for Scholastic, the publisher of children's books founded in 1920, resembles many of Rossi's other designs that boil architecture down to its constituent parts (columns, beams, cornices, pediments), especially the 1987 Hotel II Palazzo in Japan. His approach is derived from memories—images amassed in distinctive sketches in which archetypal buildings are combined with horses, teakettles, and other assorted elements—and from his theories on the architecture of the city, which limit forms to those found in collective memory.

The main façade fronts Broadway next to the lacy 1905 Singer Building to the north. Painted red beams span the full width of the façade, alternating with green beams that are truncated by round white columns. Of course these architectural elements, including the cornice composed of three matching red girders, are decorative, standing in for the real structure behind. The overall effect is like that of looking at the Singer or another cast iron original while squinting. More dynamic are the red steel arches of the Mercer Street façade, which recall the entire area's industrial origins, not just the neighboring architecture.

19 40 MERCER RESIDENCES

ATELIERS JEAN NOUVEL with SLCE Architects, 2006

2

40 Mercer Street, at Grand Street

⑥ ⓙ ⓩ Ⓝ Ⓠ Ⓡ to Canal Street

French architect Jean Nouvel's first building in New York City can appear timid when compared to his subsequent design for 100 Eleventh Avenue (**58**) in Chelsea, but when it is seen in context, this assessment seems premature, if not irrelevant. Located in SoHo's Cast Iron Historic District—as is the Scholastic Building (**18**) by Aldo Rossi—Nouvel's design required approval by the city's Landmarks Preservation Commission. This called for a design that would respect the area's historic industrial architecture yet still express its time; otherwise why would hotelier Andre Balázs hire the Pritzker Prize–winning architect known for the ethereal Fondation Cartier and the high-tech Institut du Monde Arabe, both in Paris? Originally the project was designed as a hotel, but it was changed to condos after the events of September 11, 2001, a switch the architect admits was minor for a design generated more by site conditions than by function.

The two-part structure—base and tower—arises from zoning setback requirements but also from the architect's decision to create a garden on the northern portion of the site, spanning from Broadway to Mercer. The elevations are well-crafted compositions in glass and steel, the former dark gray and the latter a mélange of red, blue, and clear. An exclamation point on the tower slab is created by blue glass louvers reaching up and over the east end like a *brise-soleil* for a VIP. The south façade also features two vertical strips of sliding glass walls, hard to distinguish when closed but impossible to miss when open.

19 Two vertical stripes on the south feature sliding glass walls (below). Photo by Stephen Murray. **The building stands apart from its cast iron neighbors (right).**

ONE KENMARE SQUARE 20

GLUCKMAN MAYNER ARCHITECTS
with H. Thomas O'Hara Architect, 2006

210 Lafayette Street, at Kenmare Street
⑥ to Spring Street

One of three residential properties in New York City developed by hotelier Andre Balázs (see also **6** and **19**), One Kenmare Square offers through its site a rarity in Manhattan's unrelenting grid: the terminus of a T-intersection. Kenmare Street's east-west axis is a continuation of Delancey Street, the wide thoroughfare extending from the Williamsburg Bridge. A short block from the Storefront for Art and Architecture (designed by Steven Holl and Vito Acconci in 1993 and well worth a visit), the building is given additional exposure on its prominent eastern face by the triangular open space of the redesigned Lieutenant Joseph Petrosino Square. Confronted with this situation, architect Richard Gluckman designed an undulating façade "derived from the banded masonry façades of early twentieth-century warehouse construction."[3] The undulating trend can be found in other residential projects such as 497 Greenwich Street (**17**), One Astor Place (**34**), and One Jackson Square (**50**).

Before undertaking this project, Gluckman—who partnered with David Mayner in 1998—designed primarily arts facilities and retail interiors, such as two galleries for Larry Gagosian in Chelsea and a couple of Manhattan storefronts for Helmut Lang. Gluckman's minimalist aesthetic informs the ribbon-window façade of One Kenmare Square, though the gray brick and dark glass are somber in comparison to the skillful treatment of light found in his art spaces as well as the lobby, which one can peek into from Lafayette Street. The project actually comprises two buildings: eleven stories facing east and a narrow six-story piece on Crosby Street. The latter uses the same gray brick as the front, but on an unadorned flat wall with small punched openings, a standout on a street textured with fire escapes.

20 Seen from Spring Street on the north, the street widens toward Petrosino Square (above). The undulations vary slightly from floor to floor (right).
Photo by Scott Norsworthy.

A precise mapping of the different neigh-

borhoods east of SoHo is difficult, as each grows or recedes over time, as most neighborhoods do, but to a more pronounced degree here. The area bounded by Houston on the north, Lafayette on the west, Canal Street and the Manhattan Bridge on the south, and the East River on the east is sometimes referred to simply as the Lower East Side. Yet certainly distinctions abound. The smells from the sidewalk stalls and the sights in the shop windows color the pedestrian's experience of these different neighborhoods defined by nationality (Chinese, Italian) or culture (hipster, glitterati). Tying these small parts of the larger Lower East Side together are their history as destinations for immigrants and as a consistent urban fabric of five- and six-story tenements housing the steady stream of newcomers to the city.

Chinatown started out as a six-block area between the Bowery, Mulberry, Canal, and Worth Streets as early as the 1840s, after the Transcontinental Railroad was completed. Not until after the repeal of the 1882 Chinese Exclusion Act in the 1960s did Chinatown break through these streets into adjacent parts of Little Italy and the Lower East Side. As much a tourist attraction today as a functioning community, Chinatown, centered on Canal and Mott Streets, abounds with activity during the day, as stores spill out onto the sidewalks.

Just above Chinatown is Little Italy. The destination in the nine-teenth and twentieth centuries for Italian immigrants, it has shrunk to a symbol of its former self, concentrated on a strip of Mulberry Street best known for the San Gennaro festival each September. This street fair extends to Houston Street, but for the rest of the year the area north of Broome Street is all fashionable boutiques and trendy eateries. Nolita (*N*orth of *Li*ttle *Ita*ly) may take its name from the traditional neighborhood to the south, but the newbie's ground-floor retail spaces are more in tune with fashionable SoHo; if anything, the boutiques that once called the Cast Iron District home now have a place in Nolita, where the small retail spaces below the old tenements aren't as conducive to fit-outs by national chains.

To the east of the Bowery, the area now considered the Lower East Side has been home to waves of immigrants from Ireland, eastern Europe, and more recently Puerto Rico. The current and historical presence of these cultures can still be found in the tenements themselves, the religious structures dotting the area, and the stores and restaurants resistant to the gentrification personified in the young hipsters found throughout "Loisada." This last process has dramatically reshaped the skyline with hotels and condos puncturing the previous six-story limit (as far as people were willing to trudge up without an elevator). In response to a number of these "pencil buildings," the Department of City Planning rezoned the area in 2008 to limit the height of new buildings to the neighborhood's traditional scale.

21 MUSEUM OF CHINESE IN AMERICA
MAYA LIN STUDIO with Bialosky + Partners, 2009

211–215 Centre Street, between Howard and Grand Streets
⑥ Ⓙ Ⓩ Ⓝ Ⓠ Ⓡ to Canal Street

MOCA was founded in 1980 as a community-based organization, the New York Chinatown History Project, by historian John Kuo Wei Tchen and activist Charles Lai as a way to keep the memories of Chinese Americans alive through oral histories, documentation, and research. While representing Chinese people all over the United States, Manhattan's Chinatown—one of the largest and most visible Chinese communities outside Asia—helps to give the museum a strong identity and presence, particularly in its new space on the SoHo border. Occupying an early-1900s industrial warehouse space between Centre and Lafayette Streets, the museum has storefronts on both streets. The main access is from Centre, under a wood canopy that continues inside to become the ceiling and the donor wall of the lobby; the studio access on Lafayette is more restrained but features a glimpse into one of the core exhibits: a reconstructed "general store."

Maya Lin—still widely known, even decades later, for her design of the Vietnam Veterans Memorial in Washington, D.C.—infuses the museum's interiors with the minimalism found in her memorials, artwork, and other architectural projects. The brick of the existing building is left exposed, particularly in a central multistory space, an old skylit courtyard. This space takes on importance as the gallery spaces circle it, occasionally peering into it from selective openings that also receive projected images, the faces of the people the museum celebrates and remembers.

21 The framed Centre Street entrance.

THE NOLITAN **22**
GRZYWINSKI + PONS, 2011

30 Kenmare Street, at Elizabeth Street
J **Z** to Bowery; **4** to Spring Street

3

Before moving to New York City in 2006, my wife and I used to visit at least once a year, staying at a cheap but decent hotel on Broome Street for under $100 a night. The overnight rate at the nearby nine-story, fifty-five-room Nolitan, by contrast, hovers around $500, a testament to the area's quick rise in popularity and the price of architecture with

22 What looks like two buildings is actually one hotel. Photo by Jackie Caradonio.

a capital A. Matthew Grzywinski and Amador Pons certainly are no strangers to hotels. Their design for the Hotel on Rivington (THOR) helped make the place a popular destination in the Lower East Side after its 2004 opening. Yet while that earlier tower is covered in milky glass, the design for The Nolitan has a split personality: dark metal panels erode into glass on the corner, a grid of balconies behind clear glass railings hangs to the west, and translucent channel glass unites these two parts. THOR may sprout way above its neighbors, but The Nolitan rises only a couple of floors above adjacent buildings in the Little Italy Historic District, giving guests at the top unobstructed views over the surrounding rooftops.

30 ORCHARD STREET **23**
OGAWA/DEPARDON ARCHITECTS, 2010

30 Orchard Street, between Hester and Canal Streets
F to East Broadway

Cor-Ten steel is the trademarked but common name for weathered steel, in which alloyed sheets of the material are coated in a distinctive protective layer of rust. The most prominent use of the material is in the artwork of Richard Serra. His monumental sculptures are found primarily in museums such as Dia:Beacon (in Beacon, New York, two hours north of Manhattan on Metro North) and sculpture parks around the world. Perhaps inspired by Serra, Kathryn Ogawa and Gilles Depardon's design for a twelve-story condo building in the Lower East Side uses Cor-Ten steel to elevate what is typically an afterthought—the usually solid party walls—closer to something artistic. Here the walls step back as they rise, clearly illustrating the required setbacks of the zoning envelope. The "urban rust" that covers these walls gives the tall building added prominence in its low-rise context and threatens to overshadow the rest of the design. Thankfully the glass and wood frames of the street wall are a suitable match for the weathered steel, giving a strong presence to the building even at street level when the side walls are out of sight.

23 Seen from the north, "urban rust" rises in the Lower East Side. Photo © Aaron Dougherty.

24 Looking north across Delancey Street, with THOR in the distance at left (left). Photo © Peter Aaron/Esto. **A pixelated wrapper in shades of blue (right).** Photo by Scott Norsworthy.

24 BLUE CONDOMINIUM

BERNARD TSCHUMI ARCHITECTS, with SLCE Architects, 2007

105 Norfolk Street, between Delancey and Rivington Streets
Ⓕ Ⓜ Ⓙ Ⓩ to Delancey Street–Essex Street

In 2008 the New York City Council adopted the Department of City Planning's rezoning of more than one hundred blocks in the East Village and Lower East Side to, among other things, "preserve the established neighborhood scale and character by establishing … height limits."[1] What the DCP deemed "out-of-scale tower developments"[2] includes the nearby Hotel on Rivington and most strikingly the seventeen-story Blue Condominium, which towers above its surroundings and stands out for its unique form and namesake multihued cladding. Depending on one's location, the building's volume angles out, angles back, or is cut away as it rises. The dappled blue is like a cover that wraps the whole, indifferent to any variations that may exist across the sides.

Architect Bernard Tschumi attests that the numerous sloping walls and pixelated façade "negotiate the varying setback rules" in the first case and "reflect both the internal arrangement of spaces and the multi-faceted character of the neighborhood below"[3] in the second case. These angles and notches can also be seen as a means of maximizing the allowable square footage while simultaneously creating a prominent building, thus increasing desirability and maximizing profits for the developer. This reading may apply to most if not all of the high-profile condominiums in Manhattan of the last decade or so, but the resulting design also prompted the City Council's decision to downzone the area, ensuring Blue's prominence on the Lower East Side skyline for a long time to come.

SWITCH BUILDING **25**
nARCHITECTS, 2007

109 Norfolk Street, between Delancey
and Rivington Streets
ⓕ ⓜ ⓙ ⓩ to Delancey Street–Essex Street

3

Just north of the seventeen-story Blue Condominium (**24**) sits a seven-story apartment building completed the same year, designed by Brooklyn-based nARCHITECTS. Whereas the former calls for attention with its color and bulk, the Switch Building subtly expresses the qualities of its full-floor apartments above a ground-floor art gallery. The angled projections are reinterpreted bay windows, allowing views alternately up and down Norfolk Street from wood-lined seats. In Eric Bunge and Mimi Hoang's design, these projections also set up a design motif that integrates the omnipresent air conditioner units behind angled louvers oriented vertically. These "switches" are synthesized into a façade system, an important differentiation from building skins that uniformly cover a structural frame. Here the exterior ambitiously integrates non-architectural systems and frames experiences. The building may be small in stature, but it is big on ideas.

115 NORFOLK RESIDENCES **26**
GRZYWINSKI + PONS, 2011

115 Norfolk Street, between Delancey and
Rivington Streets
ⓕ ⓜ ⓙ ⓩ to Delancey Street–Essex Street

25 The normal treatment of AC units is found in both of the Switch Building's neighbors (top). Photo by Scott Norsworthy. **26** A narrow space subtly reveals itself behind the flat glass elevation (above). Photo by Jackie Caradonio.

On this one-block stretch of Norfolk Street, home to the Blue Condominium (**24**) and the Switch Building (**25**), a more recent addition is an infill building with a flat glass curtain wall, a façade that is not expressive of its contents. Housing twenty-four residential units, the eight-story project follows the rezoning sparked by tall buildings in the area, such as Blue Condominium and Matthew Grzywinski and Amador Pons' own Hotel on Rivington around the corner. Yet with a smaller scale, the glass wall and its sloping horizontal mullions are still a departure from the area's predominant masonry character, even on this block being taken over by contemporary architecture. But the great surprise lies behind this façade: a courtyard, though given its small scale, a more accurate term might be light well. In the early morning hours, and especially at night, when floodlights are turned on, this off-center space is revealed. Lining the void are walls with punched openings akin to those in the surrounding masonry buildings.

27 NEW MUSEUM OF CONTEMPORARY ART

SANAA with Gensler Associates, 2007

235 Bowery, between Stanton and Rivington Streets

J **Z** to Bowery; **F** to Second Avenue

The day after leaving her curator post at the Whitney Museum of American Art in 1977, so the story goes, Marcia Tucker founded the New Museum, an entity "somewhere between grassroots alternative spaces for contemporary art and major museums that show only artists of proven historical value."[4] In 1983 the museum moved into its longtime home in SoHo, inside a historic building on Broadway between Houston and Prince Streets, next to what was the Guggenheim's SoHo branch and what is now the city's flagship Prada boutique (see page 77). Over the years the museum expanded in square footage and programming, but the limitations of the old building—renovated above into luxury condos in 1994—necessitated that continued expansion would eventually require new facilities. In 2002, under a new director, Lisa Phillips, the museum announced plans to relocate to a new building on the Bowery, doubling its size to approximately 60,000 square feet. A search for an architect led to a design competition, won the following year by Kazuyo Sejima + Ryue Nishizawa/ SANAA, a duo known for a minimalist aesthetic and ethereal buildings rendered in glass and metal. Their designs for numerous buildings in Japan, for the Glass Pavilion at the Toledo Museum of Art, and for the New Museum itself, contributed to their winning the 2010 Pritzker Architecture Prize.

SANAA's winning design for the New Museum stands in stark contrast to its context on the Bowery, a street stretching from the East Village to Chinatown whose name even today brings to mind the image of flophouses and their occupants; in fact the Bowery Mission still stands two doors to the south. The gleaming cubes—offset slightly from one another in a nod to the required zoning setbacks and a means of creating skylights to light the galleries naturally—herald the beginning of the gentrification of the strip, an in-between zone sharing the borders of the Lower East Side, Nolita, the East Village, and NoHo but belonging to none. Other developments along the Bowery include Avalon Bowery Place, the Cooper Square Hotel (**33**), and the nearby Sperone Westwater Gallery (**28**).

As built, SANAA's design stacks the six offset "bento boxes" above a transparent lobby that is a visual continuation of the sidewalk; loading occurs at the north end of this level, putting on display what is usually hidden. Looking up at the building's exterior skin from the sidewalk, one can see the façade's composition of aluminum mesh projected in front of solid white metal panels. The custom mesh reflects sunlight, allowing the building to glow or, alternatively, to appear muted and gray, depending on the weather, time of day, and one's position relative to the building.

A gallery space at the rear of the ground floor draws people into the museum; its white walls and bare fluorescent lighting hint at the minimal gallery spaces above. Best reached by elevator, these spaces are disappointing after one has taken in the layering of the building's exterior, but their sizes allow the curators to display large-scale artworks, something that was impossible at the old Broadway location. These galleries are an extreme contrast to a trend Frank Lloyd Wright started at the Guggenheim on Fifth Avenue in 1959, namely, the imposition—not accommodation—of architecture upon artists. SANAA's architecture makes every concession to the artists and their work on display, whatever the size, medium, or subject may be. The seventh-floor terrace with dramatic views downtown and a narrow stair linking the fifth and sixth floors on the north side offer a couple of respites from these sparse open galleries. Yet the barren quality of the gallery spaces is hardly an issue, as most people visit the New Museum to gaze at the art, not at the walls themselves.

27 The stacked "bento boxes" seen from Prince Street (opposite). Photo by Scott Norsworthy. The tall, long, and narrow stair on the building's south side (below left). Photo by Dean Kaufman. Looking toward the Bowery from the lobby (below). Photo by Dean Kaufman. Detail of façade and artwork by Ugo Rondinone, since removed (bottom). Photo by Scott Norsworthy.

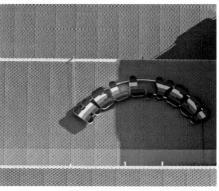

28 SPERONE WESTWATER GALLERY

FOSTER + PARTNERS with Adamson Associates Architects, 2010

257 Bowery, between Stanton and Houston Streets
J Z to Bowery; F to Second Avenue

Sperone Westwater Fischer was established in 1975, named for its three founders, who aimed to showcase European artists with little or no stateside recognition, though American artists were not excluded. The third name was dropped in 1982, but it would be another twenty years before the gallery moved from its Greene Street location in SoHo to a 10,000-square-foot space in the Meatpacking District. Yet a mere six years later, in 2008, Gian Enzo Sperone and Angela Westwater announced that they would relocate to the Bowery, to a new building designed by Norman Foster. The nine-story building—street-level lobby, three floors of public galleries, two floors of private galleries, two floors of offices, and a one-story library—sits one block north of the New Museum of Contemporary Art (**27**); minimal like SANAA's design, it is revealing where the former is shrouded.

Foster's design is basic at first glance: laminated glass in a vertical expression covers the 20-foot-wide façade; black corrugated metal siding covers the north and south walls and clearly expresses a setback at the sixth floor. The one element that sets this building apart from the myriad other infill glass buildings constructed in recent years is the full-width, 12-foot-deep "moving room" located behind the freestanding glass wall. Ferrari red, the lift/room can move people and objects up and down the building or be docked on a particular floor to extend the area of that gallery. Whatever its justification, the gimmick literally activates the street wall via architectural means, something rare in cities. Access the sparse and intimate white galleries through the lobby space situated literally underneath the moving room, an experience initially unsettling yet wholly unique.

28 Looking down the Bowery with the New Museum in the distance (left). Detail of the Ferrari-red "moving room" (below). Photos by Amy Barkow. **The lobby is also the base of the elevator shaft (below, left).**

290 Mulberry Street, at Houston Street
Ⓑ Ⓓ Ⓕ Ⓜ to Broadway–Lafayette Street;
⑥ to Bleecker Street

Confronted with a site right across the street from the nineteenth-century landmark Puck Building (designed by Albert Wagner, restored by Beyer Blinder Belle in 1995) on the north edge of Nolita, SHoP Architects opted for a design that was resolutely technical, indebted to but at odds with its predecessor in a number of ways: Puck is red brick, 290 is gray brick; Puck gives emphasis to the corner through curves and statuary, 290 does the same by wrapping windows around the corner; Puck's redbrick elevations are articulated in a traditional base-middle-top composition, but 290 uniformly covers the elevations above the ground floor with diagonals and undulations of brick.

SHoP pulled off the un-bricklike appearance of the two main façades through two technical achievements, one part of the design process and one part of the construction. First, the architects used the project to segue from CAD (computer-aided design/drafting) to BIM (building information modeling), a process many firms are undergoing. The latter treats the design in the computer environment like a 3-D model of the building, while the former is basically a computerized version of traditional drafting, consisting of lines on paper, or in this case on screen. BIM further allows manufacturers' details to be imported into the 3-D model and information from the architect's model to be shared with engineers, consultants and, most significantly, with the contractor, who can fabricate certain assemblies directly from the model rather than from intermediate drawings created by subcontractors. In other words, BIM is a networked system based on collaboration and the ability to realize complex forms generated by architects, not just a means of cutting costs.

The complex geometry of the façade at 290 Mulberry was realized by using BIM and a second technique: bricks are set in precast concrete panels formed directly from the architect's 3-D model, instead of being stacked in the traditional manner. To observe this construction, take in the building from the south, looking up Mulberry: you'll see that wafer-thin panels and smaller-than-average bricks are suspended in front of a narrow gap of windows.

29 Looking across Houston, with the Puck building at right (right). Photo © Aaron Dougherty. **The undulating brick façade on Mulberry Street (top).**

THRESHOLDS

In the years since September 11, 2001, the heightened security measures taken not just by airports but by offices and other types of buildings have put most lobby spaces—once extensions of the public realm—off limits, barriers to the more stringent keycard checkpoints manned by security personnel. Recently constructed office buildings like the New York Times Building (**93**) and One Bryant Park (**90**) have been designed with both security and public passage in mind, and they offer unique experiences to those traversing their lobbies. Other types of new buildings present highly complex entrance halls with the now expected restrictions of access: 41 Cooper Square (**35**) and the Sheila C. Johnson Design Center (**38**) are but two examples in academia. Presented here are some examples of lobby spaces in various kinds of noninstitutional buildings that illustrate the diverse ways architects approach these thresholds between the public life of the street and the private realm beyond.

3LD ART & TECHNOLOGY CENTER
LEESER ARCHITECTURE, 2003

**80 Greenwich Street, between
Rector and Edgar Streets (Map 1)**

The new facilities for the 3-Legged Dog media and theater group—replacing those lost on September 11, 2001—sit underneath a Brutalist 1950s parking garage. Thomas Leeser cut back the glass storefront, revealing theatrical spaces normally hidden from the public gaze. Most striking is the portal entry/hallway that extends from the façade to the recesses of the floor space; it's best seen after the sun goes down, when the hallway softly glows. Photo courtesy Leeser Architecture.

PROJECTED IMAGE
WORKSHOP/APD, 2009

**58 White Street, between Broadway
and Church Street (Map 2)**

In this lobby and façade renovation for a cast iron building housing co-op residences, the desire for a contemporary design was tempered by restrictions arising from its location in the Tribeca East Historic District. The architects inserted aluminum louvers in front of the glass walls and entry doors to cut down on light entering the south-facing lobby. Cutouts in the transom louvers signal the building's address, spelling out "58" with shadows in the bright green lobby when the sun hits the façade. Photo courtesy workshop/apd.

505 FIFTH AVENUE
KOHN PEDERSEN FOX
ASSOCIATES with James Turrell,
2005
505 Fifth Avenue,
at 42nd Street (Map 8)

Cater-corner to the landmark Carrère and Hastings New York Public Library sits a speculative office building whose client wanted the lobby space to be a collaboration between the building's architect, Kohn Pedersen Fox, and an artist. Given an L-shaped lobby space, James Turrell, known for his skyspaces (one can be found at P.S.1 in Long Island City) and massive Roden Crater project in Arizona, inserted bands of recessed cove lighting where the walls meet the floor and ceiling. The effect is ethereal and ever changing as day gives way to night. Photo by H. G. Esch.

METROPOLITAN TOWER
PUBLIC PASSAGE
ROGERS MARVEL ARCHITECTS, 2007
146 West 57th Street, between Sixth and
Seventh Avenues (Map 8)

This dark yet dramatically lit lobby space is the northernmost of a series of aligned through-block passages just east of Seventh Avenue, starting at 51st Street. These Privately Owned Public Spaces (POPS), used by developers to gain extra square footage in the towers above, vary in character (outside, inside) and level of design consideration. This sleek black and blue insertion is a highlight, but its design—from its materials and lighting to the long row of small television screens in the east wall—definitely encourages passage, not rest. Photo © Paul Warchol.

HUDSON NEW YORK
PHILIPPE STARCK, 2000
356 West 58th Street, between Eighth
and Ninth Avenues (Map 9)

A stark stucco façade a few steps west of Columbus Circle barely hints at the eclectic spaces French designer-of-all-trades Philippe Starck created for hotelier Ian Schrager in the last of their New York collaborations. The yellow-green ribbon and square windows of the exterior are echoed in the glass-enclosed escalators that transport people to a hunting lodge–cum–greenhouse lobby. Off this space are a "library" complete with inaccessible books, a surreal guests-only bar with a ceiling fresco by Francesco Clemente, and an open-air courtyard ringed by the twenty-six floors of rooms above.

See Map
6
Chelsea

See Map
7
Gramercy Park

See Map
5
West Village

See Map
2
SoHo

See Map
3
Lower East Side

Seventh Av

Greenwich Av

Christopher St

W 4th St

Sixth Av

MacDougal St

Sullivan St

Thompson St

Laguardia Pl

Bleecker St

Mercer St

Houston St

University Village •

W 12th St

W 13th St

W 14th St

New School University Center •

Sheila C. Johnson Design Center 38•

W 11th St

W 10th St

W 9th St

W 8th St

Fifth Av

University Pl

Union
Square
Park

•**37** 39 East 13th Street Building

E 14th St

E 13th St

East Village Brownstone 36•

4th Av

E 12th St

E 11th St

3rd Av

•**41** Infinity Chapel

Washington
Square Park

Waverly Pl

1/4-mile
radius

E 10th St

E 9th St

E 8th St

NYU Wilf Hall •

NYU Center for Academic
and Spiritual Life

Kimmel Center

Washington Pl

•**34** One Astor Place

St Marks Pl

•**42** The Townhomes of Downing Street

•**39** NYU Department
of Philosophy

Cooper Square

W 4th St

•**40** Center for Architecture

W 3rd St

Broadway

Lafayette St

Great Jones St

•**35** 41 Cooper Square

•**33** Cooper Square Hotel

E 7th St

E 6th St

E 5th St

22 Bond Street •

25 Bond Street **31•**

•**30** 40 Bond

Bond St

•**32** 48 Bond Street

E 4th St

2nd Av

1st Av

Bowery

E 3rd St

E 2nd St

E 1st St

Houston St

The various "Villages" stretch from river to river, from Houston Street on the south to 14th Street on the north. Washington Square Park sits roughly in the center of this swath, between the east-west-oriented blocks of the East Village and the eighteenth-century diagonal grid of the West Village (covered in the next chapter). This rectangular park is surrounded by the expanding NYU campus and the charming historic streets of Greenwich Village, but the situation would have been very different if Jane Jacobs and her compatriots had not successfully, and famously, stopped Robert Moses's plan to extend Fifth Avenue through the park, what would have been a ramp in his equally unsuccessful attempt to bulldoze parts of SoHo for the Lower Manhattan Expressway. In 1969 the Landmark Preservation Commission designated a huge area north and west of Washington Square Park as the Greenwich Village Historic District. This cemented the area's network of low-scale buildings dating back to the 1820s, when the rural village of Greenwich began to be urbanized.

Other historic districts were added in the Villages in the ensuing years, including three in NoHo, a narrow triangular area "North of Houston" between the Bowery and Broadway. Less a neighborhood than a real estate label, NoHo is marked by some impressive old loft and warehouse buildings, similar to but more varied than those in its more famous neighbor to the south. Regardless, a cluster of new high-profile buildings were realized on Bond Street before that and a couple of surrounding blocks were protected by LPC in 2008.

Continuing east, beyond the Bowery, we come to the East Village, a now trendy area retaining traces of its nineteenth- and early-twentieth-century eastern European past, but with stronger social roots in the 1960s counterculture and the punk movement of the following decade. A symbol of the last, the music club CBGB, was located on the Bowery, a thoroughfare long associated with drunks and the homeless. Although the neighborhood had held out against the gentrification sweeping around it on all sides, a recent spate of luxury condos and hotels has risen north of Houston, while to the south can be found the New Museum of Contemporary Art (**27**) and Sperone Westwater Gallery (**28**).

30 Looking west toward 40 Bond (left), with 48 Bond on the far right. A detail of the "graffiti gates" fronting the town houses (right).

30 40 BOND

HERZOG & DE MEURON with Handel Architects, 2007

40 Bond Street, between Bowery and Lafayette Street
6 to Bleecker Street

Bond Street is a short two-block extension of 2nd Street running west from the Bowery to Broadway, through NoHo. The stretch of Bond between the Bowery and Lafayette Street has evolved into a dense block of high-profile architecture, most of it residences catering to the superrich. If one building can be credited with making the block so desirable, it is surely 40 Bond, an Ian Schrager development designed by the Pritzker Prize–winning Swiss architects Jacques Herzog and Pierre de Meuron. Schrager is best known for his part in creating the disco Studio 54 in the 1970s, but he subsequently focused on developing "boutique hotels" and expanded into residential developments with a John Pawson–designed project overlooking Gramercy Park.

Schrager's second residential undertaking, 40 Bond stacks eight floors of apartments above three-story town houses; the former sit behind large windows framed by a grid of curved glass, and the latter are screened by graffiti-like gates crafted of cast aluminum. The Herzog & de Meuron design is a reinterpretation of historic cast iron architecture, replacing the namesake material with laminated glass that, combined with a metal backing, reflects sunlight and covers the concrete structural frame. The graffiti base, grid of curved glass, and upper-level setback root the design in a traditional tripartite division, even as it strives to distinguish itself from its predecessors in any way possible.

31 The view east down Bond Street, a layered composition of stone and bronze.
Photo © Paul Warchol.

25 BOND STREET **31**
BKSK ARCHITECTS, 2007

25 Bond Street, between Bowery and Lafayette Street
⑥ to Bleecker Street

Across the street from Herzog & de Meuron's grid of curving green glass (**30**) sits its formal antithesis: a layered, asymmetrical façade of two types of stone fronting variously sized windows. A close look reveals the distinctive "bush hammered" finish of the stone and the window frames made of bronze, a metal used infrequently in such applications today. A walk around the corner to Bleecker Street reveals what BKSK Architects call the "accidental façade" of glass and more bronze, the latter reminiscent of the iconic Seagram Building by Mies van der Rohe, which is draped in the material. The project also diverges from its neighbors on Bond in its development process; instead of being built as a speculative project for unknown owners, the building was conceived when seven individuals teamed up with a developer to create their new homes. The resulting design may relate to its historic neighbors in its use of masonry, but it stands out as much as its glassy contemporaries.

48 BOND STREET **32**
DEBORAH BERKE & PARTNERS with GF55 Partners, 2008

48 Bond Street, between Bowery and Lafayette Street
⑥ to Bleecker Street

The most recent of three ground-up buildings on this one-block stretch of Bond Street is flat and smooth where the façades by Herzog & de Meuron (**30**) and BKSK Architects (**31**) are curving and layered, respectively. Windows set flush with the charcoal-gray granite are punctuated by canted vertical lights placed randomly across the façade. These angled pieces resemble the operable awning windows one occasionally sees poking out from all-glass curtain walls around the city, but they are fixed protuberances more decorative than functional (though the squareish windows open for ventilation). Architect Deborah Berke contends that the "windows projecting from the taut façade provide a play of shadows…throughout the course of the day."[1] Like 40 Bond, the eleven-story building is set back above the cornice line it shares with its neighbors, a contextual nod from an alien presence.

32 The canted projections give relief to the flat elevation.
Photo © Aaron Dougherty.

33 Looking south down Third Avenue, with the edge of 41 Cooper Square at left (left). A frontal view illustrates the tower curving over its neighbor on the right (right). Photos © Aaron Dougherty.

33 COOPER SQUARE HOTEL

STUDIO CARLOS ZAPATA with Perkins Eastman, 2009

25 Cooper Square, at East 5th Street
⑥ to Astor Place; Ⓝ Ⓡ to 8th Street–NYU

An obvious first impression on seeing the Cooper Square Hotel is the huge jump in scale between the Bowery context and the twenty-one-story tower, an impression made all the more apparent by the old three- and four-story neighbors immediately to the north and south, respectively. These brick buildings appear to pinch the tower, directing its slenderness as much as the impulses of architect Carlos Zapata. Apparently splaying out above these neighbors, the milky white façade billows away from the Bowery as it rises, as in much of Zapata's oeuvre, be it a grocery store in Miami or the infamous stadium bowl atop Soldier Field's neoclassical colonnade in Chicago.

While the hotel's presence is defined by grand gestures—its height, a curved profile, fritted glass recalling Frank Gehry's IAC Building (**59**) in Chelsea—it is a nuanced design when one actually interacts with it. For such a tall building it is surprisingly intimate at sidewalk level, for example, in the path from the Bowery to the second-floor bar and terrace carved from the podium, a path that splits apart the lobby and its own bar. Around the corner on 5th Street is another entrance and a garden terrace at grade. Purportedly these outdoor spaces were inspired by the backyards common to the East Village, but unfortunately they afford glimpses of the tower's less flattering west-facing side. Interiors by Italian designer Antonio Citterio round out the influx of high design in this Bowery locale, where decades earlier the idea of a hotel would hardly have been entertained.

ONE ASTOR PLACE 34
GWATHMEY SIEGEL & ASSOCIATES ARCHITECTS, 2006

One Astor Place, at Lafayette Street
6 to Astor Place; **N** **R** to 8th Street–NYU

A surface parking lot for years, the property on Lafayette, Astor, and Cooper Square across from the Foundation Building at Cooper Union (the owner of the lot) was an architect's dream site. Frontage on three sides and a prominence arising from the triangular open space to the north (anchored by Tony Rosenthal's *Alamo* sculpture) are just two reasons among many. A proposal in 2000 for a hotel and theater designed by Rem Koolhaas and Herzog & de Meuron for developer Ian Shrager raised the hopes of admirers of contemporary architecture, but the cheese grater–like design was shelved after September 11, 2001 (see **66** for a cheese grater realized by Handel Architects). Related Companies stepped into the picture a few years later, hiring Charles Gwathmey to design a twenty-one-story apartment tower with close to forty units above a retail base.

Gwathmey's design—an undulating glass tower wrapping a gridded rectangular volume atop a two-story base—was blasted by *New Yorker* critic Paul Goldberger as fussy and garishly reflective—Mies van der Rohe as filtered through Donald Trump."[2] Goldberger's biting words were supposedly single-handedly responsible for slow sales, but in the pre-bust economy, those words didn't resonate for long. A public plaza to the southeast enables the tower to be seen in three dimensions, an obelisk as envisioned by the architect, who also strove for contrast with the surrounding masonry buildings. Bordering the entrance to a parking garage, this new public space feels as if it's in the wrong location; little used, it might have had a better chance of success if it had faced the triangle to the north. A failure or a wasted opportunity to some, the building still manages to make a strong impression and is a memorable insertion in the city below 14th Street.

34 Looking south down Lafayette Street, with Cooper Square Hotel in the distance. Photo by Adam Friedberg.

35 41 COOPER SQUARE

MORPHOSIS ARCHITECTS with Gruzen Samton, 2009

41 Cooper Square, at East 7th Street
6 to Astor Place; N R to 8th Street–NYU

The Cooper Union for the Advancement of Science and Art was founded in 1859 by businessman Peter Cooper as a college, private but "free as air and water" (well, water *was* free 150 years ago) and available to all who qualify. The full-tuition scholarships given to all students define the school's image as much as—or even more than—its East Village setting, its excellent academic reputation, and the historical events held in the school's Great Hall. These "free rides," which have made the school even more desirable during periods of economic recession, are made possible in part by the rent from The Cooper Union's numerous properties in the area, such as One Astor Place (**34**). One such property, the former home of the engineering department, played a large part in the ability of the school to construct this $111 million academic building, its new home for engineering, humanities, and the arts. The Cooper Union intends to develop the former engineering department site a couple of blocks north as a commercial property, shifting air rights to that property from 41 Cooper Square. Coincidentally, this maneuver resulted in a building about the same size as the school's Foundation Building across the street, which dates to the year of The Cooper Union's founding.

In 2003 Thom Mayne's Morphosis was selected from a pool of 150 architects to design the new academic building. The result, completed six years later, can best be described as a Morphosis building, because it strongly recalls other idiosyncratic designs by Pritzker Prize–winner Mayne, especially the Caltrans District 7 Headquarters (2004) in Los Angeles and the San Francisco Federal Building (2007). Like his design for The Cooper Union, these buildings veil their mass behind perforated metal panels, which serve a dual purpose, cutting down on direct sunlight into the largely glass buildings while creating the primary means of expression for the architecture. At Cooper Union this expression is equal parts angular and flowing, like a metallic garment covered in random white pixels, lest the gray metal surface become unrelenting. The main façade overlooking triangular Cooper Square is marked by a deep incision that echoes the angular atrium rising from the corner entrance at East 7th Street. At sidewalk level the building is most revealing, as the first-floor glass walls angle back and provide an "underskirt" peek at the projection of the complex perforated wall in front of the simple glass box.

Access to the LEED Platinum building is limited, but it is worth taking a couple of steps inside to glimpse the dynamic thrust of the stairs up and away from the street. Mayne claims that the "vertical piazza" will foster "informal social, intellectual and creative exchange,"[3] a fairly common trend in secondary education today (see New York Law School [**14**] and the Diana Center [**121**]). Here the space, like the façade, clearly wants to break from the building's basic structure of stacked rectangular floor plates: irregular openings are enveloped by an "undulating lattice," also the architect's term. This inner realm may be limited to those benefiting from Peter Cooper's lasting free rides, but the impressive façade on Cooper Square lets the presence of this space be known to all.

35 Looking southeast from Cooper Union's Foundation Building (opposite). Photo by Adam Friedberg. **Angles abound, even where the building meets the ground (below, left).** Photo © Aaron Dougherty. **The façade bends up into a canopy with subtle cutout signage by Pentagram (below, center).** Photo © Aaron Dougherty. **Inside the lattice-wrapped atrium (below, right).** Photo by Scott Norsworthy.

36 EAST VILLAGE BROWNSTONE
BILL PETERSON ARCHITECT, 2004

224 East 14th Street, between Second and Third Avenues
🅛 **to Third Avenue**

Among the bars and cheap eateries catering to students and East Village hipsters on a stretch of 14th Street sits a brownstone with a perforated metal storefront, also brown, that exudes a certain Zen-like calm. This CNC-milled screen is a treat in and of itself, but it is even subtler than the surprise (barely) visible one floor above. The seven-story building is basically a formal reconstruction of the nineteenth-century brownstone that formerly occupied the site, but the gap around the two second-floor windows reveals that the 16-by-12-foot section actually retracts into the residence like a garage door. At the click of a button, the living space opens to the street and its trees (and traffic and bugs and other elements kept at bay by an air curtain), a contemporary device layered over the historical exterior. That the façade actually opens points to another contemporary maneuver: the brownstone appearance is just a thin veneer to reduce the weight of the wall.

36 Outside goes inside and inside becomes outside.
Photo © David Sundberg/Esto.

37 39 EAST 13TH STREET BUILDING
IO ARCHITECTS, 2008

39 East 13th Street, at University Place
④ ⑤ ⑥ 🅛 Ⓝ Ⓠ Ⓡ **to 14th Street–Union Square**

Like the East Village Brownstone (**36**) a few blocks east, this three-story addition by Philip Wu of io Architects attempts to meld old and new. Confronted with an existing four-story warehouse, the architect opted to restore the nineteenth-century cast iron building rather than demolish it and create anew from the ground up. The expansion above mimics the columns below, but instead of cast iron, the addition's "columns" are rendered in translucent channel glass, a gesture that privileges its predecessor as the generator of form. This front façade gives the impression that the glass wall rests on the wall below, but it actually cantilevers forward and floats above the existing structure. Visible from the intersection of 13th Street and University Place is the top-floor terrace, which takes advantage of views over the low neighbor all the way to the Hudson River.

37 Seen from University Place to the south,
a translucent glass box floats.

SHEILA C. JOHNSON DESIGN CENTER **38**

LYN RICE ARCHITECTS, 2008

66 Fifth Avenue, at 13th Street

④ ⑤ ⑥ Ⓛ Ⓝ Ⓠ Ⓡ to

14th Street–Union Square

4

38 Angular storefront windows project from the existing building.
Photo © Michael Moran.

A campus map of Parsons The New School for Design pinpoints buildings scattered in and around Greenwich Village, converging on the intersection of Fifth Avenue and 13th Street. Not surprisingly, this is the location of the school's campus center, a melding of four existing buildings dating back to the early 1900s. The Sheila C. Johnson Design Center can be seen as an internal campus quad for the 115-year-old institution, a better-late-than-never consolidation of studios, galleries, auditorium, and other spaces. It exposes some of these functions to the street, though most of the facilities are off limits to the public. Lyn Rice's design is a jumble of gestures (a diamond glazed skylight, a bark wall, a metal mesh elevator enclosure, white box galleries) that gel through the open spaces he knits together. Most notable from the street are the tilted and turned storefront windows and graphic canopies on both 13th Street and Fifth Avenue which spell out the name of the school and signal its presence in the city.

NYU DEPARTMENT OF PHILOSOPHY **39**

STEVEN HOLL ARCHITECTS, 2007

5 Washington Place, at Mercer Street

Ⓝ Ⓡ to 8th Street–NYU

New York University's Department of Philosophy occupies an impressive 1890 orange brick and stone building on the northeast corner of Washington Place and Mercer Street, in the NoHo Historic District. In this interior renovation of the six-story building, Steven Holl focused on the stairwell rising up the easternmost bay on Mercer. A peek into the lobby from the corner reveals the design's recurrent gesture: white walls with Swiss cheese–like openings allowing light to spill out from the stair (and vice versa). Porosity like this has been a theme of Holl's over the years, in combination with a core focus on the phenomenological properties of light and materials. Here light spans the vertical circulation and the different floors, anchoring the stair in the plan like a lantern leading the way. For visitors seeing the building from the street, a trip after sundown is best, but for the building's users, daytime is most striking when the prismatic film on the windows splits sunlight into its constituent colors, enlivening the all-white vertical space.

39 The stair's porous walls reach out into the lobby (far left). Inside the stairway, color is "applied" to the surfaces by light (left). Photos by Scott Norsworthy.

40 CENTER FOR ARCHITECTURE
ANDREW BERMAN ARCHITECT, 2003

536 LaGuardia Place, between Bleecker and West 3rd Streets
Ⓐ Ⓒ Ⓔ Ⓑ Ⓓ Ⓕ Ⓜ **to West 4th Street;**
Ⓖ **to Bleecker Street;** Ⓝ Ⓡ **to 8th Street–NYU**

The Center for Architecture houses the American Institute of Architects' (AIA) New York Chapter and the Center for Architecture Foundation, two nonprofit organizations that, respectively, provide resources for member architects and promote an appreciation of the built environment to the broader public. On any given weekday evening a number of events may be happening at The Center, be it AIA board meetings, lectures by and for architects, exhibition openings, or even performances. A quick glance from the sidewalk raises doubt whether this storefront can accommodate all of these at once, not to mention the office space for the two organizations. But a closer look at the center bay of the storefront reveals two additional floors below grade, visible through openings in the first floor and the one below, which create a diagonal vista from the street to the main lecture hall. It is actually possible to watch a lecture from the sidewalk!

Andrew Berman's competition-winning design is spatially complex—connecting the interior spaces to the public realm and bringing natural daylight into the deepest spaces—but simple in terms of surface and materials, enabling the exhibitions and other events to come to the fore. The architecture does not assert itself as something unique or different. It instead illustrates how an architect can shape space to reap the greatest benefit from certain conditions and restrictions, a subtle but fitting vehicle for clients promoting architecture. Heating and cooling are achieved with a geothermal heat pump system, novel at the time but more common with today's green architecture. Visitors can peek at the tip of the quarter-mile-deep wells from a windowed door on the first level below grade.

40 From the street the depth of the spaces is evident, here through the word "center" (left). Photo by Sam Lahoz. **Looking toward the street from the first-floor gallery (above).** Photo by Björn Wallander.

INFINITY CHAPEL **41**
HANRAHAN MEYERS ARCHITECTS, 2010

171 MacDougal Street,
between Waverly Place and West 8th Street
Ⓐ Ⓒ Ⓔ Ⓑ Ⓓ Ⓕ Ⓜ to West 4th Street;
Ⓖ to Bleecker Street; Ⓝ Ⓡ to 8th Street;
❶ to Christopher Street–Sheridan Square

41 The chapel's complex play of curves.

Photo © Michael Moran.

The date 1891, mounted on the brick just below the upper floor of this façade, marks the completion of the original Romanesque loft building at 171 MacDougal Street. But if the brick looks too new to be over a hundred years old that's because it is a recent "interpretive design" by TRA Studio. The architects peeled off the windowless brick shell from a 1966 redesign for the Tenth Church of Christ, Scientist, after the church decided to sell the unused upper floors to a developer, using the funds to redesign the chapel and other spaces below. Beyond the new orange brick façade, architects Thomas Hanrahan and Victoria Meyers have created a light-filled sacred space composed of curving walls. Referencing the endless loop of a Moebius strip, the complex yet serene chapel is reached through the lobby/reading room they also designed. Look for the book pedestals with glass tops, used to bring natural light into the duo's third and last contribution, the Sunday school in the basement.

THE TOWNHOMES OF DOWNING STREET **42**
1100: ARCHITECT, 2011

22–26 Downing Street
❶ to Houston Street

Most of the attention given to boom-time residential developments at the beginning of the twenty-first century focused on iconic high-rise buildings, stacked luxury condos with innovative skins of glass and metal. Nevertheless, participants in the residential building boom include small-scale insertions into the city, such as these three town houses on quiet Downing Street, half a block removed from Sixth Avenue. Developed on vacant lots by Urban Muse—responsible for the "Sky Garages" at 200 Eleventh Avenue (**61**)—and designed by David Piscuskas and Juergen Riehm, the roughly 6,000-square-foot town houses have a singular expression: flat sandstone cladding with dark window frames projecting slightly from the minimalist surface; only a shallow vertical reveal separates the entity into a trio. Each town house features three windows across, with variation coming in groupings of windows on the two ends. It is an elegant ensemble that does not try to make a statement with over-the-top flourishes. Regardless, the structure stands out in the Greenwich Village Historic District.

42 Three town houses, one elevation.
Photo by Jackie Caradonio.

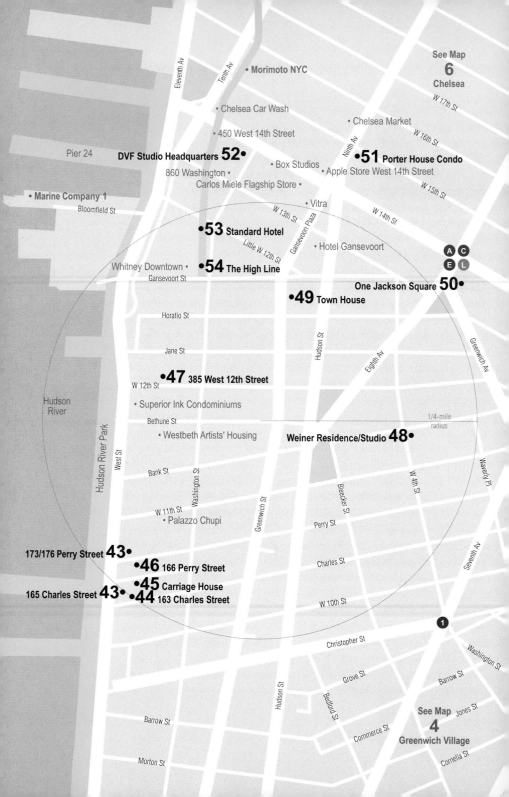

The West Village, spanning from Sixth or Seventh
Avenue to the Hudson River, and from Houston Street to 14th Street, is best known for being different, mainly because it does not follow the 1811 gridiron plan that can be found to its north; this makes sense since the streets predate the plan. Furthermore, much of the population was sick with yellow fever and cholera around that time, so the city gladly skipped the area in its implementation of the plan. Most of the West Village falls within the Greenwich Village Historic District and its extensions, minus the formerly industrial strip along the waterfront—sometimes referred to as the Far West Village—which has seen the majority of recent development in the area. The combination of the off-the-grid street plan and a well-preserved residential fabric make this part of the Village one of the most popular places in Manhattan with residents and tourists alike.

To see the changes wrought by new construction in the Far West Village, a stroll or bike ride up the Hudson River Walk is recommended. The park underfoot is one spark that ignited what's been dubbed the "new condo coast," a strip where developers have built higher than is possible anywhere else in the immediate area, thanks to generous commercial zoning. A 2005 rezoning of the area toward retaining the low-scale fabric should ironically keep the early-2000s skyline as well preserved as the historic district behind it.

Even more dramatic is the transformation of the Meatpacking District in the last few decades, a shift from industrial to commercial use. From Gansevoort Street to West 15th Street west of Ninth Avenue, boutiques, galleries, restaurants, clubs, hotels, and offices occupy the buildings that long ago housed the area's namesake businesses. The nineteenth-century Gansevoort Market—the district's official moniker— became the largest location for the slaughtering and packing of meat in the city well before the 1950 opening of the Gansevoort Meat Center, which gained the area the status of "the largest meat and poultry receiving market in the world," according to the *New York Times*. A gradual decline followed this peak, and now only a handful of the meatpackers still operate in the area, easily overshadowed by the high-end commercial establishments and fashion shoots on the cobblestone streets.

The Meatpacking District may be small, but it is well stocked with high-profile buildings and interiors. This density of design stems from the area's popularity as a nighttime destination but also from the

5

redevelopment of the High Line railway viaduct into an elevated linear park; the southern tip is located in the district. The area is marked by a mix of old and new, a contrast of brick and cobblestone against steel and glass. The city's 2003 designation of Gansevoort Market as a historic district helped cement this diversity.

43 173–176 PERRY STREET, 165 CHARLES STREET

5

RICHARD MEIER & PARTNERS ARCHITECTS, 2002, 2006

173–176 Perry Street and 165 Charles Street, at West Street
❶ to Christopher Street–Sheridan Square

This trio of glass towers facing the Hudson River and its new park were designed and built in two phases: the two Perry Street towers were built simultaneously, and the Charles Street tower followed four years later. They were designed by Richard Meier for different clients, and there are slight but noticeable differences between the former and the latter that point to the separate developers and the changing market conditions—even for the super-rich—in the years in between. Each of the sixteen-story Perry Street towers features one unit per floor with 270-degree views; these are accommodated by placing the elevator and stair cores on the east, turning their backs on the low-scale West Village. Furthermore, a ladder-like white metal armature is poised in front of the Perry Street façades overlooking the Hudson, and the balconies are guarded by translucent glass panels. The Charles Street tower differs from its predecessors in all of these characteristics except the height (also sixteen stories) and the core placement: each floor is split between two units, expressed in a vertical reveal in the middle of the west façade. Gone is the metal grid fronting the glass wall. And finally, clear glass guardrails offer unobstructed views.

Just as the twentieth-century glass office towers in New York and other cities paled in comparison to High Modernism, most notably that of Mies van der Rohe, Meier set the bar fairly high for developers and their architects in the ensuing condo boom. Uninspired examples followed, many of which lacked the

important combination of glass walls and name-brand architect that the Perry Street duo initiated. (To compare these towers to Meier's first Manhattan project, walk north a few blocks to Bethune Street for a glance at the courtyard of the introverted Westbeth artists' housing.)

43 The three towers reflect the Hudson River sunset (above). Photo by Scott Norsworthy. **Looking up West Street with the Charles Street tower in the foreground (left).**

163 CHARLES STREET 44
DANIEL GOLDNER ARCHITECTS, 2008

163 Charles Street, between
Washington and West Streets
❶ to Christopher
Street-Sheridan Square

Immediately next door to Richard Meier's third sixteen-story glass tower (**43**) fronting the Hudson River is this condo building, half as tall, and only 22 feet wide, yet targeting the same ultra-exclusive buyers. Housing three units on eight floors, Daniel Goldner's design staggers deep balconies to give punch to the narrow façade on Charles Street. The first two floors meet the sidewalk and the older neighbor to the east, while the upper floors are set back to meet the neighbor on the west; in this sense the design mediates between the historical Village context and the glass towers. A continuous ribbon of metal and white brick seems to form a question mark, but as ceiling and wall it serves to draw residents and visitors back to the lobby along a side walkway. A trip around back to Charles Lane is recommended for a view of the rear of the building and its small neighbor to the east (**45**).

44 A question mark sits below the alternating balconies. Photo by David Joseph.

CARRIAGE HOUSE 45
CHRISTOFF:FINIO ARCHITECTURE, 2006

12 Charles Lane, between Washington and West Streets
❶ to Christopher Street-Sheridan Square

Charles Lane is a one-block-long alley that separates two of Richard Meier's sixteen-story towers (**43**) at its western terminus, but its Belgian block paving harks back to another era. The twenty-first-century Modernism extends west down the alley with the backs of buildings by Daniel Goldner Architects (**44**) and Asymptote Architecture (**46**), but a two-story carriage house by Taryn Christoff and Martin Finio (who also designed the same building's penthouse addition facing Charles Street) commands as much attention as its bigger neighbors. A simple glazed upper story sits above a wall screening a shallow "urban garage" housing bikes and garbage cans. Defining the latter are metal bands that twist 90 degrees as they span from top to bottom, each one perpendicular to the next. The effect is solid at an oblique angle but porous head-on. The design elevates the mundane and is a gem to discover.

45 Light filters through the twisting screen onto Charles Lane. Photo by Jan Staller.

46

166 PERRY STREET
ASYMPTOTE ARCHITECTURE, 2010

166 Perry Street, between Washington and West Streets
❶ to Christopher Street–Sheridan Square

Before construction on this eight-story condo building began, the avant-garde designers Hani Rashid and LiseAnn Couture had realized only a few projects in New York City, all small interiors: an "advanced trading floor" for the New York Stock Exchange, the Carlos Miele flagship store on West 14th Street in the Meatpacking District, and the SoHo café and store for the Italian design company Alessi. These environments fused technology, innovative materials, and non-Euclidean geometries to create spaces that felt like the not-too-distant future when unveiled. The same can be said of their first building in the city, twenty-one residences directly next door to Richard Meier's first ground-up project (**43**) in the district.

Proximity to the Perry and Charles Street towers naturally draws comparisons, but that trio is also a point of departure for Rashid and Couture, who admit their design is "an antidotal design and a formal and tectonic play off of Meier's buildings."[1] This effort is expended on the north and south façades, composed of angled glass panes that alternately reflect the sky and buildings opposite. As with Jean Nouvel's tower in Chelsea (**58**), the articulation of the glass and metal elements discourages a reading of the stacked floors, something that is readily apparent with most exterior walls, be they masonry or glass. Like a waterfall, the façade exudes movement, capturing a moment in time both as a physical metaphor and as a marker of early-twenty-first-century contemporary architecture.

46 The building as seen from the west, with the concrete core of Meier's building on the right (left). Close-up of the entry seen from the east (right).

385 WEST 12TH STREET **47**
FLANK ARCHITECTURE, 2010

385 West 12th Street, between
Washington and West Streets
🚈 to Christopher Street–Sheridan
Square; 🅐 🅒 🅔 to 14th Street;
🅛 to Eighth Avenue

5

47 The building seems to rise
almost naturally toward its
stepped profile.

On one of the few true east-west streets in
Manhattan sits a twelve-unit condo building
co-developed by Peter Moore with frequent
collaborator FLANK. The design is articulated
like an organic assemblage of vertical bays
rising to different heights and with different
profiles. Its size, massing, and variegated façade recall the Hudson Hill Condominium (**97**), but in contrast to the artificial longevity of the Clinton condo's
wood-grain laminate panels, this copper skin will slowly patinate over time from
brown to green. (Even as construction was nearing completion, some green
could be found on water-prone areas around windows.) This anticipated patina
explains the narrow vertical bands of green glass that stripe much of the façade.
On this tree-lined street near the Hudson River, the slow transformation over time
will lend the building a more monolithic appearance as it blends in with its natural
neighbors. Nature's entropy is embraced, not denied.

WEINER RESIDENCE/STUDIO **48**
LOT-EK, 2007

297 West 4th Street, between
West 11th and Bank Streets
🚈 to Christopher Street–Sheridan Square

LOT-EK's Ada Tolle and Giuseppe Lignano—designers
known for their reuse of shipping containers and other
industrial artifacts—seem to have tempered their usual
tendencies in this renovation and expansion of a two-
story 1910 building in the Greenwich Village Historic
District. But a closer look at the three projecting windows
reveals some atypical details: diamond tread sills and
projecting handles on the jambs. The bay windows are
actually the rear frames of truck bodies, repurposed to
function as a bench, nook, or platform bed on different
floors of the artist's studio and living spaces. Not visible
from the street is more industrial reuse: a vertical service
core fashioned from sheet metal ducts and two more
truck bodies—in full—making up the penthouse.

48 Old truck bays project from a brick wall.
Photo by Nikolas Koenig.

49 Looking northwest, with Morris Adjmi's home for Theory next door (left). The narrow windows give peeks at the glass and green of the rear façade (right).

49 TOWN HOUSE
MATTHEW BAIRD ARCHITECTS, 2005

829 Greenwich Street, between Horatio and Gansevoort Streets
Ⓐ Ⓒ Ⓔ to 14th St; Ⓛ to Eighth Avenue

Cor-Ten, or weathering steel, is a material that found a brief popularity in architecture in the 1960s—see the Ford Foundation Building on East 42nd Street—but is primarily associated with the artist Richard Serra. His sometimes monumental sculptures almost exclusively utilize rust-covered sheets; curving, coiling, leaning, they approach architecture in their scale and definition of space. The contemporary use of Cor-Ten in architecture can be attributed to Serra's influence. Here the material is used in unarticulated solid sheets. The residential development at 30 Orchard Street (**23**) is in this vein, as is this town house in the Greenwich Village Historic District.

Matthew Baird's design replaces a dilapidated old building that actually fell in on itself shortly after the clients bought the property. A single sheet of Cor-Ten steel an inch and a quarter thick—14 feet wide by 34 feet high—hangs across the four-story façade. (A portion of the George Washington Bridge had to be closed so it could be trucked into Manhattan!) Narrow vertical bands of glass on either side of the steel bring daylight into the 5,000-square-foot interior, but most of the natural lighting in the house arrives through the fully glazed rear façade and through skylights. Given the location within a historic district, the design was subject to review by the Landmarks Preservation Commission. Its approval is evidence of a preference for contemporary buildings that differentiate themselves from older neighbors. Nevertheless, the design is symbolic of the rift between those who appreciate contemporary difference and those who prefer to respect historic neighbors by copying them.

ONE JACKSON SQUARE 50

KOHN PEDERSEN FOX ASSOCIATES with SLCE Architects, 2009

122 Greenwich Avenue, at Eighth Avenue

Ⓐ Ⓒ Ⓔ to 14th St; Ⓛ to Eighth Avenue

Since the 1920s, when a series of row houses was demolished to accommodate the Eighth Avenue subway beneath it, this six-sided, wedge-shaped site, located across from Jackson Square and within the Greenwich Village Historic District, was used as a parking lot. The area's desirability made the difficult underground conditions worth tackling in order to build on the site. Like Schermerhorn House in Brooklyn (**130**), this thirty-five-unit condominium building uses a supersized foundation to cantilever over the subway tunnel.

Above ground the building's design is influenced by the obtuse angle formed by Greenwich and Eighth Avenues and their respective zoning districts that split the site in two. The volume of the building follows the angle of the site but undulates like "a found object, like a rock in a rushing stream that influences the shape and form of the water flowing over it,"[2] according to the architects. Each stacked floor has its own shape irrespective of the ones above and/or below, basically reflecting the architects' words. Curved glass buildings often appear faceted and angular instead of flowing, but the relative success of this iteration is aided by the narrow panes of full-height glass and the varied spacing of the vertical mullions, further integrated with operable windows. These undulations unite the two otherwise distinct volumes that follow from the different zoning allowances: eleven stories on Eighth and seven stories on Greenwich across from the park. At the crux of the two volumes, behind a glass storefront the lobby features striated bamboo panels, a 220-foot-long installation by Brooklyn's Situ Studio.

50 The view north up Greenwich Avenue; the eleven-story volume projects in the distance (left). Undulating wood walls curl into the lobby (above). Photos by Paúl Rivera/Archphoto.

51 PORTER HOUSE CONDO

SHoP ARCHITECTS, 2003

366 West 15th Street, at Ninth Avenue
Ⓐ Ⓒ Ⓔ to 14th St; Ⓛ to Eighth Avenue

Like many of the recent interventions in the Meatpacking District, Porter House, named for the cut of meat—recalling the area's ever-dwindling namesake enterprises—is a renovation, in this case of a six-story, 30,000-square-foot warehouse. In a move that recall's Winka Dubbeldam's 497 Greenwich Street **(17)**, this residential development adds floors above the existing structure, also cantilevering over its neighbors to the south. Definitely the most striking aspect of SHoP Architects' design is the façade, made up of three components: zinc metal panels (in four thousand unique shapes), full-height windows, and internally mounted light boxes. This last element gives the project its image. It's best seen at night from Gansevoort Plaza south of 14th Street, when the area shifts from daytime shopping to nighttime partying, as revelers hit the numerous bars, restaurants, and clubs. A canopy, resembling the type once ubiquitous over the meatpackers' loading docks, caps the building's first floor and further refers to the area's history.

While the condo entrance is on Ninth Avenue, a vertical band of zinc, glass, and light boxes on 15th Street links the ground floor to the new floors above. This less than subtle integration of dark zinc and yellow brick reveals the latter to be exactly what it is: a shallow skin. As new confronts old, the architects exploit their similarities (both exteriors are hung off the structural frame) and differences (the addition's computer-created custom panels contrast with the existing building's modular bricks), creating a striking addition of dark and light.

51 Seen from the south, the addition bridges historical buildings of various sizes (above). Seen from the west across Ninth Avenue, the cantilever is most apparent (right).

DVF STUDIO HEADQUARTERS **52**
WORK ARCHITECTURE COMPANY, 2007

440 West 14th Street, at Washington Street
Ⓐ Ⓒ Ⓔ to 14th St; Ⓛ to Eighth Avenue

The headquarters of the Diane von Furstenberg fashion design company, DVF Studio is a transformation of two landmark brick buildings. Given their status, the exterior only hints at the changes inside, most overtly through a crystalline structure atop the roof, visible from the street and the High Line (**54**) to the south. A staircase climbs diagonally from the entrance on West 14th Street toward this skylight structure, uniting a diverse mix of public and private spaces—a store on the ground floor (the extent of public access), offices and showroom above, an apartment at the top. Envisioned by architects Dan Wood and Amale Andraos as a "shaft of light" through the now combined existing buildings, the open stair is lined with glass crystals on steel cables. The "stairdelier," as the architects dubbed it, is illuminated by heliostats mounted to the roof.

The headquarters was the first renovation in the Gansevoort Market Historic District. In order to receive Landmarks Preservation Commission approval, the architects argued that their design promised "new life in the district," at the same time restoring the main façades of the existing building while adding a new canopy across both façades. This example of "façadectomy" is more sensitive to the existing structure than in buildings like Hearst Tower (**99**) that transplant taller buildings on top of low-rise bases. Here the crystal "growth" signals something new and fresh without overpowering the shell within which it sits.

52 Looking up the "stairdelier" lined in glass crystals (left). The diagonal shaft of light cuts from the penthouse down to the entrance (below). Photos by Elizabeth Felicella.

53 STANDARD HOTEL
ENNEAD ARCHITECTS, 2009

848 Washington Street, at Little West 12th Street
Ⓐ Ⓒ Ⓔ to 14th St; Ⓛ to Eighth Avenue

The redevelopment of the mile-and-a-half-long stretch of the High Line (**54**) into a park has spurred loads of development, but none as daring as André Balazs's stylish boutique hotel which actually straddles the old railway viaduct. At eighteen stories the hotel is short by Manhattan standards, but it is tall for the area, and its location one block north of the southernmost entry to the elevated park solidifies its visibility, as strollers pass under it daily. Furthermore, the kink at the plan's midpoint—emphasizing the building's freedom from the city grid—gives the hotel a distinctive skyline presence.

Todd Schliemann of Ennead Architects (formerly Polshek Partnership) crafted the hotel from concrete and glass. The former, occasionally blended with gray brick, is finished raw, emphasizing its structural role in raising the building fifty-seven feet above the sidewalk. The full-height glazing of the curtain wall at each floor covers the majority of the north- and south-facing elevations, giving the hotel its reputation as a "voyeur's delight." For people not lucky or daring enough to stay in one of the 337 see-and-be-seen rooms (interiors were designed by Roman and Williams), the entry plaza/café and a beer garden, added later, are respectively pleasing and raucous spaces nestled beneath the High Line and one of the hotel's tapering concrete piers.

53 The hotel acts as a gateway to the High Line near its southern entrance (top). Photo by Richard Anderson. **Looking up at the concrete and glass building bridging the old rail viaduct (above).**

54 The plantings are striking year-round; looking south toward the Gansevoort entrance in the fall.

HIGH LINE **54**

JAMES CORNER FIELD OPERATIONS with Diller Scofidio + Renfro, 2009

Entry at Gansevoort and Washington Streets

Ⓐ Ⓒ Ⓔ to 14th St; Ⓛ to Eighth Avenue

After nearly eighty years of accidents caused by freight trains chugging along Manhattan's West Side, an elevated railway was constructed and completed in 1934. In its functioning years, the High Line ran from 34th Street to Spring Street— primarily along Tenth Avenue and Washington Streets—serving the numerous industrial buildings it passed alongside and in many case through. But with the rise of trucking in the 1950s, the railway was no longer necessary. Train operations ceased in 1980, about fifteen years after the section south of Gansevoort Street was demolished. (A remnant can be seen at the eastern end of the Westbeth artists' housing.)

Inspired by the Promenade Plantée in Paris, in 1999 Joshua David and Robert Hammond established the nonprofit Friends of the High Line (FHL) to advocate for reuse of the viaduct as a public park instead of its demolition, requested by the owners of adjacent buildings at the time. The efforts of FHL led the city to file for railbanking—turning over unused lines for recreational purposes—to save the structure. Later the nonprofit held a design competition and selected landscape architect James Corner and architects Elizabeth Diller, Ricardo Scofidio, and Charles Renfro as the design team for the park. Construction began in 2006 after the city took ownership of the portion of the High Line below 30th Street.

The designers' plan for the abandoned elevated railway spanning twenty-two city blocks was inspired by what they called "the melancholic, found beauty of the High Line, where nature has reclaimed a once-vital piece of urban infrastructure."[3] They combined organic matter and building materials into a blend that blurs the typical hard line between the two. Custom-made tapered pavers

54 The Tenth Avenue amphitheater at dusk. Photo by Scott Norsworthy.

allow the plantings to poke through and create a gradient where hard and soft are enmeshed. Native vegetation, carried out with planting designer Piet Oudolf, recalls the photographs of Joel Sternfeld, who captured the High Line's "found beauty" and helped FHL spur public interest in the project and raise millions of dollars toward the cause.

The park is being realized in phases. The first phase, from Gansevoort to 20th Street, opened in 2009; at the time of writing in late 2010 the second phase, extending northward to 30th Street, is set to open in the spring; and the last section, wrapping around the Hudson Yards and terminating along 34th Street, is in the process of being acquired by the city, so its future remains uncertain, though supporters are optimistic about its eventual integration into the park. As the park continues uptown, so do adjacent developments, sparked by the success of this one-of-a-kind urban amenity.

Overall the design consists of access points, walkways with border vegetation, and nodes of activity or repose. In detail the design features stairs framed in Cor-Ten steel, glass-walled elevators, precast concrete plank walkways, wood benches rising from the walkways, preserved railway tracks and ties, public art, native plantings, and subtle lighting. The pockets of space or nodes that invite stopping during a slow stroll are treated uniquely. For example, where the High Line crosses Tenth Avenue, visitors can gaze southward from a grove of trees to the Statue of Liberty or descend a ramped amphitheater to "inhabit the structure" and catch views of Midtown to the north. These and other site-specific microclimates create an experience both varied and memorable, rewarding repeat visits and boosting anticipation for the park's extension.

54 Benches curl up from the precast pavers (right). Photo by Scott Norsworthy. **Gehry. Nouvel. Shigeru.** The High Line spurred big money and big names (below).

DESIGNER SHOPPING

The relationship between fashion and architecture is an important and multifaceted one in contemporary society. Each influences the other through their articulation of form and surface; personalities from one field are clients of the other; and most important, a search for the new and innovative is a trait shared by both. The influence of fashion can be found in buildings with fabric-like skins, such as Frank Gehry's 8 Spruce Street (**9**) and SANAA's New Museum (**27**), but a more direct relationship between the two realms is found in the design of retail spaces for high-end fashion houses. Centered in areas such as SoHo and Chelsea, and along Fifth Avenue, the following interiors illustrate what happens when architects are faced with creating spaces that bring out the best in the designer duds on display.

TRIBECA ISSEYMIYAKE
GEHRY PARTNERS with G TECTS, 2001
119 Hudson Street, at North Moore Street (Map 2)

Creating a miniature of his large-scale buildings popular since the Guggenheim in Bilbao (1997), Frank Gehry uses flowing sheets of metal inside this Tribeca storefront as a fitting wrapper for the clothes springing from the innovative techniques of Japanese fashion designer Issey Miyake. Like his garments made from only one piece of cloth, the titanium winds through the space in an apparently continuous band. Here the flows frame not only the clothes but occasional events held in the space as well.

DEREK LAM
SANAA, 2009
10–12 Crosby Street, between Howard and Grand Streets (Map 2)

A couple of years after the Japanese duo Kazuyo Sejima and Ryue Nishizawa made a splash in Manhattan with the New Museum of Contemporary Art on the Bowery (**27**), their boutique for San Francisco-based designer Derek Lam opened. The brick and cobblestone of this block of Crosby Street is juxtaposed with curved walls of glass, transparent containers for Lam's fashions. At 2,700 square feet, the design is like a small-scale version of the pair's Glass Pavilion at the Toledo Museum of Art (2006) in Ohio. Photo courtesy Derek Lam.

PRADA
OFFICE FOR METROPOLITAN
ARCHITECTURE, 2001
575 Broadway, at Prince Street (Map 2)

Prada invested $40 million in this renovation of the 23,000-square-foot former Guggenheim SoHo space at the area's busiest intersection. The Italian fashion label entrusted the project to Rem Koolhaas and OMA*AMO, whose research with the Harvard University Graduate School of Design on the ubiquity of shopping and consumption treated the commission as a thesis project on reinventing retail. The wave and changing mural blend into a memorable space, but the shopping—aided by technology—actually happens in the basement. Photo by Scott Norsworthy.

LONGCHAMP SOHO
HEATHERWICK STUDIO, 2006
132 Spring Street, between Greene and Wooster Streets (Map 2)

Glass doors in an otherwise blank brick wall barely hint at the dramatic space for French leather goods company Longchamp that lies beyond. A ribbon-like stair is the defining element that ties the ground floor with the larger second floor above. Longchamp makes handbags, among other things, so appropriately the continuous treads appear to be made of leather (they are rubber on steel plate). Glass guardrails—fabricated the same way as car windshields— look like billowing fabric frozen in motion. All is skylit, like a luxury stairway to heaven. Photo by Scott Norsworthy.

ARMANI FIFTH AVENUE
MASSIMILIANO FUKSAS ARCHITETTO, 2009
717 Fifth Avenue, at 56th Street (Map 8)

Italy's Doriana and Massimiliano Fuksas designed three stores for their countryman Giorgio Armani, one in China, one in Japan, and the last a few blocks south of Central Park. A central staircase winds up four flights like a ribbon unfurled, recalling Frank Lloyd Wright's Guggenheim thirty blocks up Fifth Avenue. Spiraling, overlapping, and flowing like fabric, the complex insertion makes its predecessor look tame.

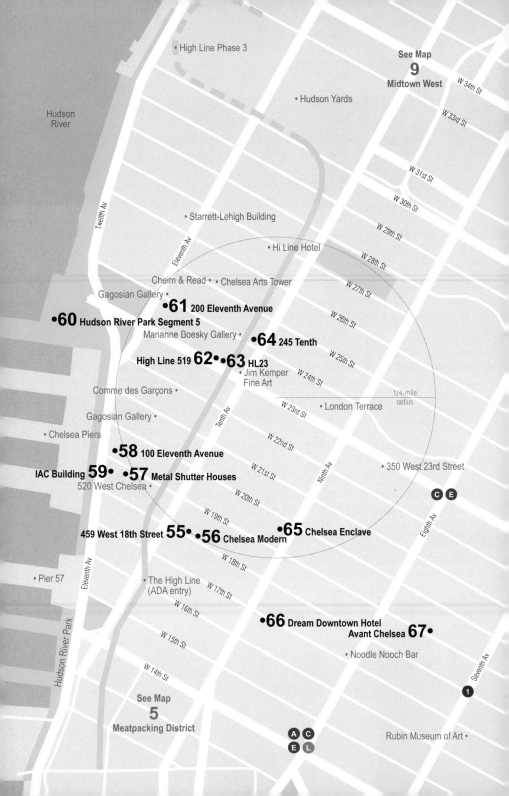

High Line Phase 3

See Map
9
Midtown West

W 34th St
W 33rd St
W 31st St
W 30th St
W 29th St
W 28th St
W 27th St
W 26th St
W 25th St
W 24th St
W 23rd St
W 22nd St
W 21st St
W 20th St
W 19th St
W 18th St
W 17th St
W 16th St
W 15th St
W 14th St

Hudson Yards

Hudson
River

Twelfth Av
Eleventh Av
Tenth Av
Ninth Av
Eighth Av
Seventh Av

Starrett-Lehigh Building

Hi Line Hotel

Cheim & Read • • Chelsea Arts Tower

Gagosian Gallery •

•**61** 200 Eleventh Avenue

•**60** Hudson River Park Segment 5

Marianne Boesky Gallery •

•**64** 245 Tenth

High Line 519 **62**••**63** HL23

• Jim Kemper
Fine Art

Comme des Garçons •

1/4-mile
radius

• London Terrace

Gagosian Gallery •

• Chelsea Piers

•**58** 100 Eleventh Avenue

IAC Building **59**• •**57** Metal Shutter Houses
520 West Chelsea •

• 350 West 23rd Street

C **E**

459 West 18th Street **55**• •**56** Chelsea Modern

•**65** Chelsea Enclave

• Pier 57

The High Line
(ADA entry)

Hudson River Park

Eleventh Av

•**66** Dream Downtown Hotel
Avant Chelsea **67**•

• Noodle Nooch Bar

See Map
5
Meatpacking District

A **C**
E **L**

Rubin Museum of Art •

1

While the name Chelsea for the section of Man-

hattan west of Eighth Avenue between 14th and 30th Streets dates back to the eighteenth-century estate of British Major Thomas Clarke, it was not until the 1811 platting of Manhattan into its grid of blocks that development really got started by his grandson Clement Clarke Moore, best known as the author of the "night before Christmas" poem, "A Visit from St. Nicholas." Residential blocks filled the streets between Eighth and Tenth Avenues, but west of here an industrial zone took shape, served by waterfront access and the Hudson River Railroad freight line. The railroad was elevated in the early 1930s in response to accidents and deaths at the dangerous grade crossings; this is the rail line that, after sitting dormant since its closure in 1980, is being transformed piece by piece into the mile-and-a-half-long High Line (**54**).

6

Before the reuse of the High Line as a linear park even took its first steps, the former industrial area in West Chelsea had undergone substantial change. As rising rents in SoHo forced out artists and then galleries, and as industrial buildings in Chelsea sat vacant after shipping moved from the adjacent waterways and piers to distant container ports and highways, the center of the New York City art scene shifted to this area west of Tenth Avenue. The Dia Center for the Arts opened on West 22nd Street near Eleventh Avenue in 1987, and galleries slowly followed, rising in number to an estimated three hundred by 2010. (Dia: Chelsea closed in 2004, initially eyeing the spot next to the High Line's Gansevoort entrance, a location soon to be the home of the downtown branch of the Whitney Museum of American Art, but at this writing Dia planned on reopening in its old location.)

The infusion of galleries into West Chelsea involved small bits of new construction, but most of the change was internal, happening within the large former warehouse spaces. A more substantial physical transformation of the area can be attributed to the reuse of the High Line as a park—the process started in 1999, and the first phase opened in 2009—and the related Special West Chelsea District zoning created by the Department of City Planning. The first gave the area a unique amenity paralleling the nearby Hudson River Park, and the second aimed to "provide opportunities for new residential and commercial development,"[1] among other goals. A walk along the High Line testifies to this combo's success.

55, 56 Seen from the High Line are 459 West 18th (left) and Chelsea Modern (right).

55 459 WEST 18TH
DELLA VALLE BERNHEIMER, 2009

459 West 18th Street, between Ninth and Tenth Avenues
① to 18th Street; **C** **E** to 23rd Street

It is not uncommon for properties to fall into more than one zoning district, leading to unique and sometimes irreconcilable bulk and height restrictions for as-of-right developments. Some architects find inspiration in these conditions, visible in Loadingdock5's 904 Pacific Street (**143**), and this eleven-story condo building on West 18th Street, designed and developed by Jared Della Valle and Andrew Bernheimer. The duo composed the form to assume "the shape of the idealized zoning diagram ... articulated as a pair of linked or nested dualities."[2] Eschewing the prevailing trend of all-glass skins, black and white aluminum-clad volumes interlock with large horizontal expanses of glass. Compare and contrast the design with their building six blocks north at 245 Tenth Avenue (**64**).

56 CHELSEA MODERN
AUDREY MATLOCK ARCHITECT, 2009

447 West 18th Street, between Ninth and Tenth Avenues
① to 18th Street; **C** **E** to 23rd Street

When seen from the High Line, the developments at 447 and 459 West 18th Street read like one project, albeit one with a split personality. The former with its ripples of blue glass and the latter with its interlocking black and white volumes may not physically resemble each other, but their shouts for attention link them as much as the property line they share. The horizontal glass planes of the Chelsea Modern are grouped into five alternating zigzag bands rising twelve stories, with the last four floors set back in respect to the zoning requirements. So the basic volume dictated by zoning is made dynamic through the articulation of the exterior wall, a common technique at the beginning of the twenty-first century for developers looking to draw attention to their properties, be it in Chelsea, the West Village (**46**), Clinton (**95**), or even Brooklyn (**136**).

524 West 19th Street, between Tenth and Eleventh Avenues
1 to 18th Street; **C E** to 23rd Street

Japanese architect Shigeru Ban veers between two extremes: high-budget houses, primarily in his home country, and disaster relief shelters constructed from cardboard and other inexpensive materials for displaced peoples around the globe. His experiments with paper tubes typically used to form concrete columns found their way to New York City in an archway over MoMA's courtyard in 2000 and the Nomadic Museum five years later, which traveled to California and Tokyo inside the shipping containers that also made up its walls. Ban's first permanent commission in the city straddles the pricey minimalism of his residential commissions and the low-budget experiments that constitute a good chunk of the architect's oeuvre.

This nine-unit condominium development steps from the High Line (**54**) takes its name from the motorized screens that face West 19th Street; the perforated metal shutters act as privacy screens for the double-height living spaces behind. Folding glass walls also enable the interiors to be opened entirely to the outside. The shutters and glass walls combine to create a gradient of possibilities for the façade: open, closed, or a number of positions and combinations in between. The building is bracketed by Frank Gehry's IAC Building (**59**) to the west and a condo development designed by Annabelle Selldorf to the east; Ban's design occupies a realm between the predominantly glassy exterior of the latter and the fritted glass obscuring Gehry's flowing exterior. As executed, the metal shutters only occasionally exhibit the minimalist appeal of early renderings. More often they resemble the ubiquitous storefront shutters, an appealing contextual reference but hardly one to emulate in high-priced residential architecture.

57 The translucency of the shutters is evident in the evening.
Photo © Albert Vecerka/Esto.

58 Trees "float" in the interstitial space at the corner (left). Detail of the modular curtain wall and foreground screen (above). Photo by Scott Norsworthy.

58 100 ELEVENTH AVENUE

ATELIERS JEAN NOUVEL with Beyer Blinder Belle, 2010

100 Eleventh Avenue, at 19th Street
1 to 18th Street; **C** **E** to 23rd Street

At the start of construction for Jean Nouvel's second building in Manhattan, the twenty-year-old Institut du Monde Arabe in Paris—striking for its glass wall with mechanical apertures—was noted as an antecedent to his design for Chelsea's "vision machine." But it is actually his Fondation Cartier, also in Paris, that is a more direct influence on the twenty-three-story glass tower across the street from Frank Gehry's IAC Building (**59**). Most overtly this influence occurs at the six-story base, which stands fifteen feet in front of the building's façade and screens the vertical garden at the corner, just as the glass street wall of the Fondation Cartier screens a mature cedar in front of the building proper. This interstitial space features custom hanging planters with mature trees and plants suspended over the planned lobby restaurant. It is landscape as sculpture, trees as elements of beauty and representations of nature, not functioning parts of natural processes.

The curving glass façade of the tower is as striking a composition as any recent building in New York City, or elsewhere for that matter. Close to 1,700 uniquely sized and uniquely oriented panes of colorless glass make up the two main elevations that wrap around the corner from West 19th Street to Eleventh Avenue. Like abstract art lifted onto a building, the effect eschews the stacking that makes floors readable as such, even though the curtain wall is built from bays assembled off site and lifted into place. (Double mullions separated by small gaps in the horizontal and vertical directions illustrate this means of construction.) The rear of the building is hardly an afterthought; seen from the High Line (**54**), openings of various sizes are punched into black brick walls, like a sampling of the glass panes facing Gehry's IAC Building and the Hudson River.

555 West 18th Street, at Eleventh Avenue
❶ to 18th Street; ⒞ ⒠ to 23rd Street

Frank Gehry—the most famous architect in the world at the turn of the century thanks to the attention claimed by his Guggenheim Museum (1997) in Bilbao, Spain—realized his first ground-up building in New York City in 2007, at the age of seventy-eight. This headquarters for Barry Diller's Internet conglomerate IAC/InterActiveCorp fits into the post-Bilbao phase of the architect's sculptural buildings: curves, curves, and more curves. But instead of the sheets of titanium or stainless steel that define most of Gehry's twenty-first-century oeuvre, glass exclusively covers this exterior, over 1,300 unique panes actually shaped on site. Gradients of fritted dots on the insulated glass are used in lieu of traditionally solid spandrel glass, avoiding the hard-edged banding of modern glass boxes and "acting as an integrated sunscreen," according to IAC's literature.

The flowing and twisting curves do not rise unimpeded from the sidewalk to the top; a setback splits the building into top and bottom zones in deference to zoning, but it is an abrupt break at odds with the design. Regardless, the greater torque of the top gives the building a sensuality that belies the fact that it is constructed from a usually flat material. Unfortunately the lower portion fails to reconcile itself with the sidewalk or its surroundings. The mostly impenetrable ground floor does not offer anything to passersby but glances of the video art in the semi-public lobby. A narrow outdoor space east of the building also teases people with a screened view into an inaccessible bamboo garden. Born of a desire on the part of Diller to improve this area of Chelsea, the building falls short in failing to interact with the neighborhood beyond adding a pretty building by a famous name.

59 After sunset the fritted dots disappear (left). The building's beauty is best appreciated from below (right). Photos by Scott Norsworthy.

60 HUDSON RIVER PARK SEGMENT 5
MICHAEL VAN VALKENBURGH ASSOCIATES, 2010

Hudson River from Gansevoort Street to 24th Street
C **E** to 23rd Street

In 1999 the Hudson River Park Trust began work on a string of green spaces extending from Battery Park to 59th Street on Manhattan's West Side, an area once home to more than fifty piers for freight and passenger ships. The decline of commercial shipping in the middle of the twentieth century led to the Westway plan of the 1970s, which proposed a buried interstate highway to be accommodated in a land-filled strip of the Hudson River. Luckily for residents and fish alike, Westway fizzled, and thereafter plans for a park slowly materialized. The creation of the trust in 1998 cemented the park's eventual realization, formed in response to the changing residential demographics of areas along the park and in Tribeca, the West Village, Chelsea, and Clinton. After about a dozen years of construction, approximately 80 percent of the five-mile park—partitioned into six segments—was built and open for use. Segment 5, stretching from Gansevoort Street (Pier 52) to 24th Street (Pier 64), is described in detail here.

Different architects and landscape architects are responsible for the various segments: Sasaki Associates and Matthews Nielsen (Segments 2 and 3), Abel Bainnson Butz (Segment 4), and Richard Dattner Architects with Miceli Kulik Williams (Segment 6). The landscape architect responsible for Segment 5, Michael Van Valkenburgh Associates (MVVA), christened the area just north of Chelsea Piers Chelsea Cove, which opened in summer 2010. This area features an expansive lawn—the largest open space in Hudson River Park—bracketed by Pier 64 to the north and Pier 62 to the south. Pier 64 provides for repose and taking in views of the Hudson River on one side and Chelsea's new high-rises on

60 The expansive lawn with skyline beyond (opposite). The dynamic structure of the Pier 62 Carousel (top). Looking north at Chelsea Cove's waterfront walkways (above). Photos © Albert Vecerka/Esto.

the other, while the skate park and carousel of Pier 62 are all about activity, as if in deference to the neighboring Chelsea Piers complex. Designed by CR Studio, the Pier 62 Carousel features five large trusses propping up a green roof that also incorporates solar panels, providing power to spin the thirty-three hand-carved wood figures. CR Studio also contributed to Segment 5 with its design of the Marine Company 1 (see page 160) farther south on Pier 53.

Reaching Chelsea Cove from the east means crossing the busy and wide West Side Highway. MVVA's landscape design manages to mitigate the road noise in the bucolic park spaces; one feels removed from the speeding cars and the neighborhood's galleries and nightlife beyond. In addition to the open lawn, the landscape features tables and seating around ornamental flowers adjacent to Chelsea Piers, a walkway along the waterfront, and intimate paths connecting these various spaces. Other design elements in this segment planned at the time of writing include a work by artist Justen Ladda on Pier 54, marking the ghostly presence of the Lusitania before its ill-fated 1915 voyage, and a transformation of the historic Pier 57 (see **NYC 2020**) into an urban market and cultural center by LOT-EK. This last piece should bring a dose of cultural vitality to the recreation and leisure spaces of the linear park. Combined with Riverside Park farther north and planned parks and promenades along the East River, the 550-acre Hudson River Park creates the equivalent of another Central Park on the island's periphery, replacing long-gone industries and serving the city's present-day residents.

61 200 ELEVENTH AVENUE
SELLDORF ARCHITECTS, 2011

200 Eleventh Avenue, at 24th Street
Ⓒ Ⓔ to 23rd Street

The "suburbanization of New York," as lamented by Jerilou and Kingsley Hammett in the book of the same name, can take many forms, least of which is the single-family house surrounded by grass and white picket fencing. The phenomenon is represented by this high-rise condo tower, much like others in the city but with one difference: an elevator for delivering cars to "En-Suite Sky Garages" and the front doors of select residents of the nineteen-story building. This device can be seen as the arrival of the suburbs because it eliminates one thing that makes the city so special: the interactions—intentional and accidental—that take place on New York's streets. Instead of at least walking back and

61 The stainless steel spandrels ripple across the west façade.
Photo © Albert Vecerka.

forth to the subway, residents get in the car, take the elevator down, drive to work, park in the garage, and do the reverse in the evening. Unfortunately, in Annabelle Selldorf's design for developer Peter Moore, the elevator and garages on the west façade are not expressed with the stainless steel or terracotta of the rest of the building; they are hidden behind tinted glass and leuvers.

62 HIGH LINE 519
ROY DESIGN, 2007

519 West 23rd Street, between Tenth and Eleventh Avenues
Ⓒ Ⓔ to 23rd Street

Of the numerous high-profile residential developments spurred by the transformation of the High Line railroad viaduct into a linear park, High Line 519 reached the checkered flag first, realized three years before its neighbor to the east (**63**) filled the narrow gap bordering the High Line (**54**). An even narrower site confronted Lindy Roy in her design for the eleven-story building. The façade layers perforated embossed stainless steel balustrades in amorphous, semi-continuous shapes across the glass front. At the rear similar panels act as guardrails for balconies projecting like drawers from the slender building. Like two slightly different sides of one coin, these stainless steel pieces subtly express the full-floor units that fill the spaces behind the façades.

62 High Line 519 is squeezed between bigger buildings of brick and glass.

515–517 West 23rd Street, between Tenth and Eleventh Avenues
C E to 23rd Street

Between Lindy Roy's sliver of a building (**62**) and the High Line (**54**) sat a roughly 40-foot-wide by 100-foot-deep plot of land, waiting for a building able to address its unique conditions: a relatively narrow site for high-end residences and a proximity to the throng of strollers on the High Line. Los Angles–based architect Neil Denari overcame the constraints of the site by shaping the eastern façade of the fourteen-story building over the linear park below, adding square footage to the upper floors and giving park-goers something to ogle. HL23 is best seen from the north and the south along the High Line, where the slenderness of the building, its stepped cantilever (like a wheelchair ramp turned on its side), and the structural bracing required to achieve the latter are clearly expressed. Seen from the east on 23rd Street, the building appears portly, and its solidity seems more conventional than the glassy views from the elevated-park.

After decades of teaching and designing distinctive interiors in California and Japan, Denari became known for projects with a fluidity of form and surface, certainly evident here in the undulating façade of stamped stainless steel facing the High Line. This fluidity extends to small details, such as the articulation of the bracing on the glass walls which graphically depict the structure, even as it is hidden behind curtains. The stainless steel panels may be echoed at 245 Tenth (**64**) a block away, but the cantilevered form is a striking and singular presence among the numerous developments along the High Line.

63 Seen from the south, the building angles over the High Line (left). Seen from the north, High Line 519's rear façade is also visible (right). Photo courtesy NMDA.

64

245 TENTH
DELLA VALLE BERNHEIMER, 2009

245 Tenth Avenue, at 24th Street
Ⓒ Ⓔ to 23rd Street

Jared Della Valle and Andrew Bernheimer's second residential tower in Chelsea (see also 55) is shaped by two neighbors: the corner gas station the tower wraps itself around and the High Line (**54**) it sits beside. The former may limit the building to its L-shaped plan and dictate solid walls facing south and east, but the old rail viaduct inspires the treatment of these surfaces: diamond patterns on the stainless steel panels replicate clouds billowing from old steam engines. Depending on the angle of the sun (sometimes blinding!) and one's location, the effect is occasionally visible. A similar smoke-like dissipation occurs on the glass façades fronting Tenth Avenue and the High Line. The building cantilevers slightly over the latter to gain some square footage, but not as dramatically as its neighbor to the south, HL23 (**63**).

64 An early photo before construction began on the High Line's second phase (left). A slight angle gives the impression of being squeezed between the High Line and a gas station (top).
Photos by Frank Oudeman.

65

CHELSEA ENCLAVE
ENNEAD ARCHITECTS, 2010

177 Ninth Avenue, at 21st Street
Ⓒ Ⓔ to 23rd Street

This seven-story condominium building caps the east end of a whole Chelsea block owned and occupied by the General Theological Seminary of the Episcopal Church, its home since 1827. It was originally developed as a ten-story glass tower atop a brick base, but the Landmarks Preservation Commission successfully pushed for downsizing. The all-glass top story, set back from the masonry walls below, is basically the bottom of what might have been if the original scheme hadn't been cut short. Architecturally, Susan

65 The building is a refined addition to the seminary's close.

Rodriguez's design is a huge improvement over the ugly mid-twentieth-century building that was demolished to make way for these million-dollar condos. It relates to the neo-Gothic seminary campus in its height but also in the articulation of the matching orange brick and the asymmetrical Ninth Avenue massing, which recall the chimneys found throughout the rest of the block. Examples of contrasting new designs in historic contexts abound in the city, but this building shows that a balance can be struck between the historical and the contemporary.

DREAM DOWNTOWN HOTEL 66
HANDEL ARCHITECTS, 2011
346 West 17th Street, at Ninth Avenue
① to 18th Street

Designed by Albert C. Ledner and built in the 1960s, the National Maritime Union's pair of buildings in Chelsea expressed the nautical nature of the organization in porthole windows that dotted the rectangular slab on Ninth Avenue and the sloping wall that followed the zoning envelope on West 17th Street. With minimal exterior alterations, the first was turned into the Maritime Hotel in the early 2000s, and its success surely inspired the transformation of the latter into another hotel, this time by the international boutique hotel chain Dream. With the exterior now clad in stainless steel panels, the regular grid of portholes has been contemporized into irregularly staggered circles in two sizes. The slope, cladding, and windows create the image of an oversized cheese grater, a welcome addition to those disappointed by the outcome at One Astor Place (**34**). On West 18th Street more circles can be found, puncturing a metal veil in front of glass walls. On all sides, the architects found inspiration in Ledner's geometries.

66 The 17th Street "cheese grater" shortly before completion.
Photo © Albert Vecerka/Esto.

6

AVANT CHELSEA 67
1100: ARCHITECT, 2008
245 West 19th Street, between Seventh and Eighth Avenues
① to 18th Street

One side effect of building taller in areas with older building stock is the blank side walls that rise over smaller neighbors. With most of the expense lavished on the street façade, those party walls are too often left unadorned, an afterthought, waiting to be covered in time by an equally tall building. In some cases, like the Orchard Street Residential Development (**23**) and this twelve-story condo building, the extra effort expended on treating these solid walls can actually overshadow the street façade and give a project its character. Six shades of indigo in a mosaic of 2,500 metal panels cover the east elevation, like a burst of light that trickles down from the penthouse ribbon windows. Seen from the street, the fully glazed front façade steps up from west to east, as if to prop up the indigo canvas.

67 The east-facing wall steals the show.

See Map
8
Midtown East

Seventh Av

Broadway

① ② ③

B **D**
F **M**
N Q R

400 Fifth Avenue •

E 42nd St

E 41st St **④ ⑤ ⑥**

⑦ S

E 40th St

E 39th St

E 38th St

Morgan Library Expansion 76• E 37th St **•75** Scandinavia House

E 36th St

Empire State Building •

E 35th St

E 34th St

Sixth Av

Madison Av

Fifth Av

The Ace Hotel •

⑥

•74 M127

Park Av South

E 33rd St

E 32nd St

3rd Av

E 31st St

Lexington Av

⑥

400 Park Avenue South •

E 30th St

Madison
Square
Park

⑥

1/4-mile
radius

E 29th St

• Kips Bay Towers

2nd Av

E 28th St

• Van Alen
Institute

N R

•73 Shake Shack

Flatiron Building •

•72 One Madison Park

23 East 22nd Street •

1st Av

E 27th St

E 26th St

•71 Baruch College Vertical Campus

E 25th St

East River Science Park •

⑥

Bellevue Hospital Center •

E 24th St

• NYC OCME

50 Gramercy Park North •

E 23rd St

Gramercy
Park

Broadway

E 22nd St

E 20th St

E 21st St

• **Union Square Park North End Expansion**

Union Square
Park

•69 Irving Place

E 19th St

•70 LearningSpring School

•68 15 Union Square West

E 18th St

L N

Q R

E 17th St

④ ⑤ ⑥

Irving Place

E 16th St

Peter Cooper
Village

Ea
Riv

E 15th St

• Friends Seminary School

Stuyvesant
Town

L

E 14th St

See Map
4
East Village

L

This chapter includes buildings in the neighborhoods east of Broadway from 14th Street to 42nd Street. Much of the area is defined by its parks: Union Square Park at 14th and Broadway; Madison Square Park up Broadway at 23rd Street; and Gramercy Park about halfway between those, at the southern end of Lexington Avenue. The first two are public parks of widely varying character, and the third is the only privately owned park in Manhattan.

Union Square Park is named for the convergence of Broadway and Fourth Avenue, not for labor unions commonly using the space to protest, as is widely believed. To this day the park—in particular its southern tip—is a gathering spot for demonstrations and expressions of free speech that are hard to find elsewhere in the city; it was the site of many informal memorials and reunions within days after the September 11, 2001, attacks. Union Square is also the starting point for the Critical Mass bike rides, in which cyclists take over the streets from cars to foster alternative modes of transportation, and it is the site of a popular farmer's market four days a week.

A short walk up Broadway is Madison Square Park, a well-known name mainly because of the sports venue that used to be located along its edge but which now sits on top of the old Pennsylvania Station. The space is further overshadowed by two of its neighbors: the Met Life Building, with its clock tower facing the park, and the instantly recognizable Flatiron Building, which lends the immediate area its name. Throughout the year the park is used as a canvas for artists; past installations include Tadashi Kawamata's *Tree Huts* and Antony Gormley's *Event Horizon*, which placed cast iron figures atop the Flatiron, Met Life, and other buildings surrounding the park.

The last, Gramercy Park, is a gated space accessible only to residents of the buildings overlooking the park, though traditionally they open the gates to others on Christmas Eve. The park dates back to the early 1830s and the surrounding buildings from roughly that time to one hundred years later, minus a twenty-first-century hotel on its northern edge. East of this area can be found Stuyvesant Town–Peter Cooper Village, a huge private residential development that looks like towers-in-a-park public housing but is home to a middle-class neighborhood; in 2006 it was sold for over $5 billion, supposedly the largest real estate deal ever in the United States. To its north is a cluster of hospital and biotechnology facilities and one of New York City's first examples of Brutalism, I. M. Pei's Kips Bay Towers from the early 1960s.

North of 34th Street is Murray Hill (park-free, unlike the neighborhoods to its south), named for an eighteenth-century merchant family who owned farmland and built a great house on, yes, a hill at what is now Park Avenue and 36th Street. The hill has since been leveled, but the area that carries the name features a canyon of prewar masonry buildings extending along Park Avenue to Grand Central Terminal, and nineteenth-century townhouses in the historic district to the east.

68 15 UNION SQUARE WEST

OFFICE FOR DESIGN & ARCHITECTURE with Perkins Eastman, 2010

15 Union Square West, at 15th Street

④ ⑤ ⑥ Ⓛ Ⓝ Ⓠ Ⓡ to 14th Street–Union Square

68 The old Tiffany arches are evident at night. Photo © Albert Vecerka/Esto.

In 1870 Charles Lewis Tiffany built a large cast iron building overlooking Union Square Park for his eponymous jewelry company. To call John Kellum's design for the five-story building ornate would be an understatement; its decorative columns, cornice, and other projections attempted to render in cast iron a symbol of the "palace of jewels" inside. Tiffany's stayed in Union Square until 1906, when it moved to Fifth Avenue and 37th Street, into a white marble building by the esteemed McKim, Mead & White. Its old building changed hands a number of times, but a 1952 death caused by a falling piece of cast iron from the façade caused then-owner Amalgamated Bank to rid the building of its abundant decoration and cover the whole in white brick.

When Eran Chen of Perkins Eastman was faced with converting and expanding the original Tiffany building to thirty-six high-end residences, he aimed to reveal the old cast iron structure after removing the brick exterior. (Chen left Perkins Eastman in 2007 to form ODA, completing the final design at his new office.) With the brick and cast iron gone, the new zinc-framed glass walls sit two feet in front of the remaining 1870 cast iron structure. From the outside this creates a glass box that subtly reveals these arched openings (especially at night), but for residents the framed views outside strike a balance between the historical and the contemporary. Seven new floors atop the existing building step back and cantilever with the same large sheets of glass and zinc, making the design—especially from across the park—appear completely new, not just a new face on an old building.

IRVING PLACE 69

AUDREY MATLOCK ARCHITECT with Helpern Architects, 2011

57 Irving Place, between 17th and 18th Streets

④ ⑤ ⑥ Ⓛ Ⓝ Ⓠ Ⓡ **to 14th Street–Union Square**

This eleven-story building, steps from Gramercy Park, is highlighted by single- and double-story glass projections that alternate as they rise and signal the nine condo units beyond. Connecting these projections are white horizontal steel members planned as tracks for louvered screens that would further make the façade a "kinetic sculpture."[1] Not visible at the time of writing, these operable elements would give residents another means of control over their enclosure, all the while activating the layered façade. Also not visible are the cloud frit patterns designed for the glass projections. While these two pieces may be victims of value engineering, the building still retains a strong presence on a street lined with buildings of brick and stone.

69 Alternating glass-box projections sit between masonry neighbors.

LEARNINGSPRING SCHOOL 70

PLATT BYARD DOVELL WHITE, 2010

247 East 20th Street, at Second Avenue

⑥ **to 23rd Street**

In 2000 the LearningSpring Foundation was created by a group of parents frustrated by the inadequate schooling available for their autistic children. Their goal of helping individuals with the disorder to "live independently, make friends, have a significant other, and become gainfully employed"[2] led to the creation of the LearningSpring Elementary School the following year. A decade later what was now the LearningSpring School—serving grades K–8—moved into this eight-story building, featuring a terracotta cladding that stands out in the area. The base and mainly solid side walls are rendered in orange, but the same material in gray is used for the highly articulated corner elevations. Here the gray bands sit below windows with integral louvers, the last providing a sense of enclosure while helping to cut down on the sunlight entering the south- and east-facing building.

70 Well-articulated exteriors of terracotta define the building. Photo by Frederick Charles.

71 BARUCH COLLEGE VERTICAL CAMPUS
KOHN PEDERSEN FOX ASSOCIATES, 2001

55 Lexington, between 24th and 25th Streets
⑥ to 23rd Street

"Vertical campus" is a fitting moniker for Baruch College's nearly full-block building, which doubled the size of the City University of New York (CUNY) classroom and administrative space with a laundry list of new facilities: over one hundred classrooms; fifty research and computer labs; a performing arts center with two auditoriums, a theater, and recital hall; an athletic center with fitness centers, a gymnasium, pool, and racquetball courts; a fine arts center with labs, studios, and rehearsal spaces; nearly fifty conference rooms and over five hundred offices for faculty and staff; a bookstore; and a food court. All of the above and a little bit more are stacked in seventeen stories and over three quarters of a million square feet.

Giving the building a strong presence is the curving metal-clad profile. Sitting atop a five-story brick base, the gentle curve immediately recalls the New York State Armory building located cater-corner to the northwest; the parapet's raised corner at Lexington and 25th Street even seems to gesture toward its predecessor. At sidewalk level the vertical campus is for the most part walled off, and access to the building is limited. The primary access is on 25th Street, marked by a canopy, a truncated cone, and a large expanse of curtain wall; the last is the culmination of a stepped atrium that cuts through the building from the south to bring sunlight into the deepest parts of the massive structure.

71 Looking east from next to the Armory (left). The glass-front atrium clearly demarcates the entrance (right). Photos © Michael Moran.

ONE MADISON PARK **72**
CETRA/RUDDY, 2010

22 East 23rd Street, at Madison Avenue

⑥ Ⓝ Ⓡ to 23rd Street

72 The new glass tower gestures towards the Met Life Building.

The periphery of Madison Square Park has been long defined by two landmarks: Daniel H. Burnham's twenty-two-story Flatiron Building from 1903 and Pierre Le Brun's fifty-four-story Metropolitan Life Insurance Company Tower, completed six years later. Situated between them, at the southern terminus of Madison Avenue, is a welcome addition to the open space, a slender fifty-story bronze and glass tower marked by seven cantilevered "pods" of clear and white glass on the northeast corner. This container for luxury residences recalls Santiago Calatrava's unbuilt proposal for a town house tower near South Street Seaport rather than its historical neighbors. A proposal by the Office for Metropolitan Architecture (OMA) for the lot on 22nd Street behind One Madison Park, dashed in the economic downturn, would have peeked around the tower to the park beyond, inverting our understanding of how New York City zoning is addressed. (It cantilevered like an oversized Whitney Museum, rather than stepping like a wedding cake.) Its omission enables this new tower to stand alone as the twenty-first-century landmark on the park.

7

SHAKE SHACK **73**
SITE, 2004

Madison Square Park, near 23rd Street

⑥ Ⓝ Ⓡ to 23rd Street

The first of Shake Shack's seven and counting "road-side" burger stands operates from within a kiosk in Madison Square Park across the street from Daniel H. Burnham's iconic Flatiron Building. That icon's triangular shape influenced designer James Wines, who boasts of having been green before green was cool. He embraced the vegetation of the park itself by capping the sloping kiosk with a green roof and incorporating a trellis for ivy (yet not very successful several years after completion). Before this small building, SITE (Sculpture In The Environment) executed primarily outdoor art installations—a parking lot where the asphalt overtakes the cars is a highlight— as well as a memorable series of big-box

73 The kiosk blends into the vege- tation and activity of the park.

showrooms in the 1970s that expressed humor and irony in architecture, by tilting up the front façade, in one case, to reveal the products within. A toned-down version of that Pop architecture is found in the three-dimensional lettering that announces the stand and the burgers, which sometimes require a one-hour wait in line.

74 M127
SHoP ARCHITECTS, 2008

127 Madison Avenue, between 30th and 31st Streets
⑥ to 33rd Street

New York City's building code allows fixed projections to extend beyond the sidewalk and/or property line, totaling no more than 10 percent of a façade's area; architectural details (cornices, louvers, sculptures) may project ten inches, and balconies are allowed to extend close to two feet. The architects at SHoP are adept at manipulating their designs to fit this section of the code. Recently adopted software enabled them to determine that the complex undulating brick façade at 290 Mulberry (**29**) did not exceed the limitations. And for this building five blocks north of Madison Square Park, the architects fit angled bay windows into the horizontal openings of an existing seven-story building to "create intimate seating nooks . . . offering expansive views down the avenue towards Madison Square Park"[3] and now the new glass tower (**72**) on the edge of the park.

Thankfully the architects preserved the highly articulated brick façade, a mix of running bond, stacked, soldier course, and recessed checkerboard panels, rendered in red brick with white vertical accents. The finely machined black steel and glass bays are a refined counterpoint to the brick. Above, the five new floors, set back from the old façade, feature larger bays angled in the opposite direction. This large-scale zig and zag definitely recalls the contemporary Switch Building (**25**) by nARCHITECTS, but here the name recalls a bus route, not a formal gesture.

74 The sliver building sits between bulkier and taller neighbors (left). The angled bays look north to Madison Square Park (above).

75 The signage peeks above trees on Park Avenue's median (left). Detail of the wood louvers integrated into the metal and glass façade (right).

SCANDINAVIA HOUSE 75
ENNEAD ARCHITECTS, 2000

58 Park Avenue, between 37th and 38th Streets
⑥ to 33rd Street; ④ ⑤ ⑥ ⑦ Ⓢ to Grand Central–42nd Street

The American-Scandinavian Foundation (ASF) was founded about a hundred years ago as an educational and cultural link between the United States and the five Nordic countries. (The flags of Denmark, Finland, Iceland, Norway, and Sweden project above the ground-floor storefront.) To this day the nonprofit organization fosters this connection through fellowships, scholarly exchange, publications, exhibitions, and performances. Its six-story home on Park Avenue a few blocks south of Grand Central Terminal is the setting for cultural activities that range from art and design exhibitions to concerts, lectures, and classes. It is fitting that the building, designed by James Stewart Polshek in Ennead Architects' previous incarnation, Polshek Partnership, expresses something of a Nordic character, a petite design among its larger masonry neighbors.

    Scandinavian design traits of restraint, refinement, elegance, and a connection to the natural world are evident in the Park Avenue façade, a vertical composition of glass, metal, and wood countered by horizontal mullions, joints, and louvers. The last are the most overtly Nordic elements, alluding to the abundant forests exploited for everything from vases and chairs to saunas and buildings. With the passage of time since the building's completion, the weathering of the wood gives it a connection to nature, an effect that many contemporary buildings try to extinguish with artificial materials and coatings. Inside, the galleries, café, auditorium, and other spaces are like the exterior: crisp and cool with a layer of warmth.

76 MORGAN LIBRARY EXPANSION

RENZO PIANO BUILDING WORKSHOP with Beyer Blinder Belle, 2006

225 Madison Avenue, between 36th and 37th Streets

⑥ to 33rd Street; ④ ⑤ ⑥ ⑦ ⑤ to Grand Central–42nd Street

The Morgan Library & Museum houses a collection of manuscripts, rare books, music, drawings, prints, and ancient artifacts begun by financier J. Pierpont Morgan in the late nineteenth century. Charles McKim of the renowned firm McKim, Mead & White designed a library for Morgan's growing collection in 1906, and in 1924 Morgan's son opened the collection to the public. The annex followed a few years later, but it was not until the early 1990s that the Morgan expanded into an old brownstone and a new atrium space connecting the three buildings. About ten years later Italian architect Renzo Piano was hired for an overhaul of what had morphed into a quasi-campus. The $106 million expansion doubles the square footage and increases the programs and facilities available to the public.

In an effort to unite the three detached structures (library, annex, brownstone) of The Morgan, Piano reached back to his country's Renaissance piazzas. His design adds three new pavilions housing exhibition facilities, a reading room, and offices, and an entry cube on Madison Avenue. An internal piazza connects everything, old and new, and is a setting for dining and other activities. The dramatic 50-foot-high court is covered by a fully glazed roof, what the architect refers to as a "flying carpet." This overhead plane, recalling many of Piano's museum commissions (the Menil Collection and Nasher Sculpture Center in Texas, and Atlanta's High Museum of Art addition, to name a few), washes the space in filtered light and gives the impression of an outdoor room, aided, no doubt, by the exterior walls of the old buildings facing the new court. Narrow glass walls fill the gaps between old and new, and a large glass wall to the east opens up the block's innards, the ubiquitous yet invisible rear yards that result from Manhattan's grid. In this indoor piazza, light is the unifier of the ensemble, not Piano's architecture.

On the exterior it is clear that the scale of Piano's renovation and expansion respects the existing buildings, all three designated landmarks by the city's Landmarks Preservation Commission. The low heights of the entrance and pavilions are achieved by placing half the program in four subterranean levels, a massive undertaking in its own right. These pavilions fill the gaps between the original buildings and further define the street walls, yet they are set back from their predecessors in a subtle sign of deference, though still not enough for detractors, who take exception to the way Piano covered the façades inside and out. Clad in metal painted a buff color similar to that used in the library and annex, their joints expressed, the panels are basically unadorned, creating an obvious contrast between Piano's façades and the landmark buildings. Yet it's the glass-covered atrium that is now the heart of the Morgan, a counterpoint in light to the darker spaces of a century ago.

76 The new Madison Avenue entrance sits between the brownstone, at left, and the annex (top, left). The new pavilion between the annex, at left, and the Morgan Library on 36th Street (top, right). Sun cascades down the new pavilion between the annex and the library (right). Looking from the library toward the café in the piazza (above).

Photos by Michel Denancé.

See Map
9
Midtown West

See Map
11
Upper East Side

· Central Park

N Q R · Carnegie 57

· Metropolitan Tower Public Passage
F

F

E 63rd St · P.S. 59

Brasserie 8 1/2 ·

N Q R

•**83** Apple Store Fifth Avenue

E 62nd St

•**82** Louis Vuitton Store
· LVMH Tower

N Q R

E 61st St

•**87** NYC Information Center

4 5 6

· **Armani Fifth Avenue**

E 60th St

MoMA Tower ·

·**81** Bloomberg Tower

· 745 Seventh Avenue

85••**86** MoMA Expansion

American Folk Art Museum

Sony Building ·

Phyto Universe ·

E 59th St

· Hoffman Auto Showroom

E 58th St

· Modulightor
Bridgemarket ·

E M · Paley Park

E 57th St

Austrian Cultural Forum New York **84**•

· Lever House

E 56th St

B D

· Rockefeller Center

E 55th St

F M

Brasserie · E M

E 54th St

Seagram Building ·

441 East 57th Street **80**•

Lipstick Building ·

E 53rd St

6 1/4-mile radius

E 52nd St

· Rockefeller Guest House

•**88** Cassa NY

E 51st St

•**89** Harvard Club of New York City

E 50th St

•**90** Bank of America Tower
at One Bryant Park

William Lescaze Residence ·

E 49th St

•**79** Urban Town House

· Number 5

E 48th St

B D

E 47th St

· 23 Beekman Place

F M E 42nd St

Bryant Park

· Trump World Tower

7 · 505 Fifth Avenue

E 46th St

•**77** NYPL South Court

· Grand Central Terminal

E 45th St

Japan Society ·

E 44th St

4 5 6

7 S

· Chrysler Building and Trylons

Permanent Mission of India to the UN

United States Mission to the United Nations **78**•

E 43rd St

Ford Foundation Building ·

E 42nd St

· United Nations Headquarters

See Map
7
Murray Hill

East River

Fifth Av
Madison Av
Park Av
Lexington Av
3rd Av
2nd Av
1st Av
Sutton Pl
Seventh Av
Sixth Av
Broadway
Queensboro Bridge

South and east of Central Park, midtown Manhattan
is the city's largest business district, containing some of the most
recognizable buildings in the world: the Empire State Building, the
Chrysler Building, Rockefeller Center. These structures dating from the
1930s took advantage of the firm and shallow bedrock on which they
stand to make the area, then considered uptown, a desirable place for
business. Decades later, corporate Modernism took hold on a stretch of
Park Avenue above Grand Central Terminal, when the Lever House by
Skidmore, Owings & Merrill and the Seagram Building by Mies van der
Rohe and Philip Johnson were completed in 1952 and 1958, respectively.
So many modern office buildings followed that this section of the island
permanently altered the skyline, balancing its height with that of the
Financial District at the southern tip of the island. Decades later Midtown
also witnessed the (temporary) dismantling of Modernism by none other
than Philip Johnson, in the AT&T (now Sony) Building, with its distinctive
Chippendale highboy crown. The last pre-twenty-first-century shift in the
styles of tall buildings took place on East 57th Street, where Christian
de Portzamparc's LVMH Tower rose like an oversized perfume bottle, a
sculpture in glass.

Turtle Bay, east of Lexington Avenue from 42nd to 53rd Streets, is
home to the United Nations Headquarters on eighteen acres of riverfront
land donated by John D. Rockefeller. Completed in 1953, the four-building
complex (now five buildings, including the temporary north lawn building)
was designed by Wallace K. Harrison with a ten-strong team that included
Le Corbusier and Oscar Niemeyer. Lately UN Headquarters has been in
the midst of a $1.8 billion renovation, the first in its history. Beyond its
eighteen-acre footprint, the United Nations spreads its influence wide,
with various missions, residences, and businesses serving the needs
of the organization throughout Turtle Bay. To the north is Sutton Place,
a small residential enclave that lies east of Second Avenue. The area's
streets are dominated by tall co-operative apartment buildings, some
dating to the 1920s.

8

77 A glass bridge links the old building and the new insertion. Stairs occupy the gap between old and new. Photos by Scott Norsworthy.

77 NYPL SOUTH COURT
DAVIS BRODY BOND AEDAS, 2002

Fifth Avenue at 42nd Street

7 to Fifth Avenue; **B D F M** to 42nd Street–Bryant Park

Originally the south courtyard of Carrère & Hastings's 1911 main New York Public Library building—considered by some to be the greatest masterpiece of Beaux-Arts architecture in the United States—was designed as a horse drop-off and featured a marble fountain at its center. Eight years later the fountain was replaced by a one-story staff lunchroom, the library's only above-ground addition until the South Court building filled what had evolved into a surface parking lot. This 40,000-square-foot addition to what is now the Stephen A. Schwarzman Building is spread across six floors, three above grade and three excavated, so the new structure does not project above the roofline of the landmark library.

The architects, who had been restoring some of the library's spaces since the early 1980s, "floated" the new floors within the courtyard, creating four- to five-foot gaps between them and the freshly cleaned marble walls. On the lower floors this gap exposes the old foundations, some from the old Croton Reservoir, which the library replaced. The addition is capped by skylights, which combine with walls, guardrails, bridges, and stairs—all of glass—to bring natural light to the Celeste Bartos Education Center, offices, and a staff lounge. From the main entrance to the library on Fifth Avenue, the South Court is found straight back and to the left.

UNITED STATES MISSION TO THE UNITED NATIONS 78

GWATHMEY SIEGEL & ASSOCIATES ARCHITECTS, 2010

799 UN Plaza, First Avenue at 45th Street
④ ⑤ ⑥ ❼ ⑤ to Grand Central–42nd Street

Four years after the 1945 formation of the United Nations Organization (UN) replaced the failed League of Nations, construction began on the permanent headquarters for the international peacekeeping organization. Its Secretariat, General Assembly, Conference, and Library buildings are located along the East River on land donated by Nelson Rockefeller, but the presence of the UN in Manhattan extends well beyond this eighteen-acre footprint. Of the numerous nearby buildings and spaces that arose from and cater to the organization, the greatest in size and stature are perhaps the missions of the various member states, especially the United States Mission to the United Nations (USUN), opposite the General Assembly. Replacing a twelve-story 1961 slab of glass faced with a cast stone screen, the new USUN is a twenty-two-story tower whose solidity brings to the fore the security criteria even more pronounced since the attacks of September 11, 2001.

One of the last buildings designed by the late Charles Gwathmey, the project is basically a rectangular tower intersecting a cylindrical core, both rising from a podium of curving and angled forms. The base presents a transparent face to passersby, but the concrete tower with its tapering windows gives the building an overriding bunker-like appearance. Certainly this factor arises from stringent blast criteria, but with advances in glass technology and construction, it is now possible to clad a building safely in glass instead of traditionally solid materials. (Good examples are the glassy replacement for the Alfred P. Murrah Federal Building in Oklahoma City and the UN Secretariat's replacement curtain wall.) So the decision to house the offices, conference rooms, and reception spaces behind concrete walls presents a fairly obvious message to the international community, especially in this highly visible location across from the UN.

78 The new U.S. Mission rises in front of the UN Plaza Hotel (left). The curved roof counters the rigid concrete tower above (above).
Photos © Aaron Dougherty.

79 URBAN TOWN HOUSE
PETER GLUCK AND PARTNERS, 2009

324 East 51st Street, between First and Second Avenues
⑥ to 51st Street; Ⓔ Ⓜ to Lexington Avenue–53rd Street

Situated between two masonry buildings, this five-story town house is located on a quite tree-lined block of three- and four-story buildings in Turtle Bay, just steps from Midtown's skyscrapers. The perforated metal rain screen of the façade incorporates random openings about the size and scale of a standard brick, giving the new town house a relationship to its neighbors even though it appears at odds with them. Barely visible behind the rain screen are larger rectangular openings that zigzag up the front; these are windows into the stairs and four-story bookcase that sit immediately behind the façade. Vertical slots of clear glass bookend the perforated metal and allow small glimpses inside this booklover's dream. The porosity of the façade is reminiscent of Edward Durell Stone's own 1956 house on 64th Street, which is fronted by decorative concrete blocks.

79 Windows following the stairs are visible at dusk.
Photo by Erik Freeland.

80 441 EAST 57TH STREET
FLANK ARCHITECTURE, 2009

441 East 57th Street, between First Avenue and Sutton Place
④ ⑤ ⑥ Ⓝ Ⓠ Ⓡ to Lexington Avenue–59th Street

A short block from Sutton Place Park and its Hollywood views of the Queensboro Bridge can be found a sliver of glass nestled between its bulkier brick neighbors. A void space immediately to the east of this fifteen-story building, and about as wide, makes the new addition stand out as much as the façade's composition of clear and white fritted glass in a puzzle-like pattern. This walled-off open space extends the full depth of the lot to give the residential building an additional façade. Here one can see how the duplexes and triplex fit together below the penthouse, like even larger puzzle pieces. The design wears European Modernist precedents on its narrow sleeve: Piet Mondrian's *Composition* paintings, the interlocking duplexes of Le Corbusier's Unité d'Habitation, and architect Pierre Chareau's glass-block Maison de Verre.

80 White fritted glass frames various clear glass openings (right). Seen from the east, the sliver sits among bulky co-ops (far right).

BLOOMBERG TOWER **81**

PELLI CLARKE PELLI ARCHITECTS with SLCE Architects, 2005

731 Lexington Avenue

④ ⑤ ⑥ Ⓝ Ⓠ Ⓡ to Lexington Avenue–59th Street

Bloomberg Tower occupies a full city block that previously housed the flagship Alexander's department store. It was bought by Vornado Realty Trust, which developed this mixed-use project, a fifty-four-story tower atop a six-story base. The latter is primarily occupied by and named for the main tenant, the financial news company Bloomberg LP, owned by Michael Bloomberg, New York City's first three-term mayor since Ed Koch in the 1980s. The architectural highlight of the project is Beacon Court (done with Adamson Associates Architects), the elliptical open space in the middle of the block, which provides access for residents of the 101-unit condo tower and a public entrance for Bloomberg LP, whose colorful offices (designed by STUDIOS Architecture) wrap around the space. A glazed beacon atop the tower shines at night, giving the building a strong presence on the skyline and marking the southeast corner of Central Park.

81 Looking up at the tower from Beacon Court.

8

LOUIS VUITTON STORE **82**

JUN AOKI, 2004

1 East 57th Street, at Fifth Avenue

Ⓝ Ⓠ Ⓡ to Fifth Avenue–59th Street

Japanese architect Jun Aoki has designed seven shops for the French fashion house Louis Vuitton; New York City is number six, at this writing the only location outside Asia. His design basically skins the 1930 New York Trust Company Building, a stepping Art Deco design clad in stone. Milky white glass fully wraps the first four floors, with another six floors at the corner covered in the same. From a distance the effect is that of a veil over the existing building, achieved by applying a checkerboard pattern of varying sizes and densities to two layers of the glass. As one walks past the shop windows, the overlapping layers shift in relation to each other, giving a moiré effect as intriguing as the view from across the street.

82 Vuitton veils an Art Deco building. Photo by Scott Norsworthy.

83 APPLE STORE FIFTH AVENUE
BOHLIN CYWINSKI JACKSON
with Moed de Armas & Shannon, 2006

767 Fifth Avenue, at 59th Street
N Q R to Fifth Avenue–59th Street

Apple Inc. opened its first retail stores in spring 2001, a half year before the company's hugely successful iPod made its debut. Within a decade New York City had become home to four of Apple's more than three hundred stores; most are inserted into shopping malls, but two of the four in Manhattan are new buildings, and the other two are transformations of old buildings. If one could be called its New York City flagship store, it's the Fifth Avenue location, open twenty-four hours a day, year round. It occupies the underground retail concourse of the General Motors Building, but it presides over the plaza as a glass cube marked by an illuminated Apple logo. Glass is also used for the round elevator and the stairway spiraling around it. The pricey use of glass allows natural light to enter the store, while at night the effect is reversed and the cube glows with the artificial lights from below. Glass is eschewed in the retail environment for stone floors, stainless steel ceilings and walls, and wooden store fixtures; these materials are consistent in the other stores in SoHo, the Meatpacking District, and the Upper West Side.

The first New York City store opened in 2002 in a 1920s building formerly occupied by the U.S. Post Office (stone carvings on the façade still spell out this original function) at Prince and Greene Streets in SoHo (Map 2). The two-story space is capped by a long skylight located above a straight-run glass stair that leads from the main entrance to a theater at the back of the store where workshops and performances are held. A similar transformation occurs at the West 14th Street store (2007) at Ninth Avenue in the Meatpacking District (Map 6), but a circular glass stair—like the one at the Fifth Avenue location but without the elevator—links the three floors. In 2009 the Upper West Side store at Broadway and 67th Street, next door to the Kaufman Center and steps away from Lincoln Center, opened its doors (Map 10). The new building features glass walls and a roof supported between stone side and rear walls. As at the Fifth Avenue cube, an illuminated Apple logo floats in the space. This is the most impressive of Apple's four Manhattan outposts; its expansive glass enclosure brings views of the surrounding buildings into the large first-floor space.

Pennsylvania-based architect Peter Bohlin's firm is responsible for the design of these and many other high-profile Apple stores. CEO Steve Jobs had hired the firm for the Pixar Studio and Headquarters in California. Impressed by Bohlin's design, he hired the architect to design stores that Jobs envisioned at the time to be social spaces more than purely retail environments. (His iPod might be seen as antisocial to some, but he was quite accurate in regard to these stores.) These four spaces are based on a material palette and standard details developed for Apple's whole fleet of stores, creating continuity and a smooth, minimal aesthetic that jibes with the computers and other devices whose design is as important as their performance.

83 The central skylight and stair at the SoHo store (top, left). The "Apple cube" seen from the north (top, right). Looking up from within the cube and cylindrical elevator (above, right). Photos by Scott Norsworthy. Inside the Upper West Side store's large skylit space (above, left).

84 AUSTRIAN CULTURAL FORUM NEW YORK
ATELIER RAIMUND ABRAHAM, 2002

11 East 52nd Street, between Fifth and Madison Avenues
Ⓔ Ⓜ to Fifth Avenue–53rd Street; Ⓖ to 51st Street

In 1992 Austria's Federal Ministry for Cultural Affairs held a design competition for the Austrian Cultural Institute, housed for four decades in a six-story town house on East 52nd Street dating back to 1905. Open to all Austrian and expatriate Austrian architects, the competition attracted 226 entries for the 25-foot-wide infill site. Raimund Abraham's winning design was chosen for its interior layout that ingeniously located the stairs (coined "The Vertebra") at the rear of the building rather than along the side, as most entries did, and for its striking façade, which the architect called "The Mask"; in between is the last of the three elementary towers, "The Core," the location of the functional spaces. A decade later the building finally opened as the Austrian Cultural Forum New York, but Abraham's design had changed very little from his winning entry.

The Vertebra, Core, and Mask compose the twenty-four-story tower—the island's first post 9/11 skyscraper—but The Mask, for good reason, steals the attention. Its guillotine-like blades of overlapping angled glass address the site's zoning envelope, but in a way that resembles nothing that came before it in the city (and probably after as well: it reportedly cost nearly $1,000 per square foot to build). Irregular yet symmetrical window openings are set into aluminum-clad areas above the canopy and atop the building, adding to the somewhat menacing appearance of the façade.

Not surprisingly, the public areas inside are small. Access is normally restricted to the gallery and theater on the lower few floors, but public tours of the rest of the building (library, offices, residences) are available and are recommended for fully absorbing the magnum opus of Raimund Abraham. The architect, known more as a passionate teacher and theoretician than a designer of buildings, died in a car accident in Los Angeles in 2010.

84 Looking up at "The Vertebra" from the gallery (above). Looking up at "The Mask"; the director's office projects from the angled glass (left). Photos by David Plakke.

AMERICAN FOLK ART MUSEUM 85

TOD WILLIAMS BILLIE TSIEN ARCHITECTS

with Helfand Myerberg Guggenheimer Architects, 2001

45 West 53rd Street, between Fifth and Sixth Avenues

E M to Fifth Avenue–53rd Street; **B D E** to Seventh Avenue

When it opened in December 2001, the new eight-level home of the American Folk Art Museum was a freestanding building, a unique presence on its block. Since it is now hemmed in by the expansion of MoMA (**86**) to the east and north (and potentially a tower to the west, designed by Jean Nouvel), the decision by husband and wife architects Tod Williams and Billie Tsien to cover the façade in folding planes of Tombasil—a form of white bronze—is a prescient one, giving the diminutive building a solid presence among its sleek glass neighbors. The Tombasil exhibits variations arising from pouring the panels on the concrete floor of the foundry—air bubbles among the swirls are most overt—and the overall appearance shifts gradually, depending on sunlight and season. The handmade façade relates to the folk art inside without mimicking the contents.

Tucked behind the panels that reach to the sidewalk are the entry doors, hidden but fairly obvious. Once the visitor is inside, the spatial and material complexity of the museum is revealed; one catches glimpses of skylit spaces above and in the distance, articulated in everything from concrete and Pietra stone to resin fiberglass and Douglas fir. Williams and Tsien approached the building as a "house of art," and it actually recalls their earlier house *with* art on East 72nd Street (see map on page 140). But the museum also melds the plan of a house with those of the Guggenheim and Whitney museums, especially in the vertical circulation that is articulated here in three flights of stairs, encouraging multiple interactions with the artwork. Most striking are the diagonal views across the galleries, accommodated by openings in walls and floors. Artworks are scattered throughout the spaces, not just in galleries but along stairs and in niches. This is a museum that rewards repeated visits, for more than just changing exhibitions. In spring 2011 the museum sold the building to MOMA, reestablishing its base of operations across from Lincoln Center.

85 The front façade from the plaza across 53rd Street (top). Photo by Scott Norsworthy. **The layering of spaces is evident all over the museum, here below the large skylight (above).** Photo © Michael Moran.

86 MOMA EXPANSION

YOSHIO TANIGUCHI with Kohn Pedersen Fox Associates, 2004

11 West 53rd Street, between Fifth and Sixth Avenues
Ⓔ Ⓜ to Fifth Avenue–53rd Street; Ⓑ Ⓓ Ⓔ to Seventh Avenue

In 1929 the Museum of Modern Art (MoMA) was founded by Abby Aldrich Rockefeller and a couple of friends to exhibit modern art exclusively; its first loan exhibition in a rented office space displayed paintings by Van Gogh and other Postimpressionist painters. Ten years later the museum moved into its permanent home on West 53rd Street, designed by Philip L. Goodwin and Edward Durell Stone, a building that embraced the "International Style" promoted in their influential 1932 museum show of the same name. Expansions to the increasingly popular museum followed in 1951, with Philip Johnson's seven-story annex to the west and a sculpture garden (named after the founding Rockefeller) two years later; in 1964, when the same architect added a new east wing and expanded his own garden; and in 1984, when Cesar Pelli added a fifty-three-story residential tower (using the museum's own air rights in an effort to raise money for itself) and doubled the gallery space in a major renovation. The last expansion's mall-like spaces (complete with escalators overlooking the sculpture garden) were not embraced by critics or museum-goers, so it's no surprise that Yoshio Taniguchi's 1997 competition-winning design for MoMA's $425 million expansion does away with much of his immediate predecessor's handiwork.

The Japanese architect's plan for another doubling of the museum's exhibition space basically adds two buildings on either side of the sculpture garden, itself expanded once again. The galleries inside the Peggy and David Rockefeller Building are on the west, and the classrooms and other educational spaces inside the Lewis B. and Dorothy Cullman Exhibition and Research Building are on the east. Taniguchi also modified the third side of the sculpture garden, replacing Pelli's bank of escalators and cascading glass atrium wall with less overt circulation and flat glass walls, behind which is The Modern restaurant by Bentel & Bentel, which spills out into the garden in decent weather. Access to the museum is now available from both 53rd and 54th Streets, into a lobby at the base of the Rockefeller Building which affords an appealing view of the sculpture garden, enticing the visitor to plunk down $20 for admission. (The museum is free on Friday afternoons, but be warned: the line can stretch from the doors on 53rd Street, up Sixth Avenue, and back around beyond its other doors on 54th Street.) The galleries above are oriented around the Marron Atrium, visible from the lobby and four floors high; windows into the space allow museum-goers to reorient themselves as they move about the expansion's more than 600,000 square feet of new and redesigned space.

86 Four buildings, one MoMA (opposite, right to left): Johnson's east wing, Goodwin and Stone's original, Pelli's tower, Taniguchi's expansion. Photo by Adam Friedberg. The Marron Atrium above the lobby, visible at bottom right (left). Light entering the atrium through the skylights is softened by scrims (below). Looking east in the restored and expanded courtyard (bottom). Photos by Scott Norsworthy.

In the final stage of MoMA's invited competition, Taniguchi beat out Swiss architects Herzog & de Meuron and Bernard Tschumi, dean of Columbia University's Graduate School of Architecture, Preservation, and Planning at the time. This occurred at the end of a year that saw the opening of the Guggenheim in Bilbao by Frank Gehry. Tame in comparison to the runners-up, the winning design in both project and completed form recalls museums executed by Taniguchi in his homeland, expressions of his precise yet powerful brand of Modernism. The Gallery of Horyuji Treasures in Tokyo, for example, features slender pilotis and a framed glass box, echoed here in the façades overlooking the sculpture garden. With miles of white drywall defining MoMA's minimalist galleries, and dreary blank elevations facing West 54th Street, the architectural highlights are centered on the garden and atrium. Yet like other museums, it's the modern art masterpieces that bring in the crowds, not the white walls.

87 NYC INFORMATION CENTER

WXY ARCHITECTURE + URBAN DESIGN and LOCAL PROJECTS, 2009

810 Seventh Avenue, between 52nd and 53rd Streets
B D E to Seventh Avenue

The guidebook that you hold in your hands is fast becoming anachronistic, displaced by digital applications that offer limitless amounts of information, constant updates, and customization. Even now, visitors and residents moving about cities most likely use smartphones instead of books to determine their destination and route, be it to find a restaurant, a museum, or a piece of architecture. Yet the digital conveniences cannot completely abolish the traditional modes of learning about a place, whether books or facilities in the city that can offer personal interaction mixing the digital and the analog.

NYC & Company's bricks-and-mortar extension of its nycgo.com Web site is located in the high-traffic area just north of Times Square in a 2,000-square-foot storefront space that looks—and functions—unlike any other visitor center. Between the curving bases and tops of the side walls is a row of gray tabletops capped by what look like chopped-off letter i's (for information). These tables give visitors a treat: interactive maps powered by small discs that highlight different sights around the city. These devices allow custom tours to be created, watched on the rear wall, and printed out or sent to smartphones for use back out on the city streets.

87 The i's draw inside people in need of information (above). Photos of custom tours can be projected on the rear wall (right).
Photos © Paul Warchol.

CASSA NY **88**
TEN ARQUITECTOS with Cetra/Ruddy, 2010

70 West 45th Street, between Fifth and Sixth Avenues
B D F M to 42nd Street–Bryant Park; 7 to Fifth Avenue

Located about halfway between Bryant Park and Rockefeller Center, this forty-seven-story condo-hotel aims to set itself apart from its neighbors and contemporaries in its profile and window composition. The north-facing 45th Street façade, referred to in promotional literature as an obelisk, slants backward after stepping back at the eighth floor, yet at an angle so subtle as to be imperceptible. The east and west elevations are primarily solid with a random pixelated pattern of windows. Corner openings wrap around the north and south façades with regular grids of windows, minus the occasional one removed here and there. The cladding is white aluminum precast panels, unadorned except for joints and windowsills. The result is not as promising (or as expensive) as suggested by early renderings, but the slender tower still stands out from the masonry and glass that prevail.

88 Looking up at the punch-card north façade. Photo © Aaron Dougherty.

8

HARVARD CLUB OF NEW YORK CITY **89**
DAVIS BRODY BOND AEDAS, 2003

35 West 44th Street, between Fifth and Sixth Avenues
B D F M to 42nd Street–Bryant Park; 7 to Fifth Avenue

The Harvard Club of New York City dates back to 1865, but it wasn't until 1893 that its permanent home opened on West 44th Street, in a building by Charles McKim of McKim, Mead & White. The same architect added space to the club in later decades, culminating in a neo-Georgian composition landmarked by the city in 1967. When in 2001 the late Max Bond revealed his design for yet another addition, this time in a modern idiom, some alumni formed a committee in opposition on the grounds that the design wasn't consistent with the "Harvard look." These opponents developed a traditional alternative, but that plan failing, they went to court to halt construction, also an unsuccessful maneuver. A Harvard graduate himself, Bond designed an eight-story glass and stone addition that places guestrooms in a vertical piece set back from the street; the bar and lounge sit above the entrance behind glass. A frame for the last aligns with bands on the existing building, but it was the Harvard Club's decision to use Modernism to open itself up visually to the street that is important here, not the abstract references.

89 A study in oppositions and relationships. Photo © Paul Warchol.

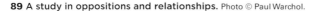

90 BANK OF AMERICA TOWER AT ONE BRYANT PARK

COOK + FOX ARCHITECTS with Adamson Associates Architects, 2009

1185 Avenue of the Americas, at 42nd Street

B D F M to 42nd Street–Bryant Park; 7 to Fifth Avenue

When 4 Times Square was completed on the cusp of the millennium, it was the greenest skyscraper anywhere, at a time when the LEED (Leadership in Energy and Environmental Design) green rating system had yet to take hold. Developed by the Durst Corporation and designed by Fox & Fowle Architects (now FXFOWLE), the forty-eight-story tower featured energy-efficient chillers, high-performance glazing, integrated photovoltaic panels, and other sustainable features not commonly used in tall buildings in the United States at the time but now becoming increasingly the norm. About five years later Durst and architects Richard Cook and Richard Fox (the Fox from Fox & Fowle, who formed Cook + Fox in 2003) unveiled designs for a fifty-five-story, 2.1-million-square-foot tower right next door to 4 Times Square, aiming to supplant its predecessor as the greenest of the green.

Success came upon its completion in the form of the first LEED Platinum Certification (the system's highest rating) for a commercial high-rise. Perhaps the most innovative sustainable element is the cogeneration plant located atop the building and in the cellar. In this system the heat produced by electrical generation is used to make steam for heating the building and heating water; at night it is used to create ice, which provides cooling the following day. In other words, the building recycles its own energy in what amounts to a closed loop, producing approximately two thirds of its power and reducing its grid demand and carbon emissions.

Rounding out the other important green features are translucent insulated glazing with optimal daylighting, rainwater harvesting, graywater recycling, waterless urinals, an under-floor fresh air system, and recycling in both construction materials and building management. The tower is an example of achieving sustainability by technological means, the prevailing trend of the new millennium. Even the building's crystalline form, which was influenced by one of the quartz crystals in the client's collection, was developed with the assistance of computer simulations to reduce wind drag against the building. This form is achieved by shearing the mass into two offset rectangular slabs and slicing them at different angles as they rise. Not surprisingly, the tower's best profile is from Bryant Park, where the spire and pointed corner are most prominent.

At its base the tower is a hodgepodge, the antithesis of the grand gestures above: a prominent corner canopy opposite the park is an extension of the wood ceiling in the Bank of America lobby; a new glass subway entry pavilion sits beneath the canopy; an "Urban Garden Room" with a "living sculpture" installation anchors the northeast corner; a terracotta-lined passage connects 42nd and 43rd Streets adjacent to 4 Times Square; and the preserved Henry Miller's Theatre (renamed the Stephen Sondheim Theatre in 2010) is incorporated into the podium on 43rd Street. These elements may not meld clearly with what is going on above, but at a time of increased security and antipathy toward banks, they are refreshing, yet still restrictive, insertions of semi-public spaces into a private development.

90 Seen from Bryant Park to the southeast, the faceted design is most striking (top, left). The southeast corner's canopy and new subway stair enclosure (top). Looking northeast in the "Urban Garden Room" (above). Inside the main Bank of America lobby (left).
Photos by Cook + Fox Architects.

EATING IN STYLE

Restaurants in New York City are an excellent barometer of trends and experimentation in architecture. The combination of small scale, tight schedules, and clients wanting to impress often results in stunning interior spaces, but the shifting tastes of foodies and the competitive nature of the business, especially in Manhattan, also means restaurants come and go, and more the latter in the wake of the 2008 economic collapse. This guidebook focuses on recent additions to the urban landscape that are more lasting and often larger in scale, but it is worth highlighting a handful of dining spaces that take stock of the diverse output of the first decade of the millennium.

MORIMOTO NYC
TADAO ANDO ARCHITECT & ASSOCIATES with Rose + Guggenheimer Studio, Stephanie Goto Design Group, 2006
88 Tenth Avenue, between 15th and 16th Streets (Map 6)

Japanese architect Tadao Ando's first New York City commission is a restaurant at the east end of the Chelsea Market for Iron Chef Masaharu Morimoto. Entry is underneath the High Line, through a gentle arch partially hung with traditional Japanese noren and framed by horizontal blackened steel siding. Inside is a light-filled two-level space set off by a wall of seventeen thousand illuminated plastic bottles. At an angle to this wall is a row of ornamental concrete columns, and above all is a fabric ceiling that recalls the raking of Japanese rock gardens.

BRASSERIE 8½
H3 HARDY COLLABORATION
ARCHITECTURE, 2000
9 West 57rd Street, between Fifth and Sixth Avenues (Map 8)

In the basement of the sloping glass-walled Solow Building (SOM, Gordon Bunshaft, 1974) is an unlikely inhabitant: a dining room with a grand entry and curving staircase befitting a 1940s Hollywood musical. The rich red floors and walls repeat Ivan Chermayeff's famous "9" in front and beckon a visit to the bar adjacent to the circular two-story space. It's a great place to watch the glamorous make an entrance. Photo © Peter Aaron/Esto.

BRASSERIE

DILLER SCOFIDIO + RENFRO, 2000

100 East 53rd Street, between Lexington and Park Avenues (Map 8)

The renovation by Elizabeth Diller and Ricardo Scofidio (now with Charles Renfro) of the Brasserie restaurant in Mies van der Rohe's classic modernist Seagram Building is an eclectic mix of shapes, surfaces, and materials. A scalloped wood ceiling wraps around the ends of the main space, penetrated at the front by the entry stair that deposits one gracefully in the middle of the space, like a sloping catwalk. A back room features objects suspended behind partially obscured glass panels. As in many well-appointed Manhattan eateries, the bathroom is a must-see. Photo © Michael Moran.

PIO PIO RESTAURANT

SEBASTIAN MARISCAL STUDIO, 2009

604 Tenth Avenue, between 43rd and 44th Streets (Map 9)

An awkward plan is exploited to great effect in the Hell's Kitchen location of the local Peruvian restaurant chain Pio Pio. The well-choreographed design by San Diego–based architect Sebastian Mariscal moves diners from the narrow entrance and the city's usual hustle-bustle into an impressive two-story dining room tucked deep inside the building. Covered with branches from desert shrubs, the space also includes sensuous surfaces of rough-formed concrete, reclaimed wood, and untreated brass panels.

THE WRIGHT

ANDRE KIKOSKI ARCHITECT, 2009

1071 Fifth Avenue, at 88th Street (Map 11)

Faced with the daunting task of designing a restaurant in Frank Lloyd Wright's iconic Guggenheim Museum, Andre Kikoski created an elegant space oriented about a curving white ceiling that follows the L-shaped plan, a design gesture subtly inspired by the museum's swirling rotunda. Adding a jolt of color to the primarily white space is British artist Liam Gillick's site-specific work, *The horizon produced by a factory once it had stopped producing views.*

Photo © Peter Aaron/Esto.

Riverside Park South •

• Riverside Center

See Map
11
Upper West Side

Hudson
River

John Jay College of Criminal Justice **96**•

W57 •

W 59th St
W 58th St
W 57th St
W 56th St
W 55th St
W 54th St

Central Park •

•**97** Hudson Hill Condominium

Ⓐ Ⓒ Ⓑ Ⓓ ①

Hudson New York •

Columbus Circle

Clinton Park •

Alvin Ailey American Dance Foundation •

Balsley Park 98•

W 53rd St
W 52nd St

•**95** **The Dillon**

•**99** **Hearst Tower**

Ⓝ Ⓠ Ⓡ

• Hudson River Park

W 51st St
W 50th St
W 49th St
W 48th St
W 47th St
W 46th St
W 45th St
W 44th St
W 43rd St

Broadway

Ⓑ Ⓓ Ⓔ

Ⓒ Ⓔ

• Pio Pio Restaurant

1/4-mile
radius

• 785 Eighth Avenue

①

Ⓝ Ⓠ Ⓡ

• West Midtown Intermodal
Ferry Terminal

W 42nd St
W 41st St
W 40th St
W 39th St
W 38th St

Eleventh Av

Tenth Av

Ninth Av

• The Signature Center

West Side Highway

•**91** TKTS

Ⓑ Ⓓ
Ⓕ Ⓜ

• Jacob K. Javits
Convention Center

W 37th St
W 36th St
W 35th St

Triple Bridges •

Ⓐ Ⓒ Ⓔ

•**94** **Westin New York**

• Affirmation Arts

New 42nd Street Studios **92**•

Ⓐ Ⓢ

• Armed Forces Recruiting Station

37 ARTS •

New York Times Building **93**•

① ② ③

Ⓝ Ⓠ Ⓡ

• Condé Nast Building

• World Product Centre

Eighth Av

Seventh Av

Broadway

Sixth Av

Ⓑ Ⓓ
Ⓕ Ⓜ

Bryant
Park

See Map
8
Midtown East

⑦

W 34th St
W 33rd St
W 31st St
W 30th St
W 29th St
W 28th St

Ⓐ Ⓒ Ⓔ

• Moynihan Station

① ② ③

15 Penn Plaza •

Ⓑ Ⓓ
Ⓕ Ⓜ
Ⓝ Ⓠ Ⓡ

Fifth Av

Madison Av

See Map
6
Chelsea

• F.I.T. - C2

See Map
7
Murray Hill

After JFK, LaGuardia, or Newark airports, the first destination

for most visitors to New York City is Times Square, alternately called the Theatre District. This tendency stems mainly from the fact that so many large hotels can be found steps from the bowtie intersection of Broadway and Seventh Avenue, not that tourists are drawn to the famous lights of the place like moths to a flame. Of course, staying in Times Square was not so desirable decades ago, in the days between the area's boom as *the* place to go in the city for entertainment and its current resurgence as a brighter, sanitized version of its former self. The *New York Times* moved to 42nd Street in 1904, giving the area its name, but it was the opening of the subway the same year that first brought crowds to the area, which subsequently filled with theaters.

As a result of the decline in theatergoing brought on by the popularity of movies and television in the middle of the century, many theaters were either demolished or transformed into "adult" entertainment. A concerted effort on the part of the city to clean up the area starting in the 1990s found realization in the renovation of old theaters by The New 42nd Street, Inc., and a cluster of new skyscrapers around Broadway and Seventh Avenue at the turn of the millennium. In accordance with the Theatre Subdistrict requirements of the Department of City Planning, these and other new buildings must incorporate large illuminated signs into their façades "to ensure the continued brilliance of the celebrated Great White Way." This brilliance—a mix of theater billboards and corporate advertising—is now easily appreciated from the pedestrian plazas created along Broadway in 2009.

Clinton may not share many traits with its glitzy neighbor to the east, but both areas can be found guilty of mining the distant past to gloss over the negative associations of the more recent past. What Times Square did with theater renovations and marquee lights, Clinton tried to do with a name. Still called Hell's Kitchen by most residents, the area was rebranded by real estate developers in the late 1950s in reference to DeWitt Clinton, the early-nineteenth-century New York governor whose farm predated the slaughterhouse, warehouses, lumberyards, and factories that covered the area west of Eighth Avenue from 30th to 59th Streets. Developers are lining the blocks north of the Jacob Javits Convention Center with condo towers just steps from the Hudson River Park, hoping the rebranding effort succeeds.

91 Looking north toward the seats for the show that is Times Square (left).
Housed in a fiberglass pod, the ticket booths are tucked under the stairs (right).
Photos by Paúl Rivera/Archphoto.

9

91 TKTS

PERKINS EASTMAN with Choi Ropiha, 2008

Father Duffy Square, at Broadway and 47th Street
Ⓝ Ⓠ Ⓡ to 49th Street

In 1973 the Theatre Development Fund's TKTS (pronounced with each letter sounded out) ticket booth opened next to the statue of Father Francis P. Duffy in Times Square, an area then more popular with prostitutes than tourists. The decision to have a booth selling half-price day-of-performance tickets for Broadway shows was aimed at bringing a more legitimate business and patronage to the neighborhood. That change took time, but the first booth wasn't exactly built to last; the ticket booths proper were housed in a construction trailer fronted by a frame assembled from scaffolding parts that displayed white canvas signage and the letters TKTS. In response to the twenty-plus years of deterioration, the TDF and Van Alen Institute launched the TKTS2K competition for a new booth in 1999. Out of the nearly seven hundred entries submitted, Australian architects John Choi and Tai Ropiha won with a terrace of bright red steps starting at the base of Father Duffy and ending above the new ticket booths, in effect adding seats to the theater that is Time Square.

A couple of years later, Perkins Eastman started to develop Choi Ropiha's design concept to turn it into built reality. (The design of the surrounding plaza is the work of William Fellows Architects.) Glass is the primary element, as both surface and structure: the red steps (illuminated from below by LED lights) are supported by matching glass stringers, like a stairway; clear glass covers the east and west sides, doubling as guardrails. Visible behind these side walls are the TKTS-emblazoned, fiberglass-formed booths and the caps of 450-foot-deep geothermal wells that heat or cool the interior air and keep the steps ice-free in the winter, ensuring that in all seasons the inclined public space is a popular place to take in the lights and energy of the center of "the center of the world."

NEW 42ND STREET STUDIOS 92
PLATT BYARD DOVELL WHITE, 2000

229 West 42nd Street, between Broadway and Eighth Avenue
Ⓐ Ⓒ Ⓔ to 42nd Street–Port Authority;
❶ ❷ ❸ ❼ N Q R S to Times Square–42nd Street

As the twentieth century marched along, the 1920s theaters on 42nd Street between Broadway and Eighth Avenue morphed into the XXX movie houses frequented by the likes of Travis Bickle in *Taxi Driver*. In response to these conditions and a desire to transform the area for more mainstream entertainment and cultural uses, city and state officials created the 42nd Street Redevelopment Project, into which a nonprofit, The New 42nd Street, was charged with overseeing the renovation and operation of the block's historic theaters. With space for two nonprofit organizations required in the redevelopment, The New 42nd Street Studios moved into a new ten-story building containing rehearsal studios, offices, and a black-box theater, called The Duke, on 42nd Street.

Charles Platt and Ray Dovell's interpretation of the redevelopment's lighting requirements eschewed the prevailing trend (then and now) of illuminated billboards and signage. The architects, working with Vortex Lighting, instead treated the south-facing street elevation as one large abstract display of colored light. Perforated stainless steel blades are located about three feet in front of the glass and aluminum curtain wall. The blades filter sunlight entering the rehearsal spaces during the day, but at night, exterior-mounted LED lights shine onto the blades, reflecting the ever-changing lightshow to the sidewalk below. The remarkable effect is a welcome respite from the corporate imagery of the surrounding buildings on 42nd Street, Broadway, and Seventh Avenue. In other cases the light displays conceal mediocre buildings, but here the architecture really shines.

9

92 During the day the building is glass and gray (left). At night the façade is a kaleidoscope of color (above). Photos by Elliott Kaufman.

93 NEW YORK TIMES BUILDING

RENZO PIANO BUILDING WORKSHOP and FXFOWLE ARCHITECTS, 2007

620 Eighth Avenue
Ⓐ Ⓒ Ⓔ to 42nd Street-Port Authority

In 2000 The New York Times Company invited a handful of well-known architects to compete for the newspaper's seventh headquarters in its 150-year history. Italian architect Renzo Piano won with an elegant glass tower sheathed in a veil of horizontal ceramic rods, though it seemed as if more press coverage focused on Frank Gehry's withdrawal from the competition soon before the final judging. Garbed in a flowing, fabric-like skin, it might have been Gehry's first skyscraper, an honor that eventually went to 8 Spruce Street (**9**) for developer Forest City Ratner, which also developed the Times Building. Less copy was devoted to the use of eminent domain to wrest land away from property owners, and to demolish a number of buildings deemed blighted, making way for the fifty-two-story, 1.5-million-square-foot tower. (Eminent domain appears to follow Mr. Piano in the city, as his Columbia University Manhattanville expansion, under way at this writing, also involves property seizure for a much larger project.) What was clear was that the city and state wanted to forestall the *Times*'s threatened move to New Jersey and instead keep the paper's offices in its namesake area, a block and a half from its previous quarters. Directly across the street from the busy and ungainly Port Authority bus terminal, the New York Times Building occupies the southwestern corner of the Time Square Alliance's district and the southern tip of the Business Improvement District's (BID) Eighth Avenue commercial corridor, touted as the "Avenue of Architecture."

Although its history involves bullying, at ground level the structure is more inviting to the public than most Manhattan office buildings. Instead of its lobby being closed off in response to post-9/11 security concerns, people can walk throughout the H-shaped space from Eighth Avenue to the glass-walled garden (designed by HM White Site Architects) planted with birch trees and moss; linking these two areas is the wall-mounted installation *Moveable Type* by Mark Hansen and Ben Rubin. Included in the low-rise portion to the east of the tower is TheTimesCenter, a cultural center and performance space offering public programs. Back in the lobby, the walls of the two elevator cores are finished in marigold-colored plaster, a strong counterpoint to the ceramic rods and gray-painted steel and metal throughout. More splashes of color can be found in the bright red security furnishings in the lobby and in the communicating stairs (not fire stairs) of the Gensler-designed *New York Times* offices on the lower floors; these stairs are visible from the two street corners on Eighth Avenue.

Of course, most of the attention is lavished on the scrim comprised of an astonishing 186,000 white-glazed ceramic rods, each almost five feet long. This extra layer filters the sunlight entering the office floors, but for the rest of the city it is an atmospheric barometer: on gray days the building looks dull, but on sunny days it is dazzling, especially at sunset. The ladder-like characteristic of the scrim was not lost on two men—one from France and one from Brooklyn—who scaled the tower without safety devices on the same summer day in 2008. Their antics prompted the removal of some of the rods close to the sidewalk so no repetition could occur. Thankfully, over 185,000 ceramic rods still remain.

93 Looking west from alongside the Port Authority Bus Terminal (top, left). Photo by the author. The Eighth Avenue façade and red stairs at night (top, center). The lobby connecting 40th and 41st Streets (top, right). The garden is a delight in winter (above). Photos by Scott Norsworthy. A view of *Moveable Type* in the lobby (left). Photo © Francis Dzikowski/Esto.

94 WESTIN NEW YORK
ARQUITECTONICA, 2002

270 West 43rd Street, at Eighth Avenue
Ⓐ Ⓒ Ⓔ to 42nd Street–Port Authority

A cluster of glass skyscrapers around Broadway and 42nd Street were the first major vertical pieces in the recent redevelopment of Times Square, but those buildings recede into the cacophony of lights, while the Westin Hotel, close on the heels of those buildings, stands out in its location. Miami-based architects Bernardo Fort-Brescia and Laurinda Spear infused the building with different colors and stripes of reflected glass, organized about a swooping curve that is illuminated at night. A glass tower rising along 43rd Street engages a seventeen-story base on 42nd Street covered in billboards, lights, and even more color—metal painted in an abstract pattern. Critics praised and panned the design in equal parts, calling it both "a Latin jolt to the skyline"[1] and "a developer's box in drag."[2] As more restrained skyscrapers have risen nearby, a decade later the building still stands out, an embrace of Times Square that turns the building into a giant billboard for the hotel chain.

94 The Westin before construction of its new neighbors to the south. Photo by Norman McGrath.

95 THE DILLON
SMITH-MILLER + HAWKINSON ARCHITECTS, 2010

405 West 53rd Street, between Ninth and Tenth Avenues
Ⓒ Ⓔ to 50th Street; ① Ⓐ Ⓒ Ⓑ Ⓓ to 59th Street–Columbus Circle

The building boom in residential condos in the early 2000s took many forms, but most of the attention went to glass towers. These stood out from and above their older masonry neighbors, giving the few residents picture postcard views of the surrounding urban landscape. But The Dillon resists this trend in favor of a low and long orientation, like a glass tower on its side. Behind the serrated glass profile are a mix of town houses, "flats," duplexes, and penthouses—eighty-three units on seven floors. Architects Henry Smith-Miller and Laurie Hawkinson reference Jane Jacobs's classic study, *The Death and Life of Great American Cities*, and while a mix of uses and incomes is nowhere to be found in this upper-income residential development, its low-rise stature embraces what she coined "eyes on the street," something missing in high-rise living. The faceted façade guarantees that those eyes will see a lot of the street, from sunrise to sunsets over the Hudson.

95 Projecting operable windows make the serrated glass exterior even more distinctive. Photo © Michael Moran.

JOHN JAY COLLEGE OF CRIMINAL JUSTICE **96**
SKIDMORE, OWINGS & MERRILL, 2011
59th Street at Eleventh Avenue
❶ Ⓐ Ⓒ Ⓑ Ⓓ to 59th Street–Columbus Circle

John Jay College of Criminal Justice, part of the City University of New York, celebrated its fortieth anniversary with a 625,000-square-foot expansion that completes a full city block west of Columbus Circle. The design by SOM (Skidmore, Owings & Merrill) pushes the school toward the nearby Hudson River and McKim, Mead & White's massive IRT Powerhouse (now a ConEd steam plant). The "New John Jay" is a fourteen-story building linked to Haren Hall—an early-twentieth-century high school the college moved into in 1973—on three levels; this link negotiates the site's east-west grade change via cascading stairs and escalators, provides a new entrance on 59th Street, and is capped by a green roof used as the campus commons. The glass box on Eleventh Avenue houses a myriad of academic and administrative spaces behind a curtain wall with projecting fins selectively treated with color to accentuate certain views of it; special interior spaces are articulated by cuts in this exterior skin. This expansion consolidates college facilities previously dispersed throughout the area into one urban campus.

96 Seen down Eleventh Avenue, the reddish fins are subtly apparent.

HUDSON HILL CONDOMINIUM **97**
FXFOWLE ARCHITECTS, 2009
462 West 58th Street, between Ninth and Tenth Avenues
❶ Ⓐ Ⓒ Ⓑ Ⓓ to 59th Street–Columbus Circle

From a distance the sculpted façade of the Hudson Hill Condominium appears to be a painted metal interpretation of the surrounding brick buildings. As one approaches the building, a pattern on the panels starts to appear, until up close, one sees wood grain. Is the exterior covered in wood? Actually, no; it is a ventilated rain screen cladding covered with a high-pressure laminate coated in a decorative surface. This blend of wood-based fibers and resins is not new, but its use in the United States is fairly recent, in no small part because of stringent fire codes. And while this project is not the first New York City application (Chelsea Arts Tower [Map 6] takes that prize), it is the first to exploit the potential for color and pattern available in such a system. An imitation wood-grained panel building may sound unappealing, but here the result is far from your parents' station wagon.

97 Squarish openings punctuate the wood-grain façade. Photo © Aaron Dougherty.

98 BALSLEY PARK
THOMAS BALSLEY ASSOCIATES, 2000

866 Ninth Avenue, between 56th and 57th Streets
① Ⓐ Ⓒ Ⓑ Ⓓ to 59th Street–Columbus Circle

Most of the Privately Owned Public Spaces (POPS) created since the start of the 1961 zoning incentive are located adjacent to the buildings that receive the square-footage bonus. But Sheffield Plaza, the first incarnation of the POPS on this site, was built three hundred feet west of its associated high-rise residential tower, which now butts up against Hearst Tower. This situation contributed to the failure of the public space, a poorly maintained plaza with one bright spot: a greenmarket two days a week. In response to its deterioration and lack of use outside of the market (still held in the space on Wednesdays and Saturdays), the plaza's owner hired landscape architect Thomas Balsley to develop a new plan that is more park-like than its predecessor. An amphitheater tucked next to the plaza's easterly neighbor was replaced by a grass mound, turning a dead zone into a spot to soak up some of the sun's rays. This same mound also sets up a diagonal path that meanders from 57th Street to Ninth Avenue, after it splits toward a playground at the southwest corner. The northwest corner is occupied by a food kiosk and an elevated seating area overlooking the park, a response to the site's change in level from north to south.

The combination of hard and soft in the paths and plantings is certainly commendable and a big improvement over Sheffield Plaza, but Balsley's handling of the edges gives the space its strongest character. A simple fence with gates fronts the sidewalk on three sides, but inside the park, bright green corrugated metal walls undulate along the eastern edge. Overlapping these are curving screens of closely spaced red pipes that work with the green walls to define smaller spaces within the park. Its success is evinced in the naming of the park after its designer, who has designed at least fifty POPS around the city.

98 Looking north from the playground on West 56th Street (above, left). Looking south from West 57th Street along the meandering path (left). Photos by Thomas Balsley Associates.

HEARST TOWER **99**
FOSTER + PARTNERS
with Adamson Associates Architects, 2006

300 West 57th Street, at Ninth Avenue
1 **A** **C** **B** **D** to 59th Street–Columbus Circle

In late 2001 the Landmarks Preservation Commission approved a forty-story addition to the Hearst Corporation's six-story 1926 Art Deco stone landmark by architect and set designer Joseph Urban. Norman Foster's oppositional design received LPC's blessing partly because Urban's building was envisioned as the base of a taller structure that was never realized or planned. One word can be used to describe Foster's design: diagrid. The structure of the tower utilizes a triangular diagrid system to use a fifth less steel than conventional post-and-beam framing. A grid of four-story triangles is created, and the corners are pulled in and out like a series of ascending open beaks. In its reliance on a single device, the design recalls the structural inventiveness of R. Buckminster Fuller, whom Foster worked with in the 1970s, and his mentor's do-more-with-less (20 percent less, in this case) philosophy.

At sidewalk level the Urban base looks clean and a bit, well, plastic. Grime will work its way back into the stone again over time, but the effect is like that of a newly poured re-creation of the landmark. The main entry is on Eighth Avenue, but access to the six-story atrium is limited to the few feet inside the doors, in front of the security gates. On entry the vista is dominated by James Carpenter's three-story water feature of cascading cast glass obliquely split in two by the escalators to the upper lobby. The tower may embrace Bucky Fuller, but in this large atrium space of overlapping art, structure, glass, and stone, theatricality more reminiscent of Joseph Urban prevails.

99 From any angle the diamond-patterned exterior stands out (above). Photo by Scott Norsworthy. **Richard Long's fresco** *Riverlines* **adorns the wall above the water feature (left).** Photo © Francis Dzikowski/Esto. **The glass tower rises from a base eighty years its elder (right).** Photo by Scott Norsworthy.

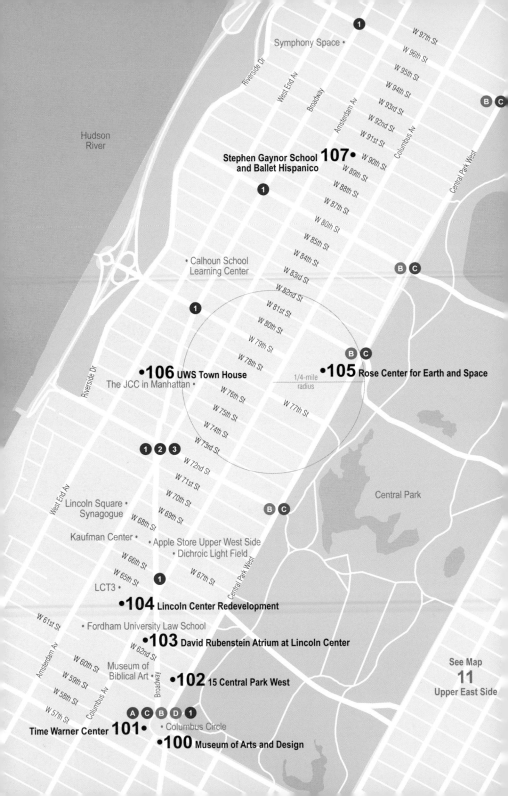

Symphony Space ●

1

W 97th St
W 96th St
W 95th St
W 94th St
W 93rd St
W 92nd St
W 91st St
W 90th St
W 89th St
W 88th St
W 87th St

B **C**

Hudson
River

Riverside Dr
West End Av
Broadway
Amsterdam Av
Columbus Av
Central Park West

**Stephen Gaynor School
and Ballet Hispanico** **107**●

1

● Calhoun School
Learning Center

W 86th St
W 85th St
W 84th St
W 83rd St

B **C**

W 82nd St
W 81st St
W 80th St
W 79th St
W 78th St

1

Riverside Dr

●**106** UWS Town House
The JCC in Manhattan ●

1/4-mile
radius

B **C**

●**105** Rose Center for Earth and Space

W 77th St
W 76th St
W 75th St
W 74th St
W 73rd St

1 **2** **3**

W 72nd St
W 71st St
W 70th St
W 69th St

West End Av

Lincoln Square ●
Synagogue

W 68th St

B **C**

Central Park

Kaufman Center ●

● Apple Store Upper West Side
● Dichroic Light Field

W 66th St
W 67th St

W 65th St

1

LCT3 ●

Central Park West

●**104** Lincoln Center Redevelopment

W 61st St

● Fordham University Law School

W 62nd St

●**103** David Rubenstein Atrium at Lincoln Center

Amsterdam Av

W 60th St
W 59th St

Museum of
Biblical Art ●

Columbus Av

Broadway

●**102** 15 Central Park West

W 58th St
W 57th St

A **C** **B** **D** **1**

**See Map
11
Upper East Side**

Time Warner Center **101**●

● Columbus Circle

●**100** Museum of Arts and Design

Forever compared with its namesake to the east

of Central Park, generally the Upper West Side is seen as liberal and artistic while the Upper East Side is more conservative and businesslike. Development of the Upper West Side lagged behind its eastern counterpart, as the area formerly known as Bloomingdale didn't bloom until after the arrival of the Ninth Avenue elevated train and the construction of the Dakota Apartments, both around 1880. Overlooking Central Park, the Dakota accurately summarizes the area's penchant for grand apartment buildings on Central Park West (it and other north-south numbered roads were given more romantic names above 59th Street at this time to attract people to the area) and up and down Broadway. Even Donald Trump contributed his own grand vision to a stretch of Riverside Drive between 59th and 72nd Streets, an undulating wall of blandness that will eventually be linked directly to Riverside Park over a buried West Side Highway. Above 72nd Street is the original Riverside Park by Central Park designers Frederick Law Olmsted and Calvert Vaux; these two green spaces bookend the Upper West Side, stretching from 59th Street to 110th Street.

10

The southeastern corner of the area is occupied by Columbus Circle, which has carried that name since the 1894 installation of a statue of the Italian explorer atop a 70-foot-high column. Like the buildings around the traffic circle, the space itself has changed; it is now easier to traverse, with a center conducive to sitting. North of the circle, with its major underground transportation node, is Lincoln Square, the neighborhood that is home to Fordham University and Lincoln Center, two urban redevelopment projects on the site of razed "slums." It would be hard to overestimate the importance of this artistic hub in the city and the country, but needless to say, its presence in the Upper West Side greatly contributes to the population that typifies the neighborhood.

100 MUSEUM OF ARTS AND DESIGN
ALLIED WORKS ARCHITECTURE, 2008

2 Columbus Circle, between Broadway and Eighth Avenue

1 A C B D to 59th Street–Columbus Circle

The Museum of Arts and Design (MAD) traces its origins back to 1942, but its tenure at 2 Columbus Circle didn't start until it moved into these new digs designed by Brad Cloepfil of Seattle-based Allied Works. Before 2008, as the Museum of Contemporary Crafts and then the American Craft Museum, it lived in various buildings near MoMA on West 53rd Street.

From 1964 to 2005 the trapezoidal site facing Columbus Circle was occupied by a marble-clad building designed by Edward Durell Stone for Huntington Hartford's Gallery of Modern Art, which later housed city offices. Stone's design became known as "the lollipop building," after critic Ada Louise Huxtable referred to the design as a "die-cut Venetian palazzo on lollipops."[1] In 2003 Cloepfil's proposed changes to the building sparked the ire of writers, artists, critics, and politicians, all unsuccessful in stopping modifications to a structure that was never landmarked. Even before MAD opened the doors to its new 50,000-square-foot home, critics lambasted the design, none more scathingly than *New York Times* architecture critic Nicolai Ouroussoff, who issued a hyperbolic call for its demolition, along with other buildings that "have a traumatic effect on the city."[2]

Traumatic, hardly, but the terracotta-clad design (iridescent in certain light) is less distinctive and memorable than its predecessor, a subtle redesign where bolder might actually have been better. About all that visibly remains of Stone's design is all but one of the lollipop columns, veiled from outside but apparent inside the lobby and store. The narrow cuts that snake up the façades are clearly composed, but they make more sense inside the galleries, where the vertical glass links up with glass strips in the floor, in effect unifying the four sides and providing sometimes unexpected views within the museum and across the newly renovated Columbus Circle.

100 Looking southeast from in front of Time Warner Center (left). Photo by Hélène Binet. **Off the lobby, a new stairway and an old lollipop (top).** Photo by Adam Friedberg.

TIME WARNER CENTER

SKIDMORE, OWINGS & MERRILL, 2004

Ten Columbus Circle, at Broadway and 59th Street

1 **A** **C** **B** **D** to 59th Street–Columbus Circle

Robert Moses was known as much for his misses as for his hits. Lincoln Center, now middle-aged (and redeveloped), is one of the "master builder's" highlights, but as Christopher Gray so eloquently put it, the windowless 1956 Coliseum exposition hall on the west side of Columbus Circle was "a low point for New York's public buildings."[3] The opening in the mid-1980s of the much larger Jacob K. Javits Convention Center on the West Side nullified the need for the Coliseum and sparked plans for its replacement. An early design by Moshe Safdie for Boston Properties was quashed by some well-coordinated opposition, but the basic ingredients were twin mixed-use towers atop a curving retail atrium.

By the time the Coliseum came down in 2000, developer Related Companies and designers David Childs and Mustafa Abadan of SOM had a considerably smaller scheme (2.8 million square feet, down from 5.25 million) and a major tenant in AOL Time Warner. Dropping the "AOL" from its name, the Time Warner Center opened a few years later, the first major building completed after the September 11, 2001 attacks; the twin tower coincidence did not go unnoticed. The project includes offices for its namesake corporation, a hotel, condo residences, a retail and restaurant complex, and Jazz at Lincoln Center, a Rafael Viñoly–designed space with a stunning Central Park backdrop, thanks to a light and highly transparent cable net glass wall designed by James Carpenter which also encloses the mall's four-story atrium below.

The design of the Time Warner Center fluctuates between two scales. From close up, one's experience benefits from the glass wall framing the park and the curving retail arcade. Yet from farther away the angled towers (following the diagonal route of Broadway) appear singular and bulky (say, from 15 Central Park West [**102**]) or distinct and slender (from Central Park South). Whatever the view, the project is a huge improvement over the previous occupant.

101 Looking west across Columbus Circle (left). From the middle of Columbus Circle, the atrium's glass wall stands out amid the large project (right). Photos by Michael Amechi.

102 15 CENTRAL PARK WEST

ROBERT A. M. STERN ARCHITECTS with SLCE Architects, 2008

15 Central Park West, at West 61st Street
① Ⓐ Ⓒ Ⓑ Ⓓ to 59th Street–Columbus Circle

Postmodern architecture—the style associated with the ironic collage of forms and elements from classical and other historic architecture—is officially dead, according to most architects and critics. A few practitioners continue to design in that vein, most notably Michael Graves, but others who took the historical references of Postmodernism to heart have embraced traditional architecture, removing irony from the equation. Robert A. M. Stern—the dean of the Yale School of Architecture, coauthor of a series of encyclopedic works on architecture and urbanism in New York City over the last 150 years, and the head of a 220-person firm in the same city—is easily the best known and most prolific of the latter.

Fifteen Central Park West is Stern's design for the brothers Zeckendorf, developers who appreciate a backward glance with their luxury apartment buildings. It sits on a full block that extends from Central Park West to Broadway, the eastern half formerly occupied by the Mayflower Hotel. Stern balances these two realms—the masonry street wall bordering Central Park and the towers marching down Broadway's diagonal—by splitting the two hundred residences into a nineteen-story "house" on the park and a thirty-five-story tower to the west; in between is a formal drop-off with a lobby in a copper-roofed rotunda, and along Broadway is a retail podium. Limestone covering every façade may put this building at odds with most high-end starchitect-designed residential towers in recent years, but this and other designs (**9**, **13**) may at last signal that all-glass architecture is not the only option.

102 The nineteen-story "house" fronts the thirty-five-story tower (above). The tower on Broadway is highly visible from Central Park (right).

10

DAVID RUBENSTEIN ATRIUM AT LINCOLN CENTER 103
TOD WILLIAMS BILLIE TSIEN ARCHITECTS, 2009

61 West 62nd Street, between Broadway and Columbus Avenue
➊ to 66th Street–Lincoln Center

In its previous incarnation this Privately Owned Public Space (POPS) at the base of a twenty-seven-story condo tower featured an oddity, a climbing wall. Those scaling the two-story wall in what was then the Harmony Atrium certainly enlivened the through-block space, but with the fiftieth-anniversary makeover of Lincoln Center taking shape across the street, a renovation was in order. Architects Tod Williams and Billie Tsien replaced one piece of pseudo-nature (rock) with another: vertical hydroponic gardens are located near the entrances to the enclosed atrium at

Broadway and Columbus Avenue. Designed with Vertical Gardens Technology, these site-specific installations are accompanied by a nearly 100-foot-long yellow and gray felt mural by Dutch artist Claudy Jongstra and a fountain designed by the architects that features twelve suspended stainless steel rods over which water slowly trickles. Other insertions into the POPS include a media wall and stage opposite the mural, a sandwich counter, bathrooms on the second floor (very nice ones), and a counter selling half-price, same-day tickets for Lincoln Center, à la TKTS (**91**) a mile down Broadway.

10

Uniting the disparate elements along the Broadway-Columbus spine are elliptical oculi in the painted yellow ceiling. A few of the openings are paired up, like a cell about to split, and two are located in the sidewalk canopies, a hint of what's inside. Helping the skylights stand out further are their white walls and the double duty they perform as housing for artificial lighting. The latter allows the ceiling surface to remain free of most openings and enables the skylights to glow, even on overcast days.

103 A space of skylights, gardens, art, and people (above). Vertical hydroponic gardens greet visitors at the two main entrances (left).

104 LINCOLN CENTER REDEVELOPMENT

DILLER SCOFIDIO + RENFRO with FXFOWLE Architects and Beyer Blinder Belle, 2009-2011

1941 Broadway, at West 66th Street
❶ to 66th Street–Lincoln Center

New York City's 1955 designation of a seventeen-block area in Lincoln Square for redevelopment was the impetus for "the nation's first cultural complex,"[4] Lincoln Center for the Performing Arts. A handful of well-known architects—Wallace K. Harrison, Philip Johnson, Pietro Belluschi, Eero Saarinen, Gordon Bunshaft of SOM—helped shape one of Robert Moses's most successful urban renewal projects, housing institutions synonymous with the city and its cultural production: the Metropolitan Opera, New York Philharmonic Orchestra, Julliard School, New York City Ballet, and others. In the multiblock plan, spanning from 62nd to 66th Streets and Columbus to Amsterdam Avenues, figure alternates with ground in hardscape plazas between large edifices of stone and glass. Together they are the embodiment of postwar urban planning and the antithesis of the supposed slums razed for what has been referred to as an "Acropolis for the cultural elite."[5]

To commemorate the fiftieth anniversary of the performing arts center, an international competition was held in 2002 for the renovation and expansion of its facilities. Elizabeth Diller and Ricardo Scofidio (now with Charles Renfro) beat out the bigger and more established architects Richard Meier, Norman Foster, and Santiago Calatrava. Up to that time the winning architects were known for a number of set designs, some temporary installations, and a restaurant in the Seagram Building (see page 117). They aimed to "turn the campus inside out by extending the spectacle within...into the mute public spaces."[6] In other words, they wanted to undo the negative connotations associated with Lincoln Center by exploiting its positive aspects, an approach born from their admitted appreciation of the place.

Their design is a patchwork, ranging from barely perceptible touches to entire building additions. In order of completion the public design elements include the extension of Alice Tully Hall and the Julliard School toward Broadway at West 65th Street, along with a grandstand, sunken public plaza, and adjacent indoor café; the Capitol Grove and its new seating; the Central Plaza fountain and access to this "front door" from Columbus Avenue by way of steps with integral LED tickertape risers and ramps covered with glass canopies, both over now submerged vehicular access; a 250-seat restaurant below the sloping and accessible Illumination Lawn midway down West 65th Street; a bridge from the adjacent plaza over 65th Street to the Julliard School; and an "Infoscape" with signs and video along this same corridor.

Peeling is a word that comes to mind when one is traversing the spaces of Lincoln Center. The lawn over the restaurant appears to peel up from the plaza and its reflecting pool; walls peel back to reveal stairs throughout, such as at the Julliard School and lower-level drop-off near Columbus Avenue; even the cantilevered glass wall of Alice Tully Hall aligned with Broadway looks as if it has peeled away from the Pietro Belluschi building rather than being an addition to it. Intentional or not, this impression of peeling is aligned with a strategy of fairly minimal interventions

104 The sunken plaza and indoor café at Alice Tully Hall (top, left). Photo by Scott Norsworthy. **Looking toward the Illumination Lawn from the Capitol Grove (top, right). One of the two canopies reaching from the plaza to Columbus Avenue (above, right).** Photo by Scott Norsworthy. **Entrance stairs/seats of the Julliard School (above, left).**

that create smaller pockets of space within the formerly barren and overwhelming plazas. Most obviously successful is the transformation of West 65th Street from a service corridor to a street that invites pedestrians. The café and sunken plaza also work well together to create a new social nexus for Lincoln Center. The entry steps to the Julliard School are a design highlight, tiered ribbons that double as seats for students and visitors. Not surprisingly, criticism has been leveled at just about every aspect of this very public project as it slowly unfurls, but at none more than the fountain (WET's design is considered too Vegas, splashing people sitting on the perimeter) and grass lawn (seen as pointless to some though in need of a partial redesign because it has been so popular with others). Regardless, I recommend that you come see for yourself how this patchwork design works with its huge Modernist canvas.

105 ROSE CENTER FOR EARTH AND SPACE
ENNEAD ARCHITECTS, 2000

81 Central Park West, at 81st Street

B C to 81st Street–Museum of Natural History

The first Hayden Planetarium opened in 1935, about sixty-five years after the founding of its parent American Museum of Natural History (AMNH). Aiming to "give the public a more lively and sincere appreciation of the magnitude of the universe," the distinctive dome housing a Zeiss star projector enabled visitors to feel "the immensity of the sky."[7] Its 2000 replacement, the Frederick Phineas and Sandra Priest Rose Center for Earth and Space, designed by Todd Schliemann and James Stewart Polshek, dramatically carries out these goals in a sphere ringed by ramps and models of planets, in effect making the space a visual representation of the solar system. This sphere hangs within a 95-foot glass cube, its walls suspended from the roof and stabilized with larger vertical trusses. The clear glass gives the addition an especially strong presence at night, when the metal skin of the sphere is lit blue.

The 2,000-ton sphere and its two high-tech theaters may get all the attention, but these are actually part of a much larger project undertaken by the AMNH to reshape its image at the end of the twentieth century. The Rose Center for Earth and Space occupies 335,000 square feet on the museum's north side; in addition to the Planetarium, it includes the Cullman Hall exhibition space, the Arthur Ross Terrace, and the Weston Pavilion. The second is located above a three hundred–space parking garage with upper access to the Rose Center, and the last is the entry from Columbus Avenue, an access point marked by Santiago Calatrava's installation *The Times Capsule*. Standing in direct contrast to its larger, historically landmarked institution, the Planetarium is a forward-thinking addition still fresh more than a decade after its construction and still inspiring young minds with the wonders of space.

105 The glass cube and metal sphere seen from the Ross Terrace (above). Photo © Francis Dzikowski/Esto. **Bridges and ramps traverse the space between sphere and cube (left).** Photo by Scott Norsworthy.

UWS TOWN HOUSE 106
WORKSHOP/APD, 2010

252 West 75th Street, between
Broadway and West End Avenue
❶ ❷ ❸ to 72nd Street

106 The terracotta color blends with the brick neighbors. Photo by Jonathan Calderon Flores.

Baguettes may be bread, but in the world of contemporary architecture they are ceramic pipes, usually in a square cross-section, in most cases integrated into larger rain screen façades. They act as sunshade devices when placed in front of windows, while also adding aesthetic interest. This residence by the firm of Matthew Berman and Andrew Kotchen covers its north-facing elevation with tightly spaced baguettes to create a terracotta veil of sorts, a design that, like Peter Gluck's Urban Town House (**79**), is contemporary in form and technique but relates to its older neighbors. The glass box behind the screen reveals itself at the west corner and in three openings that march up the façade on the east side. These north-facing baguettes, hardly justifiable as sunshades, do create a modicum of privacy, a nice alternative for people who live in glass houses.

10

STEPHEN GAYNOR SCHOOL AND BALLET HISPANICO 107
ROGERS MARVEL ARCHITECTS, 2006

148 West 90th Street, between Columbus and Amsterdam Avenues
❶ to 86th Street

In 1962 Miriam Michael and Yvette Siegel founded the Stephen Gaynor School to "address the needs of children with learning differences."[8] That fall it opened with five students in a two-and-a-half-room apartment on the Upper East Side. In 1970 the Ballet Hispanico was founded by dancer and choreographer Tina Ramirez, fusing "ballet, modern and Latin dance forms into a spirited image of the contemporary Hispanic world."[9] It moved into two rehabilitated and converted nineteenth-century carriage houses on West 89th Street twenty years later. In 2006 these two diverse groups moved into a new twelve-story building, in which the Stephen Gaynor School takes up the most of the space, while the Ballet Hispanico expanded from its home directly behind the new structure into the top three floors. Architects Rob Rogers and Jonathan Marvel express the internal functions on its façades—apparent in the different window sizes and locations—without the co-ownership being apparent. The top five floors, set back from the street wall, are rendered in brown brick, and the lower floors are clad in copper panels with a wrapping concrete frame highlighting an opening in the façade.

107 Seen from the west, the framed opening and leaning window dominate the façade. Photo © David Sundberg/Esto.

LEARNING BY DESIGN

The impact of architecture and design on learning is fairly well documented, including the importance of daylight, air quality, color, and other factors. So it's not surprising that even the smallest of learning spaces are treated with the utmost care. Here is a diverse selection of spaces and types embodying these considerations: a public library, a school library, a day care center, a public school, and a private school.

NYPL BATTERY PARK CITY BRANCH
1100: ARCHITECT, 2010

175 North End Avenue, at Murray Street (Map 1)

Think New York Public Library, and its grand Fifth Avenue edifice comes to mind; but for city residents the branch libraries are more important as learning and social spaces. Most branches are interiors, not standalone buildings, including this one inside the new Riverhouse (**12**) condo tower. NYPL's first LEED-certified (Gold) branch is spread across two floors, oriented around an oblong orange column and bench on the first floor. The ceilings are treated sculpturally with triangular panels and slots for lights and HVAC. Photo © Michael Moran.

P.S. 59, THE BEEKMAN HILL INTERNATIONAL SCHOOL
EHRENKRANTZ ECKSTUT & KUHN, 2008

213 East 63rd Street, between Second and Third Avenues (Map 8)

Manhattan's dense fabric means that room for school playgrounds is found not on the ground but up on the roof. Code requirements for these rooftop play spaces call for an enclosure at least ten feet high, both for safety and so that balls are not accidentally launched into the street below. The transformation of a ninety-year-old abandoned residence for nurses into P.S. 59 asserts the building's new identity with such a rooftop playground screen. Perforated metal in two shades of orange appears to be crawling up and over the old building.

PACKER COLLEGIATE INSTITUTE
H3 HARDY COLLABORATION ARCHITECTURE, 2004
170 Joralemon Street, at Clinton Street (Map 14)

Private schools come in all guises, but the overriding image is of old brick and stone buildings with ornate interiors, miles removed in appearance from public schools. Packer Collegiate Institute in Brooklyn Heights fits that image to a T, so much so that it stands in as the school for the privileged teens of *Gossip Girl*. Renovations by Hugh Hardy focused on one of the school's three nineteenth-century buildings, literally inserting classrooms and other facilities into the former Saint Ann's church building. A new glass atrium links the three buildings and overlooks the playground. Visible from Livingston Street, the element is a departure from the brick and stone private school image.

COMMUNITY & PARENTS DAY CARE
BECKHARD RICHLAN SZERBATY ASSOCIATES ARCHITECTS, 2005
243 South 2nd Street, between Havemeyer and Roebling Streets (Map 15)

Day care centers in New York City may vary in terms of size, affiliation, and other characteristics, but most tend to be integrated into other buildings, not standalone buildings with a strong expression of their function. This day care facility in Brooklyn's hip Williamsburg enclave is a colorful checkerboard of red, green, blue, and yellow glazed brick, intersecting with picture and clerestory windows that let plenty of sunlight into the classrooms. A generous playground fronts the building and brings the shouts and movement of kids toward the street. In the southeast corner of the playground is Moses Ros's *Mi Casita* (My Little House), a sculpture made possible by the city's Percent for Art program. Photo by Amy Barkow.

P.S. 42 ROBIN HOOD FOUNDATION LIBRARY
WEISS/MANFREDI with Pentagram, 2002
488 Beach 66th Street, at Thursby Avenue (Queens)

The Robin Hood Foundation's L!brary Initiative recognizes the importance of reading in primary education, academically and culturally, by targeting poor areas with, at this writing, fifty-six new libraries for public schools. Marion Weiss and Michael Manfredi tripled the size of P.S. 42's library in Far Rockaway, Queens, by converting a second gym into a flexible space for reading and holding classes. An undulating bookcase wall is the main element, and a flowing "storytelling" curtain emblazoned with letters partitions the space when needed. The latter is designed by Pentagram, which contributes graphic design for most of the Robin Hood Foundation libraries. Photo © Jeff Goldberg/Esto.

139

Money and class converge on the Upper East Side,

as they have since families with names like Astor, Carnegie, and Rockefeller, aided by the opening of Central Park, moved away from the immigrants encroaching on their downtown town houses in the 1800s. From 59th Street to 96th Street, doormen now stand in front of lavishly detailed apartment buildings, many resembling European palaces from the homelands of the area's first residents. The Upper East Side includes five historical districts, the majority in the western portion, from Fifth Avenue to Park Avenue. Residents are so adamant about preserving the past that the Carnegie Hill Neighbors wrote an architectural guidebook to their neighborhood along the park, north of 86th Street. To the east of Carnegie Hill is the Yorkville neighborhood, which includes Carl Schurz Park and its most famous occupant, Gracie Mansion, traditionally the residence of the mayor. Farther south along the East River is an area the *AIA Guide to New York City* calls "Hospitalia," a stretch of York Avenue that is home to hospitals and facilities for medical research, and therefore much of the Upper East Side's recent construction.

    The Upper East Side is also home to several internationally famous cultural institutions: the Metropolitan Museum of Art (technically in Central Park, but fronting the Upper East Side at 82nd Street), the Solomon R. Guggenheim Museum, the Whitney Museum of American Art, and the Cooper-Hewitt National Design Museum. Most of these museums are situated along "Museum Mile" on Fifth Avenue, which now extends into East Harlem, the neighborhood north of 96th Street known popularly as El Barrio (The Neighborhood) because of its primarily Puerto Rican and Dominican residents. Thanks to its rich soil and remove from the winds off the Hudson River, the area was originally a Dutch outpost consisting largely of farmland. The East Harlem cityscape is almost evenly divided between two extremes: old brownstones and tenements on the one hand and "towers in the park" public housing on the other.

11

108 MEMORIAL SLOAN-KETTERING MORTIMER B. ZUCKERMAN RESEARCH CENTER

SKIDMORE, OWINGS & MERRILL with Zimmer Gunsul Frasca, Architects, 2006

415 East 68th Street, between York and First Avenues
⑥ to 68th Street

Manhattan's twentieth-century glass box towers have a knack for not expressing what is happening inside. The homogeneous wrappers embody a universality that says anything could be going on behind the glass. This is not the case with the new research building at Memorial Sloan-Kettering Cancer Center, a twenty-three-story tower with two distinct faces on the east and west. The east side comprises offices and conference rooms with floor-to-ceiling vision glass and strategically placed louvers. On the west side are the facilities for the research efforts, primarily wet and dry laboratories and ancillary spaces; patterned glass minimizes the effects of the afternoon sun. A prominent terracotta wall separates the two sides and further expresses the double-loaded corridor that runs the length of the building, bringing natural light into this circulation spine. Its composition, capped by rows of exhaust flues, gives the tower a distinctive presence on the Upper East Side skyline from all sides.

At the pedestrian level, terracotta panels prevail. They turn a corner on 68th Street toward the Church of Saint Catherine of Siena, with access to its priory actually tucked beneath the tower. To the east is the seven-story second phase of the project, completed in 2010. It is clad in more glass and terracotta but also narrow coursings of rough black stone, a bit out of place with the rest of the project. Inside the lobby is an installation by LTL Architects, a porous wall with a regular grid on the front devolving into a random pattern on the back that is generated by extrapolating various viewpoints in the lobby.

108 Two distinct faces, the west is on the left and the east on the right (left). Integrated sunshades are found on the east elevation (right). Photos © David Sundberg/Esto.

WEILL GREENBERG CENTER 109
ENNEAD ARCHITECTS, with Ballinger, 2007

1305 York Avenue, at East 70th Street
Ⓖ to 68th Street

Although the Weill Cornell Medical College dates back to the end of the nineteenth century, this ambulatory care and medical education building is the school's first newly constructed freestanding building. It sits in the thick of a medical and educational corridor comprising affiliates New York Presbyterian Hospital, Memorial Sloan-Kettering Cancer Center (**108**), The Rockefeller University (**110**), and the Hospital for Special Surgery (see **NYC 2020**). Designer Todd Schliemann created a distinctive pleated curtain wall in white translucent glass with moiré patterns visible from the right angle. The overall effect is like a Modernist glass box rippling in the wind off the East River. The two main façades are glass, but a narrow sliver of white brick with horizontal windows is located on the south side. Around the corner on 69th Street the Medical Research Building (see **NYC 2020**) by the same architects will more than double the college's research space, while its similarly pleated white glass wall will unmistakably say Weill Cornell.

109 The north-facing glass skin folds and reflects.
Photo © Jeff Goldberg/Esto.

11

THE ROCKEFELLER UNIVERSITY COLLABORATIVE RESEARCH CENTER 110
MITCHELL/GIURGOLA ARCHITECTS, 2010

1230 York Avenue, between East 66th and 67th Streets
Ⓖ to 68th Street

Founded in 1901, The Rockefeller University is a biomedical research institution that prides itself on an open structure that encourages interdisciplinary collaboration toward high-risk, high-reward projects. An important piece serving this mission is the new Collaborative Research Center. Even though it acts primarily as a circulation link between two existing buildings— Flexner and Smith Halls, from 1917 and 1930, respectively—the Research Center enables its neighbors' previously unusable floor plates to be opened up for renovation into laboratories. Projecting from the six-story glass link is an inverted cone, a distinctive expression of the project, which creates an atrium space ringed by wooden slats following the elliptical plan. Access to Rockefeller's campus is limited (check the Web page of the college for public programs), but the new link is visible from the 68th Street gate east of York Avenue.

110 The new link's inverted cone boldly asserts itself. Photo by Adam Friedberg.

111 LYCÉE FRANÇAIS DE NEW YORK
ENNEAD ARCHITECTS, 2003

505 East 75th Street, between York Avenue and East River Drive
⑥ to 77th Street

Before making the decision to consolidate in 1999, the Lycée Français de New York—which celebrated its seventy-fifth anniversary in 2010—was spread across a handful of Upper East Side town houses. The 1,200 K–12 students were grouped by grade, and the faculty and staff spent a good deal of time during the day in transit from one location to another; the school lacked cohesion, to say the least.

Its new campus spans from 75th to 76th Streets. Designer Susan Rodriguez of Ennead Architects (formerly Polshek Partnership) placed the Lower and Upper Schools, respectively, on these streets in two five-story towers linked at the lower floors and capped with a landscaped courtyard. The Lower and Upper School façades are basically mirror images of each other with a regular structural grid in steel, narrow clear glass windows, a dark brick base, and an entry highlighted by the school's insignia above a canopy. Variation appears in the infill between windows; on the south-facing elevation of the Lower School, buff-colored terracotta planks reduce the impact of the sun on the classrooms, while the north façade uses similarly proportioned translucent channel glass to allow more light to filter inside. Needless to say, the latter is more striking, especially at dusk, when the interior glows.

111 Looking east at the north façade's generous glazing. Photo by Aislinn Weidele.

Twenty feet is not much wider than the typical New York City town house, but for the width of a building rising twelve stories, it is an oddity. Such is the case with this corner-lot condo building a few feet narrower than other "sliver" buildings in this book: High Line 519 (**62**), 441 East 57th Street (**80**), and the Austrian Cultural Forum New York (**84**). The all-glass building is located amidst the mass of prewar brick apartment houses along Park Avenue on the Upper East Side but outside the area's Carnegie Historic District, which preservationists are working to expand to protect this newcomer's neighbors up and down the avenue. The glass skin facing 87th Street tries to relate to the predominantly red brick prewar buildings with sections of vertically oriented terracotta-colored ceramic frits, which create privacy for residents but also let passersby know where the closets and bathrooms are located. A much bolder expression of glass colored in a similar manner can be found in The Diana Center at Barnard College (**121**).

Beyond the narrow lot size, what is also exceptional about this development is that it contains only five residential units on eleven floors: three duplexes, a triplex, and a two-story penthouse. These are located above the ground-floor lobby and library; a private gym is in the cellar. At the time of writing, only one of the units had sold, a problem even this Upper East Side standout shared with other luxury condos in the city that started or finished construction around the time the economic bubble burst.

112 A glass sliver in a brick canyon (top).
Photo by Michele Curel. **A flat glass wall with integral awning windows (right).** Photo by John Chu.

113 NEW YORK TOWN HOUSE
ALEXANDER GORLIN ARCHITECTS, 2003

**525 East 85th Street, between
York and East End Avenues**
④ ⑤ ⑥ to 86th Street

When faced with a client who desired a glass-front house back in the 1950s, architect Paul Jean Mitarachi set the building back from its masonry neighbors for privacy, behind a brick wall and front yard. Alexander Gorlin's renovation and expansion fifty years later is faithful to the existing two-story Modernist box, keeping the first floor basically as is and articulating the two upper floors with a symmetrical stacking of small windows in the center. A bright red door is a new touch that recalls the well-known Eames House in Los Angeles, but overall the house looks like an original, or at least like a contemporary interpretation of mid-century modern.

113 The Modernist renovation/ addition is tucked between its neighbors. Photo © Peter Aaron/Esto.

114 LSA FAMILY HEALTH SERVICE
PETER GLUCK AND PARTNERS, 2004

333 East 115th Street, between First and Second Avenues
⑥ to 116th Street

Before moving into this new five-story home, the Little Sisters of the Assumption (LSA) Family Health Service was scattered about East Harlem in five buildings. The consolidation provided the obvious benefits of proximity and shared spaces, but it also created a strong expression for the nonprofit community organization, which describes itself as providing home-based and center-based programs "addressing the physical, emotional, educational, and spiritual dimensions of family health." Peter Gluck utilized a standard exterior door system for the façade, with floor-to-ceiling fixed glass alternating with insulated panels in blue. The stretched checkerboard elevation is further enlivened by red fins projecting slightly from the exterior wall and awnings shading this south face. Up the ramp and behind the glass storefront on the first floor is LSA's popular thrift store, The Sharing Place.

114 A wall of standardized components that looks anything but standard. Photo © Paul Warchol.

25 East 104th Street, between Madison and Fifth Avenues
6 to 103rd Street

Founded by Ellen S. Reece in 1955 as "a non-profit special education elementary school for children who are intellectually capable but face social and educational challenges," the school bearing her name resides in a 23,000-square-foot six-story building less than a block from Museum Mile and Central Park. The school was previously housed in old brownstones. Influenced by the intimate nature of those buildings, the architects realized that the small spaces were comfortable for the students and thus conducive to learning. Therefore classrooms in the new building are sized at a fraction of the norm, at 300 square feet, with a teacher-student ratio of one to six. Other important plan considerations for the K–8 school were the lunchroom and gymnasium, the first for the school, housed below grade. All is geared toward preparing students to function in a high school environment.

The school's public face is articulated as a four-story glass curtain wall. It projects in front of a somewhat contextual orange brick wall that extends to the ground floor, under a thin steel canopy. Above, the glass wall skillfully integrates ventilation louvers into the façade, uses exposed steel sections to highlight the entry subtly while creating an asymmetrical elevation, and randomly inserts colored glass panes into the composition. These last infuse the small classrooms with splashes of orange, purple, and green sunlight, a delightful touch in an otherwise utilitarian building.

115 The glass façade resembles abstract art at dusk (right). The canopy divides glass wall from brick wall (below). Photos by Jonathan Wallen.

116 THE EAST HARLEM SCHOOL AT EXODUS HOUSE
PETER GLUCK AND PARTNERS, 2008

309 East 103rd Street, between First and Second Avenues
⑥ to 103rd Street

In 1963 the Reverend Dr. Lynn and Mrs. Leola Hageman founded Exodus House, a drug rehabilitation center that morphed about twenty years later into an after-school and summer program for children in the area. A decade after that, the Hagemans' sons Hans and Ivan opened a chartered middle school on the same site, one of only a handful of schools in the city focused on grades 5–8. Ivan, who became head of the school, is responsible for selecting Peter Gluck as the architect and construction manager (through the AR|CS arm of his firm) for the $12 million design-build project to replace the school's leaky old building. It is an optimistic design inside and out, which meshes well with the school's mission of elevating the potential of underserved children.

Of course most people who see the school will experience it only from the street. Regardless, a few things are apparent from a quick glance as one rounds the corner from Second Avenue to 103rd Street: the entrance, recessed below the wall above, isn't fenced and gated but open and inviting; the pixelated façade of white, gray, and black panels integrates with the staggered windows to play down the institutional appearance of the building. It's clear that this is a special place. Up close, the qualities of the exposed yellow ceiling, pixelated brick, and glass on the lower two floors are revealed; the translucency of the last affords glimpses of students ascending and descending the stairs inside.

116 A pixelated wall with small windows boldly asserts the school's presence (left). A strong contrast between old and new (top). Photos by Erik Freeland.

148

MUSEUM FOR AFRICAN ART 117

ROBERT A. M. STERN ARCHITECTS, 2011

1280 Fifth Avenue, at East 110th Street

Ⓖ to 116th Street

Since the 1959 completion of the Guggenheim Museum, designed by Frank Lloyd Wright, Museum Mile had consisted of ten museums spanning Fifth Avenue from 82nd to 104th Streets. The permanent home of the Museum for African Art officially adds another museum to the mix and extends the cultural cluster six blocks north to Duke Ellington Circle. Opening to the public in 1984, the museum resided first in an Upper East Side town house, then a SoHo loft space, and eventually in Long Island City. Its move to Harlem at the northeast corner of Central Park was made possible by partnering with two developers, who built a nineteen-story condo tower (designed by SLCE Architects) above the 90,000-square-foot museum. They sit on an L-shaped site that faces the circle and Central Park.

Both the tower and the museum use similar patterned precast concrete panels in a natural stone finish. The museum is distinguished by more decorative panels, more glass, and trapezoidal windows that zigzag up the lower floors. Its multistory lobby faces north, with an interior highlighted by a scalloped wood wall that curves to become the ceiling. The same glass and precast façade turns the corner toward 110th Street and a third-floor roof terrace facing the park through trapezoidal openings with a lattice infill. Stern uses the panels, glass, and lattice in fractal-like patterns that relate to traditional African weaving. At the root of the design is a fairly superficial abstraction, but one that creates a grand edifice and equally grand spaces for this recent addition to Museum Mile.

11

117 The museum occupies the lower floors of an L-shaped tower (left). Precast concrete panels and trapezoidal windows create an abstract composition on the façade (above).

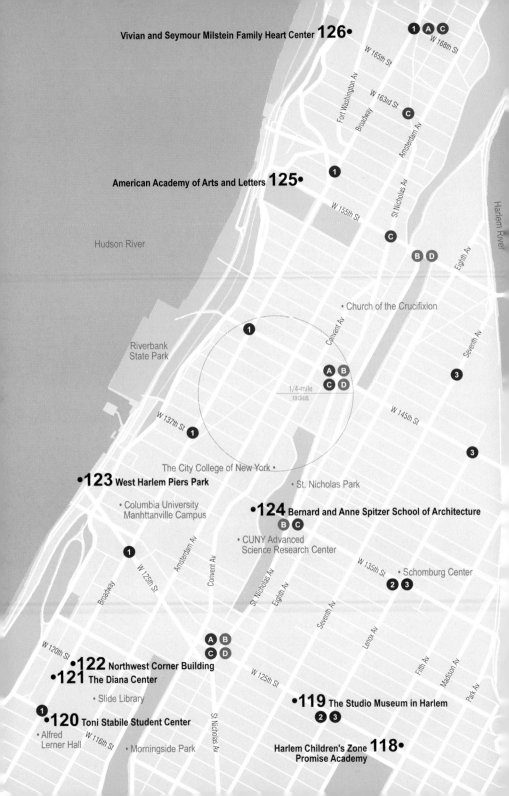

Vivian and Seymour Milstein Family Heart Center **126•**

1 A C
W 168th St

W 165th St

Fort Washington Av

Broadway

W 163rd St

C

Amsterdam Av

American Academy of Arts and Letters **125•**

1

St Nicholas Av

W 155th St

C

Eighth Av

B D

Harlem River

Hudson River

• Church of the Crucifixion

Convent Av

1

Riverbank
State Park

A B
C D

Seventh Av

1/4-mile
radius

3

W 145th St

W 137th St

1

3

The City College of New York •

•123 West Harlem Piers Park

• St. Nicholas Park

• Columbia University
Manhttanville Campus

•124 Bernard and Anne Spitzer School of Architecture

B C

Amsterdam Av

Convent Av

• CUNY Advanced
Science Research Center

1

W 135th St

• Schomburg Center

2 3

Broadway

W 125th St

St Nicholas Av

Eighth Av

Seventh Av

Lenox Av

Fifth Av

Madison Av

Park Av

W 120th St

A B
C D

•122 Northwest Corner Building
•121 The Diana Center

• Slide Library

W 125th St

•119 The Studio Museum in Harlem

2 3

1
•120 Toni Stabile Student Center

• Alfred
Lerner Hall

W 116th St

St Nicholas Av

• Morningside Park

Harlem Children's Zone **118•**
Promise Academy

North of Central Park, Manhattan's topogra-

phy—too often flattened below 110th Street—boldly asserts itself. The "heights" in the names of neighborhoods along the Hudson refers to just that, the intact hills and plateaus overlooking the river and the flat land to the east. Both the impressive IRT Broadway Line Viaduct and the equally impressive Riverside Drive Viaduct clearly illustrate the rolling topography, being situated, respectively, in a valley between the hills of Morningside and Hamilton Heights and along the strip of land west of Riverside Drive.

Running from 110th to 125th Street is Morningside Heights. This neighborhood is dominated by Columbia University, which moved to this prominent location in 1897. The McKim, Mead & White–planned campus occupies the center of the area, but since its rectangular footprint cannot contain the needs of over one hundred years of growth, Columbia is now expanding above 125th Street to Manhattanville. North of here lies Hamilton Heights, named for Alexander Hamilton and the site of his (then) country house; recently the house was relocated to St. Nicholas Park, east of the City College of New York (CCNY), the oldest (and formerly tuition-free) school in the City University of New York (CUNY) system. Northward still is Washington Heights, which starts where the 1811 Commissioner's Plan of the city stopped. The neighborhood stretches from 155th Street to roughly 183rd Street. Off the map, but worth the trek, is the George Washington Bridge and the bus station designed by Pier Luigi Nervi and built over the expressway to the east of the bridge.

Stretching to the east of these upland neighborhoods is Harlem, easily the most famous area north of Central Park. The name draws associations that are immediate and specific, mainly of the Harlem Renaissance which accompanied the African American exodus to the previously Jewish American neighborhood. Art, music, and theater flourished, but a sharp decline followed decades later, still apparent in the vacant lots that were slowly filling before the 2008 economic collapse. The heart and soul of Harlem is the 125th Street commercial corridor, a sure sign of change in the area as local stores are supplanted by national chains.

12

118 HARLEM CHILDREN'S ZONE PROMISE ACADEMY
DAVIS BRODY BOND AEDAS, 2005

35 East 125th Street, at Madison Avenue
2 3 4 5 6 to 125th Street

118 Seen from the east, the brick and glass building is a strong addition to 125th Street. Photo © Albert Vecerka/Esto.

The Harlem Children's Zone (HCZ) Project defines a one hundred–block area of Central Harlem where HCZ applies its services aimed at ending generational poverty. Its goal is predicated on educating children and getting them into college and into the job market. The effectiveness of the programs under the direction of president and CEO Geoffrey Canada led President Barack Obama to adopt the framework for his "20 Promise Neighborhoods" initiative, aimed at U.S. cities plagued by high crime rates and low academic achievement.

An important component of HCZ's efforts is the system of Promise Academy Charter Schools, and the nearly 100,000-square-foot K–12 facility in the heart of the zone gives the organization a distinctive public presence. Brick walls framing expansive glass areas rise above more glass at ground level, revealing the interiors to passersby; the below-grade gymnasium, glimpsed from the street, is especially well done. A bright red wall that slices north-south through the building, pointing playfully to the entrance, is the most memorable element of the design.

12 119 THE STUDIO MUSEUM IN HARLEM
ROGERS MARVEL ARCHITECTS, 2001

144 West 125th Street, between Lenox and Seventh Avenues
2 3 to 125th Street

The Studio Museum in Harlem is located in the heart of the area it calls home, across from the nineteen-story Adam Clayton Powell Jr. State Office Building and its large plaza on 125th Street, Harlem's main shopping strip. Founded in 1968, the museum moved to its permanent six-story home nine years later. Focused on presenting and nurturing artists of African descent, the museum offers an artist-in-residence program, education and public programs, and exhibitions. Rob Rogers and Jonathan Marvel designed exhibition space, an auditorium, and other facilities, occupying two floors, as well as an entry pavilion in a gap between the museum building and its neighbor to the east. The lower floors feature a translucent channel glass storefront and projecting steel frame, all beneath a freshly restored and painted masonry façade.

119 The museum makes its presence known on the sidewalk. Photo © Albert Vecerka/Esto.

TONI STABILE STUDENT CENTER **120**
MARBLE FAIRBANKS, 2008

2950 Broadway, at West 116th Street
① to 116th Street

Scott Marble and Karen Fairbanks have worked with Columbia University over the years to develop master plans for, and design spaces within, the Ivy League institution's various schools. Many of the spaces aren't accessible to the general public, but one exception is the slide library for the Department of Art History and Archaeology, one floor above the Wallach Art Gallery in Schermerhorn Hall.

For the Graduate School of Journalism they contributed both planning and architecture services, the latter in the form of a 10,000-square-foot student center inside the Journalism School's McKim, Mead & White building at Broadway and West 116th Street. A portion of the student center—named for investigative journalist, Columbia graduate, and donor Toni Stabile—extends outside the existing structure to fill a gap between the journalism building and the Furnald residence hall to the south. This is the public portion of the project, a brilliant insertion in the form of a café fronted by a glass wall that lifts open in favorable weather. Behind the glass, the exterior wall of the School of Journalism is left exposed. Opposite is a curving wall in felt with integral LED tickers and mounted plasma TV screens. Above is a custom corrugated metal ceiling with perforations derived from a cloud pattern.

It's worth a walk to the rear of the café to peek at the renovation portion of the project inside the Journalism School, where more perforated surfaces line the walls and ceilings. To find the student center, enter the campus at Broadway and West 115th Street between Furnald and Alfred Lerner Hall and turn left at the latter's glass-enclosed ramp, part of the building designed by Bernard Tschumi, former dean of Columbia's Graduate School of Architecture, Planning, and Preservation.

120 The glass wall in the open position reveals the interior to be what was exterior (top). The café is an inviting place for the general public as well as students (above). The slide library's wall of medium-density fibreboard with laminated glass (right). Photos by Marble Fairbanks.

12

121

DIANA CENTER
WEISS/MANFREDI, 2010

3009 Broadway, between West 116th and West 120th Streets
❶ to 116th Street

Barnard is an independent liberal arts college for women that has a unique cooperative relationship with Columbia University. Since Barnard's founding in 1889 it has shared resources with the larger university of which it is a part, with degrees awarded by Columbia. This reciprocal situation certainly benefits Barnard's students and faculty, but it also means that the college can be seen to exist in the shadow of Columbia University, regardless of its independence. At only four acres, Barnard's campus is also overshadowed by the thirty-six-acre (and counting) Columbia campus across Broadway. And even the construction of Barnard's high-profile seven-story student center was dwarfed by the contemporaneous rise of Columbia's new fourteen-story science building (**122**) right across the street. But the Diana Center, designed by Weiss/Manfredi, holds its own.

Originally called the Nexus, the building is named for donor Diana Vagelos (even though early plans to call it the Vagelos Center were scrapped, students still refer to the building as "The Vag"). It is located on the site of the 1969 McIntosh Student Center, which was demolished to make way for it. The building follows the street edge, but the campus-side face angles in plan to connect the main green space with the courtyard of Millbank Hall to the north; one can theoretically see all the way to the latter from the main gate of the college on Broadway. While the Diana replaces the McIntosh, it also adds educational spaces for art, architecture, and performance to the student center functions (lounges, computer labs, cafés, offices). These disparate elements are tied together by the skin of the building, the "slipped atria" that climb from south to north along Broadway, and the expressed exit stairs on the campus side.

Wrapping the building's four sides are panes of glass with terracotta-colored vertical frits alternating with back-painted shadow boxes in the same color. This gesture may recall the brick of older Barnard and Columbia buildings, but the varied window openings—best seen after sundown—create a whole new creature, especially in combination with the slipped atria that crawl from the patio to the green roof. This cascading space cleverly packs a lot of nonprogrammed leisure and study space into the plan while simultaneously creating intimacy and a sense of connection. One way to interpret the west campus façade with its clear glass projections is that the space of the atria forces the exit stairs outside the wedge-shaped plan. These corridors were envisioned by architects Marion Weiss and Michael Manfredi as leisurely connections between spaces, not just emergency exits. They reveal the interaction and movement that take place inside the building, just as the east side expresses the student life within.

122 The slipped atria overlooking Broadway are highly visible in the evening (opposite). Seen from the Barnard campus with Columbia's Northwest Building in the background (top). Photos © Albert Vecerka/Esto. The campus-side stair culminates in a cantilever (right). Looking down the slipped atria (above). Photos © Paul Warchol.

122 NORTHWEST CORNER BUILDING

JOSÉ RAFAEL MONEO with Moneo Brock Studio
and Davis Brody Bond Aedas, 2010

540 West 120th Street, at Broadway
❶ to 116th Street

Rising at the same time as Barnard's Diana Center
(**121**) across Broadway, the Northwest Corner
Building occupies the last available plot of land on
Columbia University's original McKim, Mead &
White–planned upper Morningside campus. Whereas
most of its buildings north of 116th Street can be
accessed only from the campus side, this building
provides entry points both from street level and
from the campus plaza above, in effect connecting
the two realms. The fourteen-story science building,
which houses a library, faculty offices, classrooms,
and research facilities for various disciplines, is
directly linked to Pupin Hall on the east and Chandler
on the south, two other science buildings in this
corner of the campus.

Fittingly for what the building houses,
Moneo's design is an expression of engineering,
the movement of natural forces, both vertical
(gravity) and lateral (wind). The design arises from
two main constraints: the fact that the building
sits over an existing gymnasium and also that the
science facilities require open, column-free spaces.
The first dictated where the vertical structure from
above could land (in only three areas); it is resolved
two floors above the campus level with a full-floor
truss over the library. As a result of the second, the
whole building works like a giant truss, expressed
in the diagonal lines crossing the modular aluminum
façade. An irregular checkerboard of diagonals,
louvered windows with horizontal openings, and
the occasional curtain wall, the composition appears
random, but it follows the load pattern determined

with structural engineer Arup. The bays are roughly 18 feet square, reflecting the
extra-tall lab spaces that face west, while the façade on the campus side is largely
a clear glass curtain wall with panes half as tall, corresponding to the height of the
office mezzanines.

122 Looking southeast toward the irregular checkerboard (top). The escalators up
to the campus are visible in the transparent lobby (above). Photos © Albert Vecerka/Esto.

WEST HARLEM PIERS PARK **123**
W ARCHITECTURE AND LANDSCAPE ARCHITECTURE, 2009

Hudson River Greenway, between West 125th and West 135th Streets
❶ to 125th Street

When Barbara Wilks's firm W Architecture and Landscape Architecture prepared the 2002 West Harlem Master Plan for the New York City Economic Development Corporation, the ten-block section of the Hudson River waterfront north of 125th Street was a gap in an otherwise unbroken strip of public open space stretching from one tip of Manhattan to the other. The site—a Borden Milk Factory many decades before and more recently a parking lot popular with prostitutes and crack addicts—was seen as an important element in the area's redevelopment, and it became the first stage in the implementation of the master plan. Its design as a park was viewed as a way to knit the waterfront public spaces together and attract people from and to the adjacent 125th Street shopping district. It is also close to Columbia University's planned Manhattanville expansion.

As executed, the narrow park features two new piers in the form of a broken diagonal that appears to peel away from the island; these provide access for fishing, boat excursions, and kayak launches, as well as a venue for permanent artwork by Nari Ward. The "inland" portion of the park includes planted areas, walkways, a bike path, and play fountains, with benches made from the old granite bulkheads scattered about "as if left by waves."[1] It is an extremely popular public space, overshadowed by the opening of the High Line (**54**) the same summer, but just as important to the community it serves.

123 Seen from the north, the diagonal juts into the water (top). A scattering of benches about the park (above). Photos by Alison Cartright.

124 BERNARD AND ANNE SPITZER SCHOOL OF ARCHITECTURE

RAFAEL VIÑOLY ARCHITECTS, 2009

160 Convent Avenue, at West 135th Street
B **C** to 135th Street; **1** to 137th Street–City College

For four decades since its founding in 1968, the School of Architecture at the City College of New York was housed in the landmark 1905 Shepard Hall, designed by George B. Post as the first of a handful of Gothic buildings on what's now considered the North Campus at the CUNY institution. Shepard's curving double-loaded corridors and small spaces were ill suited for architecture studios and left no room for expansion, so CCNY and Rafael Viñoly determined, after exploring numerous options, to reuse the structure of the 1950s Cohen Library on the South Campus for the school.

The resulting building—dubbed the Bernard and Anne Spitzer School of Architecture (SSA) after the parents of former governor Eliot Spitzer gave $25 million to CCNY—exhibits a mid-twentieth-century aesthetic, but one layered with today's features of sustainability. Precast concrete panels wrap the whole building, broken by prominent projections that frame the horizontal windows. Empty at the time of the building's opening, the large frames have since been fitted with perforated louvers on three side of the structure, which filter the sun entering the studio spaces. Inside is a dynamic full-height atrium whose dramatic impact belies the bland exterior. Created by cutting openings in the existing concrete slabs, the void is traversed by ramps and stairs set at different angles, a Piranesian space roofed in yellow. Public access is limited to the first-floor gallery at the base of the atrium.

124 A Piranesian space capped in yellow (left). The architecture occupies a commanding site atop a hill (below).

AMERICAN ACADEMY OF ARTS AND LETTERS 125

JAMES VINCENT CZAJKA
with Pei Cobb Freed & Partners, 2009

**633 West 155th Street, between
Broadway and Riverside Drive
❶ to 157th Street**

125 The almost invisible link seen from the campus side. Photo by Cody Upton.

The American Academy of Arts and Letters is tucked into the western end of a campus shared with the Hispanic Society of America and the Church of the Intercession. A previous tenant's move elsewhere allowed the academy to expand within the bounds of the campus. It now occupies three buildings, two designed by McKim, Mead & White and one by Cass Gilbert. This passageway, connecting the first two buildings at their third floors, is made up of only seven pieces of 1-inch-thick units of glass. The design features a pitched roof, an abstractly traditional form that recalls the roofs of the old buildings. Seen from 155th Street below (the link roughly coincides with the terrace level), the Wonder Woman–esque piece is easy to miss. It's an odd intervention between classical stone buildings, yet is the best solution for visually preserving the space between the existing structures.

VIVIAN AND SEYMOUR MILSTEIN FAMILY HEART CENTER 126

PEI COBB FREED & PARTNERS with daSilva Architects, 2010

**177 Fort Washington Avenue, at West 165th Street
❶ Ⓐ Ⓒ to 168th Street**

The Milstein Hospital at New York–Presbyterian Hospital spans from Fort Washington Avenue to Riverside Drive, on a block anchored by the Herbert Irving Pavilion. This addition to the Milstein Heart Center is sited between these two imposing brick buildings. Pei Cobb Freed's lead designer on the project, Ian Bader, responded to these neighbors but departed from them in just about every way possible, inserting an elegantly curving pavilion. Most curved glass façades are just that in the design phase, curved, but when built they are faceted; that is not the appearance in this well-executed curtain wall. An all-glass double-layer curtain wall incorporates vertical louvers that automatically track sunlight throughout the day and give texture to the curve. A new entry is provided on 165th Street, but the main access is from Fort Washington, where visitors move along a curving passageway toward a four-story atrium, where bridges overhead connect the floors of the new and existing buildings.

126 Looking north across 165th Street. Photo © Albert Vecerka/ Esto.

FDNYPD

The Department of Design and Construction manages the building of, among other civic facilities, New York City's firehouses and police stations. Since 2004 the department's Design and Construction Excellence (D+CE) initiative, which adopts a quality-based selection for design services, has shortlisted more than fifty architecture firms on the basis of qualifications and portfolio instead of low bids on individual projects. This program acknowledges the importance of contemporary architecture in creating civic landmarks and recognizes the role these buildings play in various neighborhoods around the city. Here is a diverse sampling of five D+CE projects for the fire department (FDNY) and police department (NYPD).

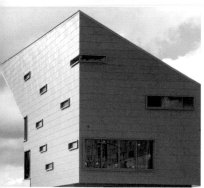

MARINE COMPANY 1
CR STUDIO ARCHITECTS, 2011
Pier 53, at Bloomfield Street (Map 5)

In addition to the New York City Fire Department's ever visible and audible fleet of trucks, a number of fireboats serve to respond to calls related to the city's 560 miles of waterfront. Marine 1 is the oldest company, currently sharing a pier with the Department of Sanitation but in the future with Hudson River Park beaches and lawn. CR Studio's design positions the gemlike zinc-covered building above a new pier that juts into the water. Nearby Pier 54 provides views of the building, and a distant glimpse can be caught from the High Line near 14th Street.

NYPD BROOKLYN TOW POUND
SPACESMITH, 2009
Sands and Navy Streets (Map 13)

Making a trip to the western edge of the Brooklyn Navy Yard to retrieve a towed car is hardly at the top of any tourist's or resident's to-do list. But the experience could be worse: the visit could have been made to the old double-wide trailers the NYPD previously used in this location. Now a trip to the "redemption center" is at least physically hospitable, in a light-filled space beyond the NYPD lattice signage and New York's Finest blue canopy. For those who don't have to make a visit to the yard, the building is highly visible from Navy Street.

ENGINE COMPANY 277
STV, INC., 2004

582 Knickerbocker Avenue, between Palmetto Street and Gates Avenue (Map 15)

This Brooklyn fire station is surrounded on three sides by the playground of the Roland Hayes School, a unique situation the architects exploited by making the building rise sculp-turally from its square base. Accentuated by burnt red side walls of cast concrete, the curving volume resembles a firefighter's helmet. *Sentinel Lanterns*—an installation that suspends an ax, Halligan bar (a tool for forcible entry), and water cannon in acrylic—is mounted next to the bay doors, a Percent for Art contribution by Julian LaVerdiere, best known for co-authoring the September 11 remembrance, *Tribute in Light*.

RESCUE COMPANY 3
ENNEAD ARCHITECTS, 2009

1655 Washington Avenue, between East 172nd and 173rd Streets (Map 17)

Unlike engine companies, which are the first responders to a fire, rescue companies deal with incidents that are more specialized, such as building collapses, subway emergencies, and even rescuing other firefighters when the situation warrants. For this firehouse in the Bronx, these specialties necessitated an almost machinelike precision for fitting the required infrastructure and equipment alongside the spaces for training, fitness, dining, and rest. In the resulting design, by partner Todd Schliemann, the zinc cladding seems to grip the bright red doors and the overhead striped aluminum and glass, putting the focus in no uncertain terms on the trucks and other equipment tucked inside. Photo by Aislinn Weidele.

ENGINE COMPANY 75
DATTNER ARCHITECTS, 2000

2175 Walton Avenue, between Cameron Place and East 182nd Street (Map 18)

This firehouse in the Bronx serves three companies (Ladder Company 33 and Battalion 19, in addition to Engine Company 75) in a 12,000-square-foot building. Richard Dattner's design reduces the scale of the building in its residential context by massing the building like a skyline in miniature. Projections at three corners house the apparatus room and areas for training and drills. And while the banded concrete block looks quite dated, it is a fitting foil to the abstract fire truck—*Honor 2000* by artist Mierle Laderman Ukeles—rendered in the same material; the Percent for Art installation also includes glass blocks etched with the names of Bronx firefighters lost in the line of duty. Photo © Francis Dzikowski/Esto.

BROOKLYN

DOWNTOWN BROOKLYN, BROOKLYN HEIGHTS, CARROLL GARDENS, GOWANUS, PARK SLOPE — **13**

PROSPECT HEIGHTS, CROWN HEIGHTS, BEDFORD-STUYVESANT, CLINTON HILL, FORT GREENE — **14**

GREENPOINT, WILLIAMSBURG, BROWNSVILLE, EAST NEW YORK — **15**

FLATBUSH, HOMECREST, CONEY ISLAND, BOROUGH PARK, SUNSET PARK — **16**

Old and new **(138)** at Grand Army Plaza. Photo © Aaron Dougherty.

Brooklyn shares many traits with Manhattan in

terms of its early history: land "bought" from an existing Indian population
by the Dutch; site of the Revolutionary War; farms; urbanization. The last
was enabled by ferry service to and from Manhattan in the early 1800s,
but it wasn't until the 1883 completion of the Brooklyn Bridge that the
future borough really started to grow. The bridge lands in what is now
Brooklyn's Downtown (as does the later Manhattan Bridge), an area
filled with civic buildings, offices, schools, a business-education campus
(MetroTech Center), cultural venues, a pedestrian retail mall (Fulton Street),
and, increasingly, condo towers. Helping steer the area's evolution is the
Downtown Brooklyn Partnership, which is focused on increasing private
commercial and residential development in the area and expanding the
Brooklyn Academy of Music (BAM) Cultural District. Its area of interest, the
perimeter of Downtown, is a triangular location bounded by the Brooklyn-
Queens Expressway (BQE) on the north, Flatbush Avenue on the east,
Atlantic Avenue to the south, and Camden Plaza West on the west. To
the north of Downtown is DUMBO (Down Under the Manhattan Bridge
Overpass), a small but touristy area with old warehouses renovated as
apartments and retail spaces and parks along the East River.

13

    Directly west of Downtown is Brooklyn Heights, a neighborhood
consisting mainly of nineteenth-century buildings, preserved in part
because of the area's designation as a historic district in 1965, the first
such designation from the city's Landmarks Preservation Commission.
Yet even before this happened, residents—admittedly more affluent and
powerful than in nearby areas—fought Robert Moses's plan to drive the
BQE through their neighborhood. They persuaded him to route it closer
to the water (note the S-like bend it takes at Atlantic Avenue as it travels
north) as a double-decker road beneath the amenity that is now the
Brooklyn Heights Esplanade.

    Below Downtown and Brooklyn Heights, to the east of the BQE,
are a few neighborhoods that are physically knit together so well that
boundaries and distinctions are difficult to discern, owing to their shared
characteristics such as low-scale buildings, lack of major thoroughfares,
and now gentrified population: Cobble Hill, Boerum Hill, and Carroll
Gardens, collectively referred to by some as BoCoCa. Across these
neighborhoods the north-south avenues are commercial, while the east-
west streets are residential, much as in Manhattan. To the east again is

Gowanus, which appropriately straddles the Gowanus Canal, called "an open cesspool" as early as 1893. Even though its present-day condition is not much better (it was recently designated a Superfund site by the federal government), residential condos that rose during the pre-2008 building boom can be found one block away. To its east is Park Slope—so named because the land slopes down from Prospect Park to the Gowanus Canal—a highly desirable neighborhood with block after block of late-nineteenth-century brownstones, most in a large historic district steps away from Prospect Park.

127 BROOKLYN BRIDGE PARK
MICHAEL VAN VALKENBURGH ASSOCIATES, 2010

East River from Fulton Street to Atlantic Avenue
F to York Street; A C to High Street;
2 3 4 5 R to Court Street–Borough Hall

Much like the transformation of Manhattan's industrial piers into the linear Hudson River Park (**60**), Brooklyn is getting its own riverfront green space where warehouses once stood, to the south and west of the Manhattan Bridge and Brooklyn-Queens Expressway. Brooklyn Bridge Park will eventually clock in at eighty-five acres and almost one and a half miles of waterfront park extending from Jay Street to Atlantic Avenue, but as of this writing only Pier 1 and portions of Pier 6 are complete; the first is a six-acre expanse just south of the Brooklyn Bridge, and the second covers seven acres at the southern extent of the park; a bike and walking lane connects the two. Access to the park is via Atlantic Avenue and Joralemon Street toward Pier 6 and Old Fulton Street in DUMBO next to Pier 1, as well as from the northern stretch at Empire–Fulton Ferry Park, the new home of Jane's Carousel (see **NYC 2020**). To appreciate the scale of the undertaking, the Brooklyn Heights Promenade offers expansive views of the unfolding park, with a vista to and between the completed piers and the Lower Manhattan skyline beyond.

Michael Van Valkenburgh has been working on the park since 1998, in the form of both a master plan and landscape design. The latter is described as weaving together civic and pastoral landscapes, exploring ideas of "urban junctions," and striving for the utmost sustainability through opportunities of "structural economy," all apparent at the completed piers. The first weaving is found in Pier 1's "civic" landscape zones: a playground, a promenade, and two lawns (split by the steps of the Granite Prospect) are geared to recreation and sweeping views of the Brooklyn Bridge, New York Harbor, and the skyscrapers across the East River. Counter to these areas are the "pastoral" paths meandering along small water pools on the

13

127 The east side of the park is marked by dense landscaping and intimate spaces (opposite). The west side of the park opens up to vistas of Manhattan (top). A walk-way along the East River and stadium seating for looking at the Financial District (above). Looking toward Pier 1, and the Brooklyn Bridge beyond, from the south (left).

13

eastern portion of the same pier, and the southern portion's large granite rocks, smooth cordgrass-planted salt marsh, and grid of over one hundred wooden piles, all supporting wildlife while the pier's western side supports leisure.

Second, the urban junctions, or activities aimed at drawing people to the park, include the playgrounds of both Pier 1 and Pier 6 (the latter has four over-the-top play areas with names like Swing Valley and Slide Mountain) and concessions at the entrance to Pier 1; later phases will include kayak launches and other water-based activities. The structural economy of the third involves the preservation and reuse of existing local and nearby structures, something found in Pier 1's Granite Prospect (the stones previously clad the Willis Avenue Bridge connecting Manhattan and the Bronx), its grid of wooden piles, and the bleachers in Pier 6's Sandbox Village, reused from an old warehouse building. Pier 2's future sports area preserves the site's original shed structure.

Future phases of the park are almost certain, but the pace of construction depends on the fate of development parcels allotted to fund construction and upkeep of the park. The first of these, the conversion of a warehouse belonging to the Jehovah's Witnesses into over four hundred condos near Pier 6, was completed before the park opened and has benefited from the proximity of the latter in the sluggish residential market. Other parcels are next to the old warehouse, east of Pier 1, and at the northernmost portion of the park. What they will become remains to be seen.

128 NEW YORK CITY OEM
SWAYNKE HAYDEN CONNELL
ARCHITECTS, 2006

**165 Cadman Plaza East,
between Tillary and Prospect Streets
Ⓐ Ⓒ to High Street**

In 1996 the New York City Office of Emergency Management (OEM) was formed to prepare the city for emergencies, coordinate emergency response and recovery, and educate and inform the public. Its offices on the **128** Limestone walls frame a rectangular opening of metal and glass. twenty-third floor of 7 World Trade Center were a victim of that building's collapse on September 11, 2001. OEM was subsequently housed at Pier 92 in Manhattan and in a warehouse under the Brooklyn Bridge before moving into this conversion of the city's former American Red Cross headquarters, a three-story freestanding 1950s building fronting Walt Whitman Park in downtown Brooklyn. Funded by post-9/11 federal aid to the city, the 65,000-square-foot building includes a southern extension of 8,000 square feet whose parkside elevation gives OEM a public face ironically reminiscent of Giuseppe Terragni's classic Casa del Fascio (House of Fascism) in Como, Italy. OEM's limestone, zinc, and glass wrapper is a careful balance of solid and void that links exterior expression with stringent functional requirements inside.

129 TOREN
SKIDMORE, OWINGS & MERRILL, 2010

13

**150 Myrtle Avenue, at Flatbush Avenue
Ⓑ Ⓠ Ⓡ to DeKalb Avenue; ❷ ❸ to Hoyt Street**

In 2004 the Department of City Planning approved the Downtown Brooklyn Redevelopment Plan to add office space and mixed residential uses to the area by rezoning over twenty blocks in the borough's core. The area just east of Flatbush Avenue was pegged for residential development, and a number of condo towers followed. Easily the most eye-catching addition is the BFC Partners–developed Toren (Dutch for "tower") on a triangular site east of MetroTech. SOM's façade design for the 240-unit, thirty-eight-story tower utilizes two types of glass (clear and tinted) interspersed with dimpled light-gray aluminum panels in irregular vertical stripes. The overall effect is a supergraphic of light splotches wrapping the corners of a dark slab. Covering the podium is the same dark glass and metal, undulating in and out to create one of the fanciest parking garages in recent years.

129 Two types of glass combine to graphically enliven the flat façades. Photo © Aaron Dougherty.

SCHERMERHORN HOUSE **130**
ENNEAD ARCHITECTS, 2009

160 Schermerhorn Street, between Hoyt and Smith Streets
Ⓐ Ⓒ Ⓖ to Hoyt-Schermerhorn; ❷ ❸ to Hoyt Street

With condo developments like Toren (**129**) bringing thousands of luxury residences to downtown Brooklyn, affordable housing can be easily forgotten, but in the case of Schermerhorn House it is mandated by the city. Common Ground, a developer of supportive housing for the homeless and people with low incomes, led a public-private collaboration with Hamlin Ventures and Time Equities, developers that donated the site as part of their adjacent market-rate, mixed-use parcel (**131**). Also involved are the Actors Fund of America, the Center for Urban Community Services, and the Brooklyn Ballet, which, respectively, serve low-income stage professionals, coordinate job training and other services, and occupy the lively ground-floor space. By 2009 Common Ground had created three thousand units of housing throughout the city, inching toward its mission of ending homelessness. Many of these units are in distinctive buildings that take into account the relationship between architectural design and social services while also embracing sustainability.

The same applies to this eleven-story building, which includes roughly two hundred affordable units, about half for formerly homeless individuals and the remainder for low-income tenants, targeted at local actors and artists. Sited

between low-rise Boerum Hill to the south and Downtown's high-density core to the north, it is also directly above a subway tunnel, necessitating that the building be cantilevered by four large trusses over this underground infrastructure. Upstairs, designer Susan Rodriguez provides daylighting, ventilation, and privacy for the occupants through a façade composed of clear and translucent glazing; the latter's channel glass is reminiscent of her earlier Lycée Français de New York (**111**). The rear façade departs from the street's pinstripes with a horizontal composition of ribbon windows and cement board planks with integral porthole-like vents.

130 Vertical stripes of translucent glass face north.
Photo © David Sundberg.

13

131

14 TOWNHOUSES

ROGERS MARVEL ARCHITECTS, 2006

267–287 State Street, between Hoyt and Smith Streets

A C G to Hoyt-Schermerhorn; **2 3** to Hoyt Street

Sharing the same block with Schermerhorn House (**130**), the 14 Townhouses, constructed as the first phase of Hamlin Equities' and Time Equities' two-acre development. could not be further from its neighbor to the north: low-rise instead of mid-rise; 4,000-square-foot residences instead of studios apartments; high-income instead of low-income; brick with punched windows instead of glass walls. Calling itself "the first major row of single-family townhouses to be developed in New York City since the 1920s," the project sits on land used as a parking lot for decades, astride five Italianate town houses listed in the National Register of Historic Places, and across the street from a row of Greek Revival town houses.

The contemporary addition to the block is influenced by its neighbors in terms of scale, solidity, and the provision for front stoops, but it is a pared-down version of these traditional buildings. Variety in the otherwise flat brick walls is found in the different colors of brick, the stone bases, and the metal protrusions. The fourteen town houses march down the street in a repeating "A-B-A-A" progression. The redbrick As are differentiated from one another by vertical reveals in gray brick, and the beige and gray Bs are highlighted by top-floor openings that frame small trees but also blank walls and exhaust flues. But not all the As are the same, and likewise the Bs; subtle idiosyncrasies make each unique. For the next phase of the development, another row of town houses on the eastern end of the block is scheduled for completion in 2012.

131 Viewed from the east, the fourteen town houses are composed in sequence (left). The exterior walls abstract adjacent town houses (above).

132 The angled bay windows peer up the street (above). The canopy follows the line of the sidewalk as the walls bend back (right). Photos © Michael Moran.

322 HICKS STREET **132**
SMITH-MILLER + HAWKINSON ARCHITECTS
with Larsen Shein Ginsberg Snyder Architects, 2006

322 Hicks Street, between State Street and Atlantic Avenue
2 3 4 5 R to Court Street–Borough Hall

13

In November 1965 Brooklyn Heights became the first of New York City's historic districts (now in the triple digits), the same year that the Landmarks Preservation Commission was established. Stretching north-south from Old Fulton Street to Atlantic Avenue and east-west from the promenade over the BQE to Henry and Clinton Streets, the area was a draw for poets and novelists who wanted to escape Manhattan but not New York City in the nineteenth and twentieth centuries. Now it is one of the most desirable areas in the city, an exclusive and pricey enclave where new buildings are minimal and contested.

One project that successfully navigated the Landmarks process is this five-story, six-unit condo building near the southern edge of the district. It is located on Hicks Street south of Joralemon, two blocks that are particularly eclectic, with carriage houses, a fire station, town houses in a variety of styles and heights, and even some relatively large new construction at State Street. In this regard the fissure at 322 Hicks is not an antagonistic neighbor in the district but a contributor to its diversity. The façade design by Henry Smith-Miller and Laurie Hawkinson breaks the street wall with its angled brick walls. Clearly and understandably the idea is to look up the street toward the rest of the historic district and away from the noisy expanse of nearby Atlantic Avenue.

133 BUTLER STREET TOWN HOUSE

TINA MANIS ASSOCIATES, 2005

112 Butler Street, between Hoyt and Smith Streets
🄵 🄶 to Bergen Street

For a previously vacant lot in Carroll Gardens, Tina Manis designed this distinctive three-story town house which places a rental apartment atop the owner's duplex. This situation necessitated two separate entries at grade, but curiously only one is evident, to the left of the central garage door; the second is actually hidden, masquerading as part of the façade's unique wood clapboard siding on the

133 The wood siding is musical in its rhythm. Photo by Russell Gera.

right side. This siding roots the building in its place (a number of houses fronted with siding are scattered about the block's predominantly masonry buildings), yet the rippling effect arising from the varied size and spacing of the planks lends the house a contemporary twist that is not alienating. A top-floor balcony for the rental unit is visible from the street, but one can only imagine the glass-walled rear façade and the owner's backyard retreat.

134 THIRD + BOND

ROGERS MARVEL ARCHITECTS, 2010

13

404–406 Bond Street, at 3rd Street
🄵 🄶 to Carroll Street

One block from the Superfund-listed Gowanus Canal may not be the ideal location for potential condo buyers, but such was the strength and pace of the residential market in the first decade of the century that development reached as far as this frontier corner of Gowanus. As the canal's cleanup is at least a decade away, light industry and manufacturing still loom over Third + Bond. But Rob Rogers and Jonathan Marvel's design of the forty-four-unit development eschews industrial inspiration, instead opting to create a transition between the town houses and canal areas by breaking up the streetscape in a manner similar to their 14 Townhouses (**131**). On 3rd Street in particular, the project reads like a series of town houses, even though each brick- or metal-clad piece is occupied by multiple condos.

134 Brick and metal façades alternate down the street.

If any architect can be credited with giving shape to the recent condo boom in Brooklyn, it is Robert M. Scarano Jr., who has referred to himself as "the architect of the new Brooklyn." The Web page of his DUMBO-based office boasts no fewer than eighty-four multifamily residential projects in the borough—from Greenpoint and Williamsburg in the north to Brighton Beach and Sheepshead Bay in the south—though reports peg a higher number: over three hundred projects at this writing. While he is certainly prolific, criticisms have been directed at the quality of his buildings, many of which are out of character and scale with their surroundings. This last trait stems from alleged abuse of zoning laws through the self-certification

135 Looking west; the almost full-block development cradles an old three-story corner building.

13

process, whereby an architect can certify that a project meets all applicable codes and laws, thus bypassing a Department of Buildings (DOB) review. Complaints against Scarano for taking advantage of the process led to his withdrawal from the self-certification program in 2006; four years later the architect was accused of "deliberately overbuilding" and was barred from filing any construction plans with the DOB. Legal issues aside, the same charges of difference and jumps in scale can be leveled at many new developments in the city, a fair number of which can be seen elsewhere in this book.

Satori—the name for the Buddhist state of enlightenment—is a development in Gowanus one block from the Gowanus Canal (like nearby **134**) that looks as if it wants to be aligned with those attention-getting buildings by other architects, not Scarano's own projects. It features what he calls a "conceptional" (conceptual and exceptional?) façade composed of randomly placed openings of different size and orientation within a wall of wood-grain panels (see **97** for more wood grain). Nevertheless the project still screams "Scarano," not for its relatively ambitious design but for its overpowering of the early-twentieth-century three-story corner building at Carroll Street.

136 580 CARROLL STREET
TEN ARQUITECTOS, 2009

580 Carroll Street, between Fourth and Fifth Avenues
Ⓜ Ⓡ to Union Street

For the most part Park Slope, block after block of well-maintained brownstones, did not take part in the condo boom that infiltrated nearby Carroll Gardens and Prospect Heights. But toward its eastern edge, where the fine-grained residential fabric meshes with the commercial and industrial uses of Gowanus, the neighborhood has witnessed some new residential construction. One such development is a five-story, seventeen-unit condo building designed by Mexico City– and New York City–based architect Enrique Norten. The project takes the name of its address on Carroll Street, yet it also fronts on Garfield Street to the south, where the building meets the sidewalk; at the former a 4,000-square-foot garden behind a wooden wall greets residents and passersby. Black House Development Company tried (unsuccessfully) to add three town houses in place of this garden, a move that would have required a variance to exceed the zoning limits the structure had already reached. As executed, the façades set back from the garden on Carroll are minimal, with clear glass walls, concrete structure, and tapering balconies. A wooden privacy screen covers the ground floor of the more urban Garfield Street façade, and diagonal bays punctuate the setback glass walls above.

136 The serrated window wall on Garfield Place (above). On Carroll Street a garden greets residents (right). Photos by Jackie Caradonio.

13

137 The rear elevation is visible through gates on Prospect Park West (above). Looking east with the Hulbert Mansion in the distance (above, right). A well-articulated wall of terracotta, steel, and glass (right). Photos by Jonathan Wallen.

POLY PREP LOWER SCHOOL **137**
PLATT BYARD DOVELL WHITE, 2007

50 Prospect Park West, at 1st Street
2 **3** to Grand Army Plaza

13

In 1854 the institution that would later become Poly Prep, then the first school for boys in Brooklyn, opened on Livingston Street in Brooklyn Heights. Before the end of the century the school split into college preparatory (Country Day) and lower schools, an arrangement that survives to this day, although since the 1970s they have admitted girls. Today the Country Day School for grades five and up is located on a twenty-five-acre campus in Dyker Heights, Brooklyn, where it has been since 1917. The Lower School sits across from Prospect Park in the Park Slope Historic District, having moved from Brooklyn Heights in 1995 with the purchase of the Woodward Park School, occupying the nineteenth-century Hulbert Mansion. Just over a decade later the mansion was reconfigured and its facilities were nearly doubled with a three-story classroom addition designed by Samuel White.

Fellow partner, the late Paul Spencer Byard, asked in a monograph on his firm, "What can old and new architecture be made to create together that will best help us understand and improve our state today?"[1] The Poly Prep Lower School is perhaps the firm's answer. The addition's 1st Street façade is a combination of limestone (rain screen panels) and glass (clear glazing and translucent channel glass); it does not attempt to refer abstractly to the Hubert Mansion, but it hardly stands in stark opposition to it or the neighboring brownstones. The restrained design instead balances the traditional vocabulary of punched windows in masonry walls and the grandiosity of the school's main building by way of small openings featuring divided lights and an asymmetrically located double-height window, respectively.

See Map
15
Williamsburg

G Flushing Av

Park Av

Myrtle Av G

Brooklyn-Queens Expy

Willoughby Av

Hart Av

•**142** Marcy Avenue Residence

•**149** Slot House

• PrattStore

•**147** Myrtle Hall

DeKalb Av

Carlton Av
Adelphi St
Clermont Av
Vanderbilt Av
Clinton Av
Waverly Av
Washington Av
Hall St

•**146** Pratt Institute Security Kiosk

•**148** Vanderbilt Studio

Lafayette Av

Tompkins Park

•**145** Juliana Curran Terian Design Center

• Fort Greene Park

G

Greene Av

Nostrand Av
Gates Av

Marcy Av

Tompkins Av

•**144** Higgins Hall Insertion

G

St James Pl
Grand Av
Classon Av
Franklin Av
Bedford Av

• Bedford-Stuyvesant YMCA

C

• Mocada

Putnam Av

Portland Av

C

Hancock Av

Atlantic Av

1/4-mile radius

Lefferts Pl

C S

Fulton St A C

•**143** Pacific Street Condominiums

Carlton Av

Vanderbilt Av
Underhill Av
Grand Av

Pacific St

Dean St

LIRR from Atlantic Termina

B Q

St Marks Av

7th Av
Flatbush Av
8th Av

2 3

S

Park Pl

Brooklyn Children's Museum **140**•

See Map
13
Park Slope

•**138** On Prospect Park

Brower Park •

Franklin Av
Bedford Av
Rogers Av
Nostrand Av
New York Av
Brooklyn Av

St Johns Pl

Brooklyn Museum Entry Pavilion **139**•
and Plaza

2 3

Classon Av

S

2 3
4 5

Eastern Pkwy 3

Brooklyn Botanic Garden •
Visitor Center

S

Union St

President St

2 5

Carroll St

•**141** Medgar Evers College
School of Science, Health, and Technology

Crown St

Montgomery St

Prospect Park West

Washington Av

Prospect Park

PROSPECT HEIGHTS, CROWN HEIGHTS, BEDFORD-
STUYVESANT, CLINTON HILL, FORT GREENE

This chapter presents projects in neighborhoods east of

Flatbush Avenue, the thoroughfare that feeds the Manhattan Bridge and
defines the northeast edge of Prospect Park. In addition to this park, two
more linked landscapes by Frederick Law Olmsted and Calvert Vaux can
be found here: Grand Army Plaza and Eastern Parkway. East of Park Slope
is the aptly named Prospect Heights, which lies just north of the park, the
Brooklyn Botanic Garden, and the Brooklyn Museum. The neighborhood's
eastern edge is Washington Avenue, and its northern boundary is defined
by Atlantic Avenue and the Atlantic Yards development, which ate up
supposedly blighted blocks just south of the avenue, despite residents'
opposition. The neighborhood's late-nineteenth-century development
declined in the 1960s, only to experience two decades later a resurgence
that continues to this day amid an eclectic population.

South of Prospect Heights is Crown Heights, home to a large
Caribbean population (the neighborhood is the site of the colorful West
Indian Carnival held annually on Labor Day) and a Lubavitcher Hasidic
community. Eastern Parkway cuts east-west through the neighborhood,
yet impressive mansions can still be found on either side of this six-
lane thoroughfare. To the north of Crown Heights is Bedford-Stuyvesant
(typically called Bed-Stuy, the last part rhymes with "eye"), the 1930s
merger of Bedford on the west and Stuyvesant Heights on the east. The
area was settled by freed slaves soon after the 1827 abolition of slavery
in New York State, making it the largest black neighborhood in New York
City, a distinction it still holds today, even as middle- to upper-class New
Yorkers eye the beautiful assemblages of brownstones that rival those
of Park Slope.

To the east of Bed-Stuy, north of Prospect Heights, are Clinton Hill
and Fort Greene. The former is home to the Pratt Institute and some
grand nineteenth-century houses, and the latter is centered on another
Olmsted-Vaux creation, Fort Greene Park. The neighborhood around the
park traces its well-established African American population back to the
days when the Brooklyn Navy Yard was churning out wartime vessels,
but now the residents' occupations lean to the artistic side, most evident
in the Brooklyn Academy of Music (BAM) on the edge of Downtown.

14

138 The glass mass presides over Grand Army Plaza and its arch (above). The south elevation belies the building's massive depth (right). Photos © Aaron Dougherty.

138 ON PROSPECT PARK
RICHARD MEIER & PARTNERS ARCHITECTS, 2009

1 Grand Army Plaza, at Eastern Parkway
2 3 to Grand Army Plaza

In 2002, two of what would eventually be three glass residential towers (**43**) designed by Pritzker Prize–winner Richard Meier were completed on the West Side Highway in Manhattan's West Village. The media coverage before and after their completion—stemming from their high-profile designs but also the record prices and celebrity owners of the condos—heralded an apparent demand in the city for glass towers designed by name architects, catering to the small percentage of people able to afford square footage prices in the thousands. During the construction of the third tower, Meier was lured by developer Mario Procida to replicate that winning formula in Brooklyn on a choice site overlooking Olmsted and Vaux's Prospect Park, Grand Army Plaza, and the Brooklyn Public Library.

In terms of volume, the fifteen-story edifice is more in line with the Soldiers' and Sailors' Arch across the street than with Meier's trio of West Side towers. Meier's exterior design for On Prospect Park recycles much of what he executed in the two Perry Street towers: large panes of full-height glass alternate with narrow operable windows; the floor slab is articulated as a white shadowbox; and frosted-glass balcony guardrails are slid in front of the same spandrel. With its proximity to Prospect Park, the 114-unit mass of glass was criticized as a "deathtrap for birds," by NYC Audubon, though the same can be said in regard to just about any tower in the city wrapped in glass, inspired by Meier's popular buildings or not.

BROOKLYN MUSEUM ENTRY PAVILION AND PLAZA

ENNEAD ARCHITECTS, 2004

200 Eastern Parkway, at Washington Avenue

2 **3** to Eastern Parkway–Brooklyn Museum

McKim, Mead & White's late-nineteenth-century Beaux-Arts design for the Brooklyn Institute of Arts and Sciences—what would later become the Brooklyn Museum, but which also encompassed the Brooklyn Academy of Music, Brooklyn Botanic Garden, and Brooklyn Children's Museum—featured a grand staircase at the museum's entrance overlooking Eastern Parkway, in the same vein as the earlier Metropolitan Museum of Art and later New York Public Library. These steps were demolished in 1934 after years of neglect, in effect creating a void in the middle of the edifice that would not be filled for another seventy years.

James Stewart Polshek's involvement with Brooklyn Museum started in 1986, when his office (formerly Polshek Partnership) won a master plan competition with Japanese architect Arata Isozaki. (More recently the office designed the triangular Elizabeth A. Sackler Gallery for Feminist Art, housing Judy Chicago's *Dinner Party* on the fourth floor.) The master plan included numerous renovations within the original building and the late 1970s service extension, but its most dramatic element is the Martha A. and Robert S. Rubin Pavilion and Lobby, along with the Eastern Parkway plaza, designed with Judith Heintz Landscape Architecture. The 15,000-square-foot pavilion recalls the original stairs, but right angles are eschewed in favor of a semicircle with shingled glass above the lower-level entry. Access to the new entry doors is on an oblique route from the northwest, between swaths of grass with concentric pavers. Yet on the axis from the Washington Avenue intersection, one passes a spray fountain and ascends steps that lead to a walkway and a small plaza atop the pavilion, allowing closer glimpses of the pavilion's shingled glass roof and the façade of the original building.

14

139 The lobby doubles as a space for displaying sculpture (above). Seen across Eastern Parkway, the plaza is capable of supporting various uses and events (right). Photos by Aislinn Weidele.

140 A bold yellow volume defines the northwest corner of Brower Park.

140 BROOKLYN CHILDREN'S MUSEUM
RAFAEL VIÑOLY ARCHITECTS, 2008

145 Brooklyn Avenue, at St. Marks Avenue
❸ to Kingston Avenue

Spawned from the nineteenth-century Brooklyn Institute of Arts and Sciences, the Brooklyn Children's Museum opened in an old house in present-day Brower Park (then Bedford Park) in 1899. The museum expanded thirty years later, but it didn't have a purpose-built home until 1977, when it moved into a Hardy Holzman Pfeiffer–designed "building" buried under the park. It was billed as the first museum in the world especially for children, though it seems now that every large city has its own children's museum—at least three hundred according to the museum's own tally. Many of these museums recognize the importance of architecture in creating special places and spaces for kids as well as a strong image for the institution; notable examples can be found as far away as San Diego or Pittsburgh, or as close as the Gwathmey Siegel–designed Jewish Children's Museum six blocks away. Not to be outdone, the Brooklyn Children's Museum commissioned Rafael Viñoly to create an adventurous design that would double its size (to 110,000 square feet) and create a strong presence in the residential Crown Heights area.

Viñoly's design certainly stands out in its Brower Park corner location, an L-shaped building covered in 8 million yellow ceramic tiles. The striking volume, which recalls Fantasia, the museum's 20-foot-long Burmese python, is propped up on glass storefronts and colored metal walls. Most of the 1977 spaces were reconfigured, with the two new floors adding a library, galleries, classrooms, and a café, all cradling a raised courtyard. The expansion is part of the Department of Design and Construction's Design and Construction Excellence program and follows the department's sustainability guidelines, making it the first green museum in New York City.

MEDGAR EVERS COLLEGE SCHOOL OF SCIENCE, HEALTH, AND TECHNOLOGY **141**

ENNEAD ARCHITECTS with Roberta Washington Architects, 2010

1632 Bedford Avenue, at Crown Street
②⑤ to President Street;
③ to Nostrand Avenue

Founded in 1970 to serve the black population of central Brooklyn, Medgar Evers College—one of twenty-three institutions that make up the City University of New York—recently saw the completion of its fourth building in Crown Heights, three of them anchoring Crown and Bedford, a mini-campus of sorts. Partner Todd Schliemann's design for the new 191,000-square-foot building accentuates this intersection by situating the entrance on the

141 A faceted glass pavilion provides entry to the long building.

corner in a faceted glass pavilion. Behind are five stories of glass and brick snaking halfway down the block. Staggered sunshades on the south-facing curtain wall sections give some visual interest to the institutional building, which sits on a plot of land formerly occupied by a Department of Sanitation garage.

MARCY AVENUE RESIDENCE **142**

JONATHAN KIRSCHENFELD ARCHITECT, 2003

614 Marcy Avenue
Ⓖ to Myrtle and Willoughby Avenues

Architect Jonathan Kirschenfeld is known primarily for the Floating Pool, which is exactly what it sounds like. It returns to the New York City waterfront every summer, usually serving an area not privileged with a local pool. The pool uniquely responds to the city's physical makeup and addresses a social need, considerations that extend to the architect's numerous projects for supportive housing. In Bedford-Stuyvesant the architect designed this simple brick building housing studio units for fifty adults with mental illness, for the nonprofit housing organization Services for the UnderServed. The L-shaped building holds the corner while creating a secure internal courtyard for the residents. Most of the units are in a three-story block raised above the ground-floor common area highlighted by columns. Similarly, the entrance on Hart Street is set off by a single round column. A double-height sun porch punctuates the elevation on Marcy Avenue. It's a simple design, but

one much better con-sidered and better executed than most of the moneymaking condo buildings that litter the borough.

142 The single column on the left marks the entry, the three on the right, the commons.

143 PACIFIC STREET CONDOMINIUMS
LOADINGDOCK5, 2007-8

**904-925-935-957 Pacific Street,
between Washington and Grand Avenues
🄲 to Clinton and Washington Avenues**

On a one-block stretch of Pacific Street in Prospect Heights, Brooklyn-based architects Loadingdock5 have designed four buildings for Hello Living, head-quartered in the same borough. Hello Living claims to create "new urban communities...of friends, family, and style," marketing lingo to be sure, but traits that seem to come across in the architects' unique and recognizable designs.

From west to east, of the four buildings the first encountered is 904 Pacific Street (dubbed Dakota by the developer), a development that straddles two zoning districts that cut diagonally through the site. The architects dealt with the different bulk requirements of the commercial (west) and residential (east) districts by splitting the project into seven-story and five-story buildings, respectively, linked by walkways punctuated with red walls. At the back is a third building containing the lobby, more condos, and vertical circulation serving the three buildings that make up the project.

Across the street are 925 (Madison) and 935 (Hudson), two similar buildings that feature double-height recessed terraces cut into elevations faced in brown panels. Also consistent in each are portal entrances, expansive glazing, wood-slat guardrails on the balconies, and jagged rooflines. Differences are seen in the balconies: those at Madison are rectangular one- and two-story spaces; Hudson's balconies are two-story L-shaped spaces, like puzzle pieces interlocking, with the windows zigzagging up from the entry.

Easternmost is 957 Pacific (Sydney), also called The Terrace House by the architects. Extending from a glass and stone first floor are what look like oversized horizontal blinds. These gray louvers shield external stairs and elevators between the large terraces fronting the apartments. By placing the vertical circulation along the prime real estate that is the street façade, the architects were able to create full-depth units optimized for cross-ventilation. A larger version of The Terrace House by the same two parties can be found one block east.

In terms of creating "new urban communities," the first and last develop-ments go furthest toward this goal, mainly through their creative use of circulation. Dakota's external yet introverted vertical circulation and corridors create an urban village. Sydney's outboard stairs serve the quality of the apartments, as mentioned, but they also promote interaction among residents as they move up and down the building and take advantage of the generous terraces. These are not buildings for city dwellers who want to sequester themselves away from their neighbors. They foster interaction among residents able to afford the price of admission.

At the time of writing, Loadingdock5 was completing what would purportedly be the first New York City building to follow Germany's stringent *Passivhaus* (passive house) green standards, in which little to no energy is used for heating and cooling the spaces; it is located at Grand Street and Bedford Avenue in Williamsburg, Brooklyn.

14

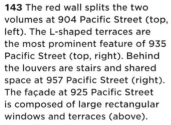

143 The red wall splits the two volumes at 904 Pacific Street (top, left). The L-shaped terraces are the most prominent feature of 935 Pacific Street (top, right). Behind the louvers are stairs and shared space at 957 Pacific Street (right). The façade at 925 Pacific Street is composed of large rectangular windows and terraces (above).

Photos © Marc Lins.

144 A striking glass box sandwiched between two landmarks (above). The complex linking of the two old buildings is written on the façade (right).

144 HIGGINS HALL INSERTION

STEVEN HOLL ARCHITECTS with Rogers Marvel Architects, 2005

65 St. James Place, at Lafayette Avenue
Ⓖ to Clinton and Washington Avenues

In 1996 Pratt Institute's Higgins Hall—home to the School of Architecture—was severely damaged in a predawn blaze that destroyed the recently completed $1.5 million renovations to the nineteenth-century building. The subsequent reconstruction and renovation of the north and south wings was overseen by Rogers Marvel Architects, but the destruction of the central wing required a new building to fill the void.

Steven Holl's standout design is set back from the street, creating a forecourt paved in bricks salvaged from the fire. Above, the façade is made up of only three materials—translucent channel glass, clear glass, and brick red steel—but it is hardly a simple composition. The horizontal lines sandwiching the milky white glass emphasize the misalignment of floor level in the north and south buildings, culminating in what Holl describes as the "dissonant zone" over the entrance. The offset floors are accommodated inside by ramps perpendicular to this zone, functionally linking the north and south wings for the first time.

The insertion also links two buildings that sit in the Clinton Hill Historic District, but Holl's design seems an unlikely recipient of approval from the Landmarks Preservation Commission. According to Rogers Marvel Architects, which collaborated with Holl's office on the insertion, the project was the first approval of an all-glass building in a historic district, signaling a shift in preservation circles from mimicry to difference while respecting a building's time period. Of course this is hardly the last all-glass building to find itself at odds with historical neighbors, as can be seen elsewhere in this book in designs by Norman Foster (**99**), Kohn Pedersen Fox (**50**), and Jean Nouvel (**19**).

HANRAHAN MEYERS ARCHITECTS, 2007

200 Willoughby Avenue (main campus entrance);
building at Dekalb and Grand Avenues
Ⓖ to Clinton and Washington Avenues

Over the roughly 125 years since its founding, Pratt Institute has evolved in the Clinton Hill neighborhood from a few scattered buildings to its current five-block campus (bounded by Willoughby, Classon, Dekalb, and Hall) with offshoots. Since the school evolved organically and within the city's block structure, the buildings are predominantly oriented toward streets that in some cases no longer exist, their backs facing the quad-like mall and sculpture park in the center of the campus. The Terian Design Center is a small addition (9,000 square feet) that plays a big role in Pratt's long-term strategy to rebrand the campus and reorient it toward this mall. The three-story insertion links the existing Pratt Studios and Steuben Hall, giving those buildings a new entrance in the heart of the campus and giving Pratt a strong image.

To accentuate the importance of this small addition, architects Thomas Hanrahan (dean of Pratt's School of Architecture) and Victoria Meyers dramatically projected the Design Center's double-height gallery over the new entrance. Clad in dark stainless steel, the cantilever is splayed in plan, giving the impression that the brick buildings are squeezing the addition. Inside, the exposed brick walls make it clear that the entrance and gallery have been literally inserted between the existing buildings. The best route to the Design Center is either from Ryerson Walk off Dekalb Avenue, one block east of Hall Street, or from Willoughby Avenue and the new Security Kiosk (**146**).

145 The projecting gallery boldly signals the new Design Center (above). Inside, the gallery window frames the campus green (right). Photos © Paul Warchol.

146 PRATT INSTITUTE SECURITY KIOSK
HANGAR DESIGN GROUP, 2006

200 Willoughby Avenue, at Grand Avenue
Ⓖ to Classon Avenue

Easily the smallest building in this guidebook, this one-room pavilion at the main entrance to Pratt Institute's five-block Clinton Hill campus serves to give security personnel a 360-degree view of the surrounding area. A cast-in-place concrete base supports the wraparound storefront glass. Above is a copper roof that dramatically cantilevers to the north and west, sheltering people interacting with security (including me, when I was interrogated for snapping some photos of the kiosk: a word of warning) and those waiting for campus buses. The copper roof panels are brought down to the ground on the campus side of the small building. As in all buildings using the material (**48**), the evolution of the kiosk as the skin patinates will make it even more intriguing when the building appears to rise from the lawn behind it.

146 A small building with a strong presence. Photo by Ty Cole.

147 MYRTLE HALL
WASA/STUDIO A, 2010

536 Myrtle Avenue, between Emerson Place and Hall Street
Ⓖ to Classon Avenue

Pratt Institute's expansion plans have drawn its facilities beyond the five-block main campus toward Myrtle Avenue, a major east-west thoroughfare. First came the PrattStore at Emerson Place, near the school's facilities department, but the adjacent Myrtle Hall is a more substantial undertaking which moves student services, some academic departments, and the nonprofit Pratt Center for Community Development to this new northern edge. WASA/Studio A's design articulates two completely different sides—a panelized masonry wall in a random pattern on Myrtle and a curtain wall with integral louvers overlooking the new plaza to the south—united by a multistory "window" and an internal atrium that stretches from one side to the other. At this writing, plans were under way to transform the four-block-long service road in front of the building into a pedestrian plaza, one of a number of public spaces along Myrtle developed by the Project for Public Spaces and the Myrtle Avenue Brooklyn Partnership.

147 The atrium window occupies the center of the Myrtle Avenue elevation (top). Photos by Amy Barkow. **The atrium window wraps around into an entry canopy on the campus side (left).**

VANDERBILT STUDIO 148

ADJAYE ASSOCIATES with David Hotson Architect, 2005

208 Vanderbilt Avenue, between Willoughby and Dekalb Avenues
Ⓖ to Clinton and Washington Avenues

This new four-story building in Fort Greene designed by London-based architect David Adjaye provides studio spaces for artists James Casebere and Lorna Simpson, who live next door. Referred to as "Pitch Black" on the architect's Web page, the street façade consists of a few glass openings flush with black polypropylene panels typically used as a lining to stabilize internal temperature in trucks. Up close, this skin, which wraps around the corner to the pitched-roof south side adjacent to a parking lot, evidences a texture that arises from screen printing the panels with black ink. It is one of the most tactically inviting façades in this book. It is also a severely private exterior that is countered by the predominantly white interiors and all-glass rear façade overlooking a terrace. In the past this privacy has been lifted a couple of times a year, when the studio is made available for the Open House New York (OHNY) and Fort Greene house tours; check the Web pages of these organizations to see if it will happen again.

148 A small but commanding presence in black.

SLOT HOUSE 149

NOROOF ARCHITECTS, 2005

134 Adelphi Street, between Park and Myrtle Avenues
Ⓖ to Clinton and Washington Avenues

14

Set back generously from the street, this distinctive Fort Greene house appears at first glance to be a new addition to the neighborhood, but the white siding bracketing the front door hints at the reality: it is a gut renovation of an existing house. Noroof's Scot Oliver and Margarita McGrath designed the small house for themselves, including a rental unit at the rear. Their two-story house is planned around the tall windows framing the maple tree that commands the space in front of the house. It is impossible to think of the house without the tree, and it is easy to see why the architects made it a driver of the interior layout. A peek inside may be possible. Whereas many architects use their offices as a display case for their design skills, Oliver and McGrath use their home, a frequent participant in OHNY and other tours.

149 The slot windows and the tree, working in harmony.

See Map
20
Long Island City

Paige St

McGuinness Blvd

Greenpoint Av

Franklin St

East River

Humbolt St

Kingsland Av

•150 Newtown Creek Wastewater Treatment Plant
•151 The Pencil Factory

Kent Av

Berry St

Bedford Av

N 7th St

McCarren Pool

•153 Loreley

Varick Av

The New Domino

Metropolitan Av

Williamsburg Bridge

• Daycare Center

Grand St

351 **152•**
Keap Street

Union Av

•154 Williamsburg Community Center

Manhattan Av

Wyckoff Exchange

Brooklyn-Queens Expy

M

Flushing Av

Broadway

DeKalb Av

Wyckoff Av

Myrtle Av

Park Av

Myrtle Av

Knickerbocker Av

Gates Av

See Map
14
Crown Heights

DeKalb Av
Lafayette Av

Lewis Av

Malcolm X Blvd

Engine Company 277

Central Av

1-mile
radius

Queens
Brooklyn

G

Bedford Av

Nostrand Av

New York Av

Bushwick Av

J Z

Saratoga Avenue
Community Center

155•

Jamaica Av

Atlantic Av

A C

Fulton St

Atlantic Av

LIRR from Atlantic Terminal

Liberty

Euclid Av

Weeksville Heritage Center •

Glenmore Gardens **156•** Glenmore Av

Van Siclen Av

Eastern Pkwy

Jewish Children's
Museum

4

Marcus Garvey Houses
Community Center

New Lots Av

3

Prospect Park •

Empire Blvd

Bedford Av

Rogers Av

Flatbush Av

Utica Av

Remsen Av

Rockaway Pkwy

Rockaway Av

Pennsylvania Av

Linden Blvd

Nehemiah Spring Creek **157•**

Linden Blvd

Kings Hwy

Flatlands Av

Belt Pkwy

Clarendon Rd

2 5

See Map
16
Flatbush

L

GREENPOINT, WILLIAMSBURG, BROWNSVILLE, EAST NEW YORK

This chapter features projects in the neighborhoods of Brooklyn that line its eastern edge, a border the borough shares with Queens. Northernmost is Greenpoint, a peninsula defined by the East River and Newtown Creek, and extending to the BQE and McCarren Park on the south. The Dutch farmed the area from 1638 until the rise of shipbuilding in the 1840s. Subsequently the area came to be defined by the "five black arts" (printing, pottery, petroleum and gas refining, glassmaking, and iron making), and to this day a mix of industry and residences prevails. The latter are occupied by a large Polish American population with origins that date to the 1930s, though diversity today is added by immigrants from South America and hipsters priced out of nearby Williamsburg to the south.

Along with Greenpoint and other neighborhoods, Williamsburg was part of the Dutch town of Bushwick. In the 1800s Williamsburg was known as the "playground of the rich" with its resort hotels, beer gardens, and private clubs. This changed as immigrants arrived, following the 1903 opening of the Williamsburg Bridge, but a present-day version of the playground exists in the bars along Bedford Avenue north of the BQE that cater to the neighborhood's hipsters. Farther south along Bedford can be found Williamsburg's Hasidic section, extending beyond the neighborhood's southern border of Flushing Avenue. The continued evolution of Williamsburg—as artists and hipsters pave the way for gentrification—will play out along the East River, where residential towers are rising on the site of former industrial tracts. The process slowed with the economic collapse, but projects on the horizon promise more development to come.

At the opposite end of the Brooklyn-Queens border sits East New York, yet another area originally farmed by the Dutch, in the borough's southeast corner, between Atlantic Avenue and Jamaica Bay. East New York incorporates smaller neighborhoods such as New Lots and Starrett City, the latter comprising nearly fifty apartment buildings, echoed in eleven public housing projects nearby. Through efforts such as community gardens and affordable housing, the area is striving to erase its association with abandonment, drugs, and sub-par adult literacy and education.

15

150 NEWTOWN CREEK WASTEWATER TREATMENT PLANT
ENNEAD ARCHITECTS, 2007 (PHASE 1)

329 Greenpoint Avenue, at Humbolt Street
Ⓖ to Greenpoint Avenue

Flush a toilet anywhere within a twenty-three-mile area encompassing roughly the tip of Manhattan below Midtown East, Greenpoint, and Williamsburg, and the effluent travels to this municipal wastewater treatment plant in northern Greenpoint. The plant takes its name from Newtown Creek, the notoriously polluted waterway separating Brooklyn from Queens, which is used to ship sludge. Over 300 million gallons a day are treated at Newtown Creek, the largest of the city's fourteen plants. It is currently in the midst of a twenty-five-year, $5 billion upgrade to bring the plant into compliance with federal standards, eliminate odors, and expand its capacity, with an expected completion date of 2017.

Richard Olcott and James Stewart Polshek of Ennead Architects (formerly Polshek Partnership) lead the master planning and architectural effort, which includes a large team of environmental engineers (Greeley and Hansen, Hazen and Sawyer, Malcolm Pirnie), landscape architect Quennell Rothschild, and the lighting designer L'Observatoire International. The last is responsible for the dramatic lighting of the eight 130-foot-tall, 80-foot-diameter digester "eggs" and their glass-enclosed walkways bridging the peaks. These eight sludge eaters are

visible from the surrounding streets and bridges, as are new buildings punctuated by splashes of color.

But as could be expected, access to the project's grounds is limited. At Greenpoint Avenue and Humboldt Street is an orange tile appendage to the main building which houses the Visitor Center at Newtown Creek. Open to the public on Friday and Saturday afternoons, it is an educational center run by the Department of Environmental Protection, featuring a great inside-outside, yin-yang fountain by artist Vito Acconci. And to the north, tucked in on the east of Paige Avenue, is the entrance to artist George Trakas's Percent for Art contribution. The curling nature walk moves people along a meandering path offering changing views of the surrounding industry and infrastructure, an entry into an otherwise inaccessible waterfront; it is a singular experience in New York City.

150 The digester eggs steal the show (below). Photo by Adam Friedberg. **The visitor center on Greenpoint Avenue (top, left). A stretch of the nature walk along Newtown Creek (left).**

151 Looking north at the new portion with the old Faber building beyond (left). A detail of the meeting of new and old (right). Photos by Amy Barkow.

THE PENCIL FACTORY **151**
DANIEL GOLDNER ARCHITECTS, 2010

122 West Street, at Kent Street
Ⓖ to Greenpoint Avenue

In 1872 Eberhard Faber moved his company's factory to Greenpoint after a fire destroyed his ten-year-old Manhattan plant that same year. After occupying a number of nineteenth- and early-twentieth-century buildings steps from the East River, the Eberhard Faber Pencil Company left Brooklyn for Pennsylvania in 1956. Its cluster of buildings spread across two blocks survived until two buildings were torn down for The Pencil Factory, a large condo development that reuses one of the Faber buildings flanked by two new buildings to its south and east. This action sparked the Landmarks Preservation Commission to designate eight factory buildings as the Eberhard Faber Pencil Company Historic District, the majority on the block south of these new condos. Faber's recurring star in a diamond motif appears on the parapets, but most distinctive are the terracotta pencils at the top of the columns at 61 Greenpoint Avenue.

    Daniel Goldner's design for the five-story buildings uses staggered colored brick panels that simultaneously stand out while being rooted in their context, as if the different colors of brick were a patchwork of the various surrounding warehouses. Set atop the new and old buildings of equal height are eight penthouse "lanterns," a repeated element that ties old and new together. Wrapped in white walls, floor, and roof, framing windows facing outward, they are so self-contained and such a break from what's happening below that they appear to have been dropped in place atop the buildings, like prefab modules for VIPs.

152 351 KEAP STREET
MICHELE BERTOMEN, 2011

351 Keap Street, between
South 3rd and South 4th Streets
🄹 🅉 🄼 to Marcy Avenue;
🄖 to Metropolitan Avenue;
🄛 to Lorimer Street

As the modular building blocks of international trade, shipping containers are ubiquitous and recognizable, but normally they can be found in the environs of New York only in Red Hook (just south of Brooklyn Bridge Park [**127**]) and near Newark Liberty International Airport in New Jersey. Made to be stacked and support loads approaching sixty thousand pounds, the inexpensive units are extremely popular with architects for use as temporary structures—the Shigeru Ban–designed Nomadic Museum, made of 148 containers, was docked on Manhattan's West Side for three months in 2005—but also increasingly for permanent offices and even dwellings. Following a few interior and backyard projects, this house in Williamsburg became the first ground-up building in the city constructed from shipping containers—seven of them, to be exact.

152 A narrow slot divides the two stacks of containers (top). Each stack of shipping containers features a rooftop garden (above). Photos by Amy Barkow.

New York Institute of Technology professor Michele Bertomen designed this three-story house for herself and her husband, who actually built it. (They creatively established a nonprofit to provide a rent-free residence for visiting scholars and students in a ground-floor "module" below theirs.) On a mid-block lot, four 40-foot-long containers are stacked next to three 20-foot-long ones on the south (each roughly 8 feet by 8 feet in section), with a 3-foot slot for vertical circulation in between. Note that two of the seven containers—one topping each stack—actually consist of a platform (the container's floor only) and a standard container with its walls removed. These alterations stem from the desire to provide rooftop access as well as the fact that containers' roofs are inherently weak. They work by transferring the loads on the floor to the corner structure; this additionally means that the walls can be punctured at will without destroying the structural stability of the unit. Although these were originally a patchwork of colors like the yards in Red Hook and New Jersey, their all-white surface tones down the industrial presence miles from the ports where these containers once belonged.

15

As computer technology expands its hold over architectural production—hand drafting was long ago replaced by computer-aided drafting (CAD)—one area of experimentation is parametric modeling. This technique utilizes sophisticated CAD modeling software that defines geometry with certain dependencies built in, so changes in one part of the 3-D model have a ripple effect, updating other parts of the model. In the case of Shawn Rickenbacker and Sam Leung's design for the Williamsburg location of the Lower East Side restaurant Loreley—a transformation of and an addition to a former gas station adjacent to the BQE—the dependencies consisted of a 50 percent openness and the structural stability of the garden wall. Variations in undulations and height arose from the parametric modeling.

The result is a billowing brick wall that appears lighter and more malleable than one would expect from the modular material. And even though the design exploits the parametric software to create a precise model, the architects acknowledged that it would be built by hand, even going so far as to create custom yet cost-effective jumbo bricks to implement the design. Structural stability and the mortar-less appearance of the wall are further achieved with a high-strength, nonshrinking adhesive that holds the bricks together. In addition to the garden enclosure, there is a taller, bulbous wall, also of brick, that ties into the existing building like an outgrowth of the new from the old.

153 A porous brick wall wraps around the beer garden (top, right). An undulating wall transitions between the existing brick wall and the courtyard's woven wall (right).
Photos by Amy Barkow.

154 WILLIAMSBURG COMMUNITY CENTER
PKSB ARCHITECTS, 2003

195 Graham Avenue, at Scholes Street
🄻 to Grand Street or Montrose Avenue

In 1938 the Williamsburg Houses' twenty four-story buildings opened, an early New York City Housing Authority (NYCHA) development that replaced more than six hundred frame structures on this twenty-three-acre multiblock site. The H-shaped buildings are angled 15 degrees to the grid and notably integrate retail storefronts—rarely found on future, taller NYCHA projects—on Graham and Bushwick Avenues. The project is seen as an early example of European Modernism transplanted to America. This is the view taken by the Landmarks Preservation Commission, which designated the public housing project a landmark in 2003, the same year this community center opened.

Serving primarily residents in the Williamsburg Houses, the 21,000-square-foot building contains a myriad of athletic and performance facilities, with outdoor courts for handball and basketball, a playground, a picnic area, and a garden for seniors. Architects PKSB (Pasanella + Klein Stolzman + Berg) utilized a modern idiom for the one-story building (plus mezzanine), but they eschewed the striated brick and concrete of the Williamsburg Houses in favor of a veiled transparency. Inspired by chain-link fencing, the exterior is wrapped in glass blocks, insulated translucent panels, and perforated metal panels fronting clear glass walls, allowing generous daylighting and aiding in security. A ribbon of clear glass sits atop these walls on all four sides, giving the impression that the roof floats on a band of light.

154 The entrance is set back from the street, beyond a small grove of trees (top). Perforated panels veil the gymnasium inside (above).

15

SARATOGA AVENUE COMMUNITY CENTER 155
GEORGE RANALLI ARCHITECT, 2008

940 Hancock Street, between Saratoga Avenue and Broadway
🚇 to Halsey Street

Both the Saratoga Avenue and Williamsburg (**154**) community centers respond to the same client (NYCHA) and serve similar users (public housing residents). But whereas the latter meets the needs of over three thousand residents in twenty buildings, the former is added to a single sixteen-story tower. Likewise Williamsburg (and the community centers, see pages 206–207) employs fashionable surfaces of glass and metal, something George Ranalli eschews in favor of carefully articulated and crafted masonry, rooted more in Frank Lloyd Wright than Mies van der Rohe. Adding 3,500 square feet to the tower's 1,500-square-foot recreation facility, the community center is a ground-up building by an architect known for his interiors and furniture, as well as his role as dean of the Bernard and Anne Spitzer School of Architecture (**124**) at City College.

Ranalli sited the community center next to a commercial building on Hancock Street, an urban gesture that continues the sidewalk edge from Broadway and its elevated tracks. By providing a narrow link to the tower on the west, the addition creates a small forecourt on the same street, but a larger plaza, playground, and athletic courts are found to the south off Halsey Street. The building stands out on all sides. Walls of narrow brick rise from a stone base, culminating in an irregular profile accentuated by copings of GFRC (glass fiber reinforced concrete), a material repeated in the lintels and scuppers. A glass box appears to pop up from within the masonry walls, hinting at the highly articulated community room inside.

155 A small plaza fronts the building on Hancock Street (left). The south-facing elevation overlooks a playground and larger plaza (right). Photos © Paul Warchol.

156 GLENMORE GARDENS

DELLA VALLE BERNHEIMER with Architecture Research Office, BriggsKnowles, LTL Architects, 2006

Glenmore and Van Siclen Avenues
🄲 to Van Siclen Avenue

156 Designs by Della Valle Bernheimer on the left and ARO in the distance (above). LTL Architects' contribution on Van Siclen Avenue (below).

In 2000 New York City's Department of Housing Preservation and Development established the New Foundations homeownership program in order, says HPD, "to develop infill sites in neighborhoods that lacked home ownership opportunities." Architects and sometimes developers Jared Della Valle and Andrew Bernheimer—responsible for both aspects on West 18th Street in Chelsea (**55**)—lamented the lack of architects' contributions to the program's typical contractor-developer initiatives, so they decided to act as developer, planner, and architect for five parcels in East New York. They invited Architecture Research Office, BriggsKnowles, and LTL Architects to collaborate on the designs of ten semidetached two-family homes that are also part of Mayor Bloomberg's New Housing Marketplace plan, aimed at creating 165,000 units of affordable housing by 2013. East New York is known as one of the poorest and most troubled neighborhoods in New York City, with no fewer than eleven public housing projects serving the primarily black and Hispanic population. This small development is certainly justified and highly commendable.

The four firms worked together to develop housing typologies (three-story slab on grade and two-story stoop with basement) and a material palette (recycled corrugated aluminum, cedar siding, fiber cement panels). As executed, each building is unique in its combination of elements, but the similarities make it clear that all the buildings have the same origins. While these additions to the neighborhood stand out from their neighbors, they are nevertheless well integrated, a counterpoint to the Nehemiah Spring Creek development (**157**) a mile and a half south.

15

157 Some stretches of the houses are close to a block long (left). Row houses with bays borrowing colors from their neighbors (right).

NEHEMIAH SPRING CREEK **157**
ALEXANDER GORLIN ARCHITECT, 2008 (PHASE 1)

Flatlands Avenue and Elton Street
③ to New Lots Avenue

In East New York between Starrett City and the Queens border sits Gateway Estates, a 227-acre development that is a roughly even split between retail and residential. The shopping takes place in the 625,000-square-foot suburban-style Gateway Center shopping mall on the southern portion of the site, completed in 2002. An anticipated 1,525 housing units are located north of the mall off Flatlands Avenue. Developed by East Brooklyn Congregations' Nehemiah Housing, the multiphase affordable housing project—the largest in the city's history—consists primarily of two- and three-story single- and two-family town houses. Four parks and a new school—the latter under construction at this writing—are also part of the neighborhood being built on a former landfill.

Distinctively, Alexander Gorlin's design utilizes prefab techniques rather than traditional on-site construction. The 20- by 40-foot units were assembled in an old Brooklyn Navy Yard foundry. Everything from the floors, walls, and windows to the kitchen cabinets and sinks was built in the controlled interior conditions and trucked to the other side of Brooklyn to be stacked, much like the smaller Bronx Box (**180**). Gorlin jazzed up what could have been mundane exteriors by selecting the boldest of the standard colors for the fiber cement siding. This patchwork quilt is arranged in rows of from five to over thirty houses, with parking tucked into rear alleys. Visiting the neighborhood in the making is quite a surreal experience, owing to the quiet, long rows of houses and a complete lack of trees (for now). A healthy dose of vitality is needed, something that should come with time.

15

•**163** Green-Wood Columbarium

Green-Wood Mausoleum 163•

•162 P.S. 69 Vincent D. Grippo School

Brooklyn College West Quad Center 158•

1-mile radius

Sephardic Community Center 159•

Stillwell Avenue Terminal 161• •**160** *Wavewall*

Prospect Park

Lakeside Center

Linden Blvd

Gowanus Expy
4th Av
7th Av
39th St
Fort Hamilton Pkwy
13th Av
New Utrecht Av
Cristoforo Colombo Blvd
65th St
75th St
Bay Pkwy
86th St
Stillwell Av
Cropsey Av

Green-Wood Cemetery

Caton Av
Church Av
Ocean Pkwy
Coney Island Av
McDonald Av
Ocean Av
Flatbush Av
Bedford Av
Nostrand Av
Ditmas Av
Foster Av

Avenue H
Avenue J
Avenue L
Avenue N
Avenue P
Kings Hwy
Avenue S
Avenue U
Avenue X

Dyker Beach Park

Belt Pkwy

Lower New York Bay

Edible Schoolyard

Ocean Pkwy
Coney Island Av
Ocean Av
Belt Pkwy

Neptune Av

Sheepshead Bay

Surf Av

Coney Island Commons

Atlantic Ocean

D N R

F G

B Q

2 5

B

D F
N Q

This chapter's projects are found in central and southern Brooklyn, neighborhoods that span from the southern end of Prospect Park all the way to the Atlantic Ocean. The immensity of Brooklyn, a borough of seventy square miles of land occupied by 2.5 million residents (the most populous of all five boroughs), is well illustrated in this area, encompassing close to twenty neighborhoods and, in its cemetery, close to a third of the borough's living population is it's dead. Buildings in this chapter can be found in Flatbush, a large neighborhood just south of the park that was incorporated into Brooklyn in 1894 and features a number of planned developments from the early part of the twentieth century; Homecrest, a residential area south of Kings Highway that reaches toward Sheepshead Bay; Coney Island, the oceanfront area world famous for early-twentieth-century amusement parks like Dreamland and Luna Park; Green-Wood Cemetery, one of the largest cemeteries in New York City, just south and east of Prospect Park; and, south of the cemetery, Sunset Park and Borough Park, two neighborhoods with populations respectively mixed (Chinese, Latin American, Indian, and so on) and Jewish.

Tying some of these diverse neighborhoods together is Ocean Parkway, running north-south from near Prospect Park to Brighton Beach, the waterfront neighborhood just east of Coney Island. Designed in the mid-1860s by Frederick Law Olmsted and Calvert Vaux as a green corridor linking the borough's open spaces, the parkway is one of two the duo designed and realized in Brooklyn, the other being Eastern Parkway, which extends eastward from the northern tip of Prospect Park. In each case the center lanes are express lanes with limited stopping (intended for pleasure driving by horse-drawn carriages and later cars, at a time when such was possible). These lanes are flanked by greenswards with trees, grass, and pedestrian and bike lanes. Outermost are service roads for local and commercial traffic. These designs no doubt influenced Robert Moses in planning scenic parkways such as the Mosholu in the Bronx, lessons quickly forgotten, most notably in the Cross Bronx Expressway, which barreled through the same borough. Olmsted and Vaux's prescience is now being appreciated, as the Department of Transportation retrofits many of the city's streets with protected bike paths and left-turn bays, among other measures that echo the layered parkways developed decades before the internal combustion engine changed everything.

16

158 The west campus entry's horizontal and vertical lines (left). On the other side of the building, the structure reaches toward the athletic fields (right).

158 BROOKLYN COLLEGE WEST QUAD CENTER
RAFAEL VIÑOLY ARCHITECTS, 2009

Bedford Avenue and Campus Road
2 **5** to Flatbush Avenue–Brooklyn College; **Q** to Avenue H

In 1930 Brooklyn College was founded, followed five years later by architect Randolph Evans's master plan for the school's twenty-six-acre site in Flatbush, which formally opened in 1937. East and west quads on either side of Bedford Avenue were envisioned, with the majority of the Georgian colonial buildings erected on the east side. Later buildings followed Evans's plan for the most part, but the west quad remained incomplete until a 1995 master plan by Gruzen Samton with Kliment & Hasland Architects called for the demolition of a couple of 1970s additions that splintered the two halves of campus: a pedestrian bridge over Bedford Avenue, and the Plaza Building occupying what would become the quad. It also suggested that a new West Quad Center complete this side of campus, something called for in the 1935 plan.

Now part of the twenty-three-strong CUNY system, this new four-story center provides athletic facilities and now centralized student services for the college; the first overlook the playing fields and the second face the quad in Rafael Viñoly's long and low design. A stair tower offset from the main axis echoes the library's recognizable steeple of knowledge to the east. Balancing and intersecting with this vertical piece is a cantilevered bar housing offices. The other side of the building is freer in expression, if repetitive: a series of projecting bars covered in corrugated metal marches down the length of the west façade. They shield the NCAA pool and basketball court from the sun's rays, but their excessive size belies this solely functional role: the projections provide a backdrop to the sports field and a strong image for the school in the twenty-first century. Student ID is required for access to the quads, so for the rest of us the two sides of the building are only visible from the adjacent streets.

SEPHARDIC COMMUNITY CENTER 159
BKSK ARCHITECTS, 2010

1901 Ocean Parkway, at Avenue S
Ⓕ to Kings Highway

For thirty years the Morris & Paulette Bailey Sephardic Community Center (SCC) provided its mix of social, cultural, recreational, and informal educational programs in a 50,000-square-foot building on Ocean Parkway in the Homecrest neighborhood. The SCC is a nonprofit organization dedicated to perpetuating the heritage, culture, and traditions of Sephardic Jews, those from the Iberian Peninsula, northern Africa, and the Middle East. Yet its textured concrete building with few openings expressed an introversion and separation from its neighbors. Now, with the ever-growing Jewish population in the area and a concomitant need to expand the center, the new Edmond and Lily Safra Building opts for transparency and an inviting openness to the community.

Actually two façades define the addition, which doubles the building's size: the four-story frosted glass entry on Ocean Parkway and the three-story stone and glass elevation on the tree-lined residential street to the east. BKSK Architects also reworked portions of the existing building, connecting it to what they call the "intricate programmatic puzzle of the interior."[1] This program consists of a gymnasium, a pool, a preschool, meeting spaces, a performance space, offices, and "a celebratory space as a repository of cultural memory," featuring ancestral images behind a centrally located glass wall. SCC is a member-based organization, so the building is not open to the public.

159 A stone façade is found on the residential street to the east (below). The veiled glass façade fronts Ocean Parkway (right). Photos by Jonathan Wallen.

16

160 WAVEWALL
ACCONCI STUDIO, 2005

West 8th Street near Surf Avenue

F Q to West 8th Street–New York Aquarium

160 Undulating panels wrap around the stairs that lead to the aquarium. Photo by Jonathan Wallen.

Most of the MTA's Arts for Transit permanent installations apply two-dimensional artwork to the subway walls or insert sculptures into their above-grade and underground spaces. Of course, examples exist that interact with the subway environments, such as Christopher Janney's easy-to-miss sound installation on the 34th Street–Herald Square station platforms and Austrian artist Vito Acconci's south façade of the West 8th Street Station in Coney Island. Done in collaboration with architect Daniel Frankfurt, this installation pulls apart the regular wall pattern to create benches and views from the Manhattan-bound platform toward the Atlantic. This wavelike effect culminates in the wrapping of the southwest exit stairs, which provide access over Surf Avenue to the New York Aquarium. Acconci's inspirations were the natural waves of water and sand, but also Coney Island's iconic roller-coasters, one of which long ago sat on the land the station and installation now occupy.

161 STILLWELL AVENUE TERMINAL
KISS + CATHCART ARCHITECTS with Jambhekar/Strauss, 2005

Stillwell Avenue at Surf Avenue

D F N Q to Coney Island–Stillwell Avenue

Near the peak of Coney Island's popularity as a playground for amusement in the early twentieth century, a new terminal was constructed that consolidated four steam train lines in one station. Starting in 2001 this, the largest aboveground transit terminal in New York City—and supposedly the world—was reconstructed. Its eight-track, four-platform glass train shed, designed by Gregory Kiss and Colin Cathcart (Sudhir Jambekhar and Mark Strauss, now with FXFOWLE Architects, were responsible for the building facing Surf Avenue), is the terminal's most impressive feature, a 76,000-square-foot enclosure that recalls the golden age of train sheds in Europe. The light-filled glass and steel overhead structure features a huge installation of building-integrated photovoltaics (PVs), a triple-laminated thin film application able to power the equivalent of thirty-three single-family houses per year, according to the architects. It is the first MTA subway station to use solar energy.

161 Under the shed, the PVs shade the space and create energy. Photo by Adam Friedberg.

162 Seen from the north, the serrated bays extend across Ninth Avenue (left). The canopy's curve follows the wall of the gymnasium (right). Photos by Elliott Kaufman.

P.S. 69 VINCENT D. GRIPPO SCHOOL

HARDY HOLZMAN PFEIFFER ASSOCIATES, 2002 **162**

6302 Ninth Avenue, at 63rd Street

Ⓝ to Eighth Avenue or Fort Hamilton Parkway

By their very nature, buildings for public schools tend to exhibit repetition in their façades, stemming primarily from the numerous classrooms that take up most of their square footage. A grid of punched openings in brick walls is the norm, relieved mainly by pieces housing gymnasiums, cafeterias, and other large spaces. Variety in New York City Department of Education schools tends to come in the form of color applied to this standard design. But in the case of this 92,000-square-foot four-story school serving pre-kindergarten to fifth-grade students in Borough Park and other parts of south Brooklyn, the articulation of the classrooms is the focus of the design by Hardy Holzman Pfeiffer Associates. (The firm split in 2004 into what are now H3 Hardy Collaborative, Holzman Moss Bottino Architecture, and Pfeiffer Partners Architects.)

Three floors of serrated classroom bays cantilever above the flat ground floor. This design gesture breaks up the long elevation on Ninth Avenue, but it also gives this east face an ever-changing appearance, depending on one's vantage point. Perhaps the most telling view is from Ninth Avenue and 63rd Street, where the corner windows of the classrooms are apparent, as are the curving wall of the auditorium-gymnasium volume and the entrance between these two perpendicular parts of the building. This entrance extends to the playground at the rear, where the warehouse-like ribbon windows are capped by sunshades that appear to lift up from the façade. In 2005 the school was named in honor of the late Vincent D. Grippo, who as superintendent of Community District 20 was the driving force behind realizing this school.

163 GREEN-WOOD COLUMBARIUM AND MAUSOLEUM
PLATT BYARD DOVELL WHITE, 2006

500 25th Street, at Fifth Avenue
R to 25th Street

Green-Wood Cemetery was one of the first rural cemeteries in the United States when it was founded in 1838, and its natural beauty made it a popular tourist destination in New York City in the subsequent decades. Brooklyn residents frequented its 478 acres for recreation until the completion in 1873 of Prospect Park by Frederick Law Olmsted and Calvert Vaux, whose "Greensward" design for Central Park won a competition actually sparked by the popularity of the cemetery. In the last century and a half, outdoor recreation has changed from idyllic strolls to a diverse mix of active and passive uses in equally diverse spaces (pocket parks, disused elevated rail lines, waterfront parks on reclaimed industrial sites), but Green-Wood remains a popular destination as an urban oasis, for bird-watching, and for the collection of New York notables among its 600,000 "permanent residents." The cemetery, lying north and east of Sunset Park, was granted National Historic Landmark status in 2006, with the National Park Service citing its "cohesive combination of dramatic landscape design and plantings," its Gothic Revival architecture, and its 360-degree panoramic views.

Yet, as in any urban cemetery, space is limited, so over time Green-Wood has added facilities for aboveground burials and cremation alongside its landscape of in-ground plots, monuments, and tombs. A couple of twenty-first-century additions come from the firm of Charles Platt, the late Paul Byard, Ray Dovell, and Samuel White: the Tranquility Garden Columbarium in the northwest corner of the cemetery, and the Hillside IV Mausoleum on its eastern edge. These contemporary additions to the grounds may differ in material and style from the predominantly nineteenth-century architecture, but they are well integrated into their respective sites and well scaled inside.

The Columbarium lies just beyond the arched Gothic entrance gates at Fifth Avenue and 25th Street, between the entrance and the Historic Chapel, dating from 1911. The horseshoe-shaped Columbarium features three pavilions surrounding a pond from which a glass obelisk rises. These low buildings are covered in glass and stone, surrounded by wood trellises propped on slender concrete columns. Skylights projecting from the flat roofs echo the obelisk and bring natural light to interiors demarcated by partial-height walls with niches for urns and memory boxes; niches are also integrated into the exterior granite walls.

Near the cemetery's Ninth Avenue entrance (at 20th Street) is the curving Hillside Mausoleum complex, used for aboveground burials. Located at the western end of the first three stone and glass buildings is a four-story standout of glass shingles between gray stone walls. But when approached from the higher grounds to the north, the addition is seen as low projecting volumes in glass and stone that blend in with the landscape of grave markers. Inside, the verticality of Hillside IV is apparent in the open stairs and blue glass waterfall culminating in planted water gardens.

163 The Columbarium with Richard Upjohn's entrance gates in the distance (top). The Columbarium's obelisk rises from the tranquil koi pond (above, right). Built into a hillside, the Mausoleum faces south (right). Detail of the Mausoleum's scalloped glass wall on the south elevation (above). Photos by Jonathan Wallen.

BUILDING COMMUNITY

One side effect of the mid-twentieth-century urban renewal schemes that cleared supposed slums and replaced them with large-scale housing projects is the loss of the mixed uses that add vitality to the daily lives of residents. The anonymity and distancing of the "towers in the park" model endanger a sense of community and interaction, and have necessitated the creation of community centers to provide amenities for amending the developments. The New York City Housing Authority (NYCHA) operates 70 of the 135 community centers in its developments, and recently has invested close to $100 million to renovate, expand, or construct over thirty new community centers in all five boroughs. Below are a handful of the new buildings, but others can be found elsewhere in this book (**154, 155**).

MARCUS GARVEY HOUSES COMMUNITY CENTER
CAPLES JEFFERSON ARCHITECTS, 2010

10 Amboy Street, between East New York and Pitkin Avenues (Map 15)

This community center sits in Brooklyn smack in between two fourteen-story towers with three-story extensions that bend in plan, in response to the diagonal of East New York Avenue to the north. The architects dealt with the site constraints by separating the functions into parallel bars and by shaping courtyards, both within the new building and between it and the housing. The brick-clad sections, otherwise windowless, gain daylight from skylights and the glass-walled courtyard. Photo by Michael Anton.

BETANCES COMMUNITY CENTER
STEPHEN YABLON ARCHITECT, 2007

465 St. Ann's Avenue, at East 146th Street (Map 17)

On a corner lot across from St. Mary's Park in Bronx's Mott Haven neighborhood, this low-slung building belies the impressive space within and the complexity of the undertaking. The design reconfigures an old warehouse-cum-gym into the home for the Betances Youth Boxing Program, linking it to a renovated ground floor of the adjacent housing. Most impressive is the three-story-high boxing ring which starts one floor down and breaks through the roof for natural light.
Photo by Frank Oudeman.

MELROSE COMMUNITY CENTER
AGREST AND GANDELSONAS ARCHITECTS
with WASA/Studio A, 2001
286 East 156th Street, at Morris Avenue (Map 17)

For a prominent corner lot in the Bronx's Melrose Houses, architects Diana Agrest and Mario Gandelsonas created a hinge in the form of an ellipse. Inside is a gymnasium, with classrooms placed in a linear bar, and the two linked by a glass-enclosed entrance. It is an early example of design excellence for NYCHA community centers, and it certainly raised the standard for subsequent designs by other architects. Photo © David Sundberg/Esto.

LATIMER GARDENS COMMUNITY CENTER
HANRAHAN MEYERS
ARCHITECTS, 2007
34–30 137th Street, between 35th Avenue and Latimer Place (Map 21)

This renovation and expansion of a community center in Flushing, Queens, is tucked among the four ten-story buildings that make up Latimer Gardens. A single space for performance and sport is sheltered under a roof that bends in two directions for reasons both acoustical and visual. Clad in stainless steel, it is a sculptural presence among the brick and concrete. Photo © Michael Moran.

WEST BRIGHTON COMMUNITY CENTER
BECKHARD RICHLAN SZERBATY ASSOCIATES ARCHITECTS, 2006
230 Broadway, between Castleton and Henderson Avenues (Map 22)

This Staten Island community center doubled in size to 12,000 square feet. Solidity is expressed by the long, low building faced in painted blue metal panels above a blue stone base; narrow ribbon windows are sandwiched between these two materials. A battered brick wall terminating the north end furthers this sense of a small but strong building fronting the housing behind.
Photo courtesy Michael Szerbaty.

The borough's urban fabric is a distinct mix of industry, buildings, and nature.
Photo © Albert Vecerko/Esto.

BRONX

MOTT HAVEN, HIGHBRIDGE, HUNTS POINT **17**

BRONX PARK, FORDHAM, NORTH RIVERDALE **18**

CASTLE HILL, THROGS NECK, **19**
MORRIS PARK, BAYCHESTER

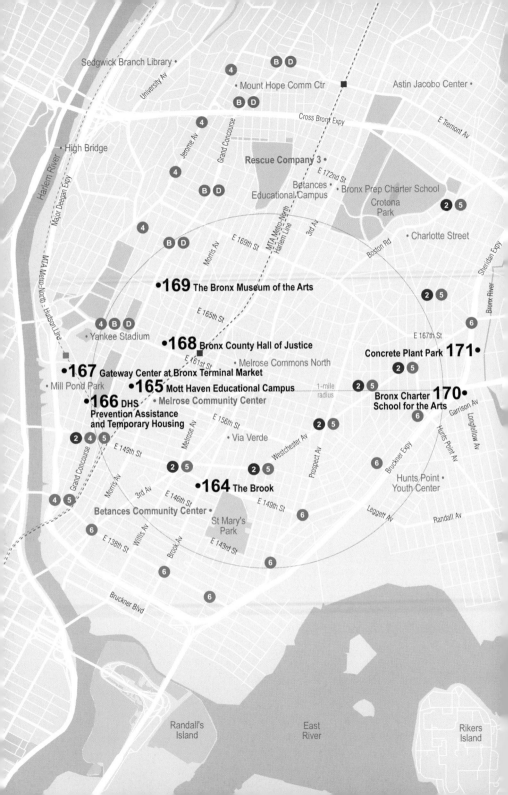

Sedgwick Branch Library •

• Mount Hope Comm Ctr

Astin Jacobo Center •

University Av

B **D**

4

B **D**

Cross Bronx Expy

E Tremont Av

4

Grand Concourse

Jerome Av

• High Bridge

E 172nd St

Bronx Prep Charter School •

Rescue Company 3 •

4

Betances •
Educational Campus

Crotona
Park

2 **5**

Harlem River

MTA Metro-North – Hudson Line

Major Deegan Expy

4

B **D**

Morris Av

E 169th St

MTA Metro-North
Harlem Line

3rd Av

• Charlotte Street

Boston Rd

Sheridan Expy

Bronx River

4

B **D**

•**169** The Bronx Museum of the Arts

E 165th St

2 **5**

6

E 167th St

4 **B** **D**

• Yankee Stadium

•**168** Bronx County Hall of Justice

Concrete Plant Park **171**•

2 **5**

E 161st St

• Melrose Commons North

•**167** Gateway Center at Bronx Terminal Market

• Mill Pond Park

•**165** Mott Haven Educational Campus

1-mile
radius

2 **5**

Bronx Charter **170**•
School for the Arts

•**166** DHS
**Prevention Assistance
and Temporary Housing**

• Melrose Community Center

2 **5**

Garrison Av

Longfellow Av

6

4 **5**

E 149th St

Grand Concourse

Morris Av

Melrose Av

E 156th St

• Via Verde

Westchester Av

Prospect Av

2 **5**

Hunts Point Av

Bruckner Expy

6

Hunts Point •
Youth Center

3rd Av

2 **5**

2 **5**

Leggett Av

Randall Av

4 **5**

•**164** The Brook

E 149th St

6

Betances Community Center •

St Mary's
Park

E 146th St

E 143rd St

6

Willis Av

E 138th St

Brook Av

6

Bruckner Blvd

6

6

Randall's
Island

East
River

Rikers
Island

The only borough that sits on the American mainland, the

Bronx features an urban fabric that dates back predominantly to the booming decades around the turn of the twentieth century. Subsequently its forty-two square miles were cut up by a patchwork of highways, public housing projects, and the aggravated destruction of the 1970s. The last is evidenced in two famous spectacles from 1977: Howard Cosell's live announcement to a national TV audience watching the Yankees play the Dodgers in the World Series that "the Bronx is burning," and President Jimmy Carter's equally famous walk atop the rubble of ruined apartment buildings on Charlotte Street. (This and adjacent streets southeast of Crotona Park are now a surreal swath of suburban tract houses in the middle of the city.)

Before this twentieth-century cycle of boom and transformation, agriculture prevailed, currently found in its industrialized version at the Hunts Point Terminal Market, the largest food distribution center in the world at over three hundred acres. Hunts Point, which juts into the East River at the mouth of the Bronx River, is part of what is now considered the South Bronx. This unofficial designation encompasses other neighborhoods between the Harlem and Bronx Rivers below the Cross Bronx Expressway, including Mott Haven, Melrose, Morrisania, and Highbridge. Historically the South Bronx has been the home of industry and low-income black and Puerto Rican residents. In response to the city's long-term plans for using the area as a site for jails and solid waste facilities, and of course the social and health effects associated with each, the environmental justice organization Sustainable South Bronx was formed by Majora Carter in 2001. Since then it has contributed to the creation of parks and green roofs in the area, as well as green educational programs for residents, making it one of the most effective and best-known urban environmental groups in the country. Through its programs, combined with a growing arts community and other grassroots efforts, Bronx residents are working to dispel the lingering impressions that have clung to the borough since the 1970s.

17

164 Red walls punctuate the cutouts in the corner volume (left). Photo © Michael Moran.
165 The buildings cradle the shared auditorium (right). Photo © Albert Vecerka/Esto.

164 THE BROOK
ALEXANDER GORLIN ARCHITECTS, 2010

455 East 148th Street, at Brook Avenue
2 **5** to Third Avenue–149th Street

Common Ground—the supportive housing developer responsible for Schermerhorn House (**130**)—realized its first construction project in the Bronx with this six-story residence in the Mott Haven neighborhood. On a former cockfighting venue, of all things, nearly two hundred units are provided for low-income workers, people with HIV/AIDS, and homeless individuals, with on-site services provide by BronxWorks. In addition to these studios, The Brook offers a large event space, a community backyard garden, an accessible green roof, and recreational spaces for the tenants. Alexander Gorlin's design breaks down the large L-shaped footprint by articulating the corner differently from the two brick arms. The metal-clad hinge piece features large terraces with bright red walls, boldly punctuating the two tones of gray that predominate and making the building visible from nearby St. Mary's Park.

165 MOTT HAVEN EDUCATIONAL CAMPUS
ALEXANDER GORLIN ARCHITECTS and PERKINS EASTMAN, 2010

780 Concourse Village West, between East 153rd and East 156th Streets
2 **4** **5** to 149th Street–Grand Concourse

In 2010 New York City's School Construction Authority opened fifteen new school buildings, none even close in size to this 280,000-square-foot four-building campus in the South Bronx; it's considered the largest school construction project in the city's history, with 2,300 seats divided among six "boutique" schools. Built on close to nine acres atop a former rail yard that required extensive environmental remediation, the site is marked by a sharp drop in grade from the street and its entry plaza to the athletic field on the east. The four buildings create a U-shaped plan, cradling the shared auditorium housed in a separate structure. Other shared facilities include a library, a cafeteria, and the playing field.

17

DHS PREVENTION ASSISTANCE AND TEMPORARY HOUSING 166

ENNEAD ARCHITECTS, 2010

151 East 151st Street, at Walton Avenue
2 4 5 to 149th Street–Grand Concourse

The Department of Homeless Services (DHS) takes a multifaceted approach toward its general mission to "overcome homelessness" in New York City: maintaining temporary shelters for individuals and families (the latter make up the majority of people housed at any one time), helping those in shelters find employment and move toward self-sufficiency, and offering prevention services aimed at reducing evictions and ensuring that people who have transitioned into permanent housing don't return to the streets. In 2003 Mayor Bloomberg announced plans for construction of this new intake center, called the PATH (Prevention Assistance and Temporary Housing) office, which addresses the two aspects of the department's goals that are specified in its acronym.

Most of the 73,000-square-foot seven-story building houses waiting areas and interview rooms for families seeking shelter, with intake and screening spaces on the lower floors and some emergency shelter on the top floor. Partner Todd Schliemann's design conceals these functions behind a uniform yet varied façade of terracotta, zinc, painted metal, and glass. This pixelated and banded composition of different materials and colors works toward establishing a certain anonymity; it's difficult to ascertain that this is a DHS facility. It goes without saying that this building is one that people don't want to be in the position of having to enter. Nevertheless, the interior aims to be welcoming for those in need, a goal furthered by Lane Twitchell's Percent for Art contribution, the *Transformation Windows* that adorn the waiting areas.

166 A terracotta flatiron building in the South Bronx.

17

167 GATEWAY CENTER AT BRONX TERMINAL MARKET
BBG-BBGM with GreenbergFarrow, 2009

560 Exterior Street, between East 150th and East 151st Streets
④ ⑧ ⑩ **to 161st Street–Yankee Stadium**

In the 2007 book, *The Suburbanization of New York*, contributors investigate the recent transformation of the city from "edgy, gritty, artistic" into "racially, ethnically, and economically separated, sanitized, and gentrified."[1] The infiltration of big-box retailers into the city—in the dense spine of Manhattan or on the fringes of the outer boroughs—is one aspect of this apparent suburbanization that is explored more than once. Three simultaneous retail developments serve as examples of this "malling" of New York City, all planned by GreenbergFarrow: Rego Park II in Queens, which features a bold red volume articulated by design architect Ehrenkrantz Eckstut & Kuhn; East River Plaza on 117th Street in Manhattan; and this million-square-foot project designed by BBG-BBGM on the site of the former Bronx Terminal Market, just south of Yankee Stadium and alongside the Major Deegan Expressway.

In 2004 Related Companies purchased the lease on the Bronx Terminal Market, where fruit and vegetable wholesalers had operated since the 1920s, and from which this Gateway Center (another was built prior to this one in southeast Brooklyn by the same developer, described in **157**) takes its name. (Not surprisingly, the retail center does not incorporate the name of the Bronx House of Detention, which it also replaces.) The project features a pair of buildings with big-box stores stacked three high, bookending a 2,600-car parking garage. Access from building to building is achieved via bridges over the streets that serve the garage and provide pedestrian access to the stores as well as Mill Pond Park, the transformation of a waterfront industrial site and part of the larger Yankee Stadium Redevelopment Project. At the southern tip of the multiblock site is "The Prow," the last remaining Bronx Terminal Market building, converted to street-level retail as part of the mall. BBG-BBGM probably won't win any design awards

for this effort, but the architects make a concerted effort to break down the scale of this massive project through the coloring and articulation of the blank walls, the incorporation of glass and remnants from the old market, and the expression of the walkways linking the three buildings. In other words, it tries to make the suburban infiltration into the city more urban.

167 A campanile-like tower punctuates the long River Avenue elevation.

BRONX COUNTY HALL OF JUSTICE

RAFAEL VIÑOLY ARCHITECTS with DMJM+Harris, 2008 **168**

265 East 161st Street, at Morris Avenue
④ ⑧ ⑩ to 161st Street–Yankee Stadium

Construction of this ten-story, 775,000-square-foot courthouse began only weeks before September 11, 2001. Heightened security concerns resulting from the terrorist attacks necessitated changes to the $421 million project's structure and glass skin, causing one delay among many—a lawsuit with the foundation contractor lost a year, contaminated subsoil conditions cost more time, and so on—that would overshadow the design's sustainability and related daylighting innovations. The latter target the courtrooms, artificially lit spaces typically buried in the middle of deep floor plates, at least in recent courthouses. Anybody who has served jury duty or seen *Law & Order* knows that these courtrooms are fed from two non-intersecting modes of circulation, the public and the judicial: the public enters the courtroom from one side, the judge and jury from the other. Here those routes are pushed to the perimeter of the relatively shallow floor plates, and then the courtrooms "borrow" sunlight over the corridor ceilings, a feature made possible by 18-foot floor-to-floor heights. Combined with artificial lighting, the resulting effect in the centralized courtrooms is a halo of sorts.

Seen from inside, the all-glass exterior by Rafael Viñoly—who previously designed the nearby Bronx Housing Court on the Grand Concourse—is more than a polemical metaphor for the transparency of the judicial process; it is the realization of a desire for daylight in spaces normally devoid of natural light, thereby reducing the need for supplemental lighting and the energy to supply it. In addition, daylighting is strongly linked with human well-being. The block-long 161st Street façade is covered in a serrated skin of frosted and clear glass, as if a billboard

made of rotating triangular panels had stopped mid-turn. The glass walls of the courtyard are flat and highly transparent, with expressed stairs overlooking the open space punctuated by the drum-shaped jury assembly room. Unfortunately, construction of the courtyard, containing the Percent for Art installation *One Stone* by Cai Guo-Qiang, has suffered from another of the delays plaguing the large project; at the time of writing, the space was still behind a construction fence and off limits to the public.

168 The L-shaped building cradles a courtyard and the cylindrical jury assembly room (top). The long 161st Street façade looking east (left).
Photos © Paul Warchol.

169 The art extends to the lobby and the occasional site-specific installation (left). Fanlike pleats greet passersby on the Grand Concourse (right). Photos by Norman McGrath.

169 THE BRONX MUSEUM OF THE ARTS
ARQUITECTONICA, 2006

1040 Grand Concourse, at East 165th Street
Ⓑ Ⓓ to 167th Street

Founded in 1971 to serve the diverse ethnic groups in the Bronx and to focus on contemporary and twentieth-century art, The Bronx Museum of the Arts has always called the Grand Concourse home. First it was housed in the rotunda of the Bronx County Courthouse at 161st Street; then a decade later it moved to its current location, into a former synagogue dating from the 1960s which the City of New York donated to the museum. This building evokes the era in which it was created, especially the cascading glass atrium in the corner. But in the museum's long-term expansion plan, developed with the Miami-based duo Bernardo Fort-Brescia and Laurinda Spear, this structure will be replaced by additional galleries, classrooms, an auditorium, a children's art center, and a residential tower (a revenue-inducer surely influenced by MoMA). For now the expansion is limited to the folded addition to the north, which includes a new entrance, galleries, administration spaces, and an outdoor sculpture court. The last is actually adjacent to the second floor, indicative of the grade changes that are typical of the Bronx.

The façade's five pleats of fritted glass and metal panels—what the architects call "architectural origami"—look up and down the Grand Concourse, two of the folds facing south and three to the north. From just the right frontal point of view, the elevation actually reads like a windowless white surface. In the long-term plan these folds continue to the corner, where they engage the undulating glass wall of the residential tower. In combination with the former synagogue, the north building looks incomplete, in need of the remainder, and of course a rebounding economy that will help make it happen.

17

BRONX CHARTER SCHOOL FOR THE ARTS **170**
WXY ARCHITECTURE + URBAN DESIGN, 2003

950 Longfellow Avenue, at Garrison Avenue
⑥ to Hunts Point Avenue

Hunts Point is a South Bronx neighborhood known for a number of industrial facilities (its best-known occupant is the huge Terminal Market), two detention centers, and a high poverty level, but recent cultural, educational, and environmental institutions point to the area's revitalization. This school is an important early piece in this process. It is the result of a transformation of a sausage factory–cum–warehouse and neighboring fur factory into a 30,000-square-foot space serving the school's philosophy that an arts education can spark academic and social

success. Claire Weisz and Mark Yoes's design for the façade of the K–6 school is composed of colorful glazed brick stripes, a flat abstract surface broken by a handful of windows and a large entry portal in the location of the old loading docks. The formerly dark interior was brightened by the addition of six skylights running perpendicular to the street, creating a learning environment far removed from the shell's industrial origins.

170 Art is expressed in the colored glazed brick striping the old industrial buildings.

CONCRETE PLANT PARK **171**
NYC DEPARTMENT OF PARKS & RECREATION, 2009

West side of Bronx River, between
Westchester Avenue and Bruckner Boulevard
⑥ to Whitlock Avenue

The transformation of obsolete and derelict industrial infrastructure into parkland is increasingly popular around the world, from Germany's Ruhr Valley to Seattle's Gas Works Park. While the High Line (**54**) is New York's most famous example of this sort of reuse, head up to the Hunts Point section of the Bronx to experience a park where industrial machinery takes center stage. The concrete plant that gives the park its name and its sculptural artifact was in operation for about forty years, until the late 1980s. The city subsequently acquired the land, setting it aside as parkland. Now the seven-acre park is part of the Bronx River Alliance's twenty-three-mile plan

17

in progress, the Bronx River Greenway. The park's simple plan includes a meandering path from Bruckner Boulevard to Westchester Avenue, salt marshes, recycled block wall bulkheads, seating, a boat launch, and of course the former concrete machinery, primed and painted in pink.

171 With such bold industrial artifacts, the park's design is secondary.

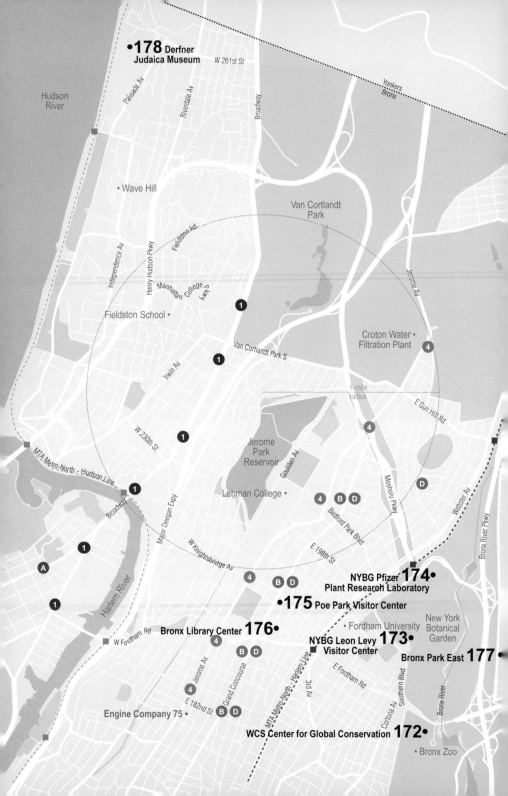

•**178** Derfner Judaica Museum

W 261st St

Palisade Av

Riverdale Av

Broadway

Yonkers
Bronx

Hudson
River

• Wave Hill

Van Cortlandt
Park

Fieldston Rd.

Independence Av

Henry Hudson Pkwy

Manhattan College Pkwy

1

Jerome Av

Fieldston School •

Croton Water •
Filtration Plant

4

Van Cortlandt Park S

1

Irwin Av

1-mile
radius

E Gun Hill Rd

W 230th St

1

Jerome
Park
Reservoir

Goulden Av

4

Mosholu Pkwy

D

MTA Metro-North - Hudson Line

Lehman College •

4 **B** **D**

Webster Av

Bronx River Pkwy

1

Broadway

Major Deegan Expy

W Knightsbridge Av

Bedford Park Blvd

E 198th St

4

B **D**

NYBG Pfizer
Plant Research Laboratory **174**•

1

A

1

Harlem River

4

B **D**

•**175** Poe Park Visitor Center

New York
Botanical
Garden

• Fordham University

Bronx Library Center **176**•

W Fordham Rd

4

NYBG Leon Levy **173**•
Visitor Center

Jerome Av

B **D**

Grand Concourse

3rd Av

E Fordham Rd

Bronx Park East **177** •

Bronx River

Engine Company 75 •

E 182nd St

B **D**

MTA Metro-North - Harlem Line

Cortona Av

Southern Blvd

WCS Center for Global Conservation **172**•

• Bronx Zoo

The Cross Bronx Expressway may effectively split

the Bronx into roughly two halves north and south, but earlier the Bronx River divided this land east and west: to the east the land slopes gently toward Long Island Sound, and to the west are found undulating hills and valleys on their way to the bluffs overlooking the Hudson River. Traversing this western section of the Bronx, one readily notes the changes in topography, negotiated via steep or winding roads but also "stair streets" that provide pedestrian-only access on thoroughfares too steep for cars. The landscape's interaction with the urban fabric also equates to a fairly loose street layout that coincides with the different neighborhoods. (Grids are localized rather than consistent across larger areas regardless of topography, as they are in Manhattan.)

The buildings in this chapter fall within the 662-acre Bronx Park, through which the Bronx River runs; the busy Fordham neighborhood to the west; and North Riverdale, in the far northwest corner of the borough on the banks of the Hudson. Bronx Park is split into two parcels by Fordham Road, which runs parallel to the Cross Bronx Expressway and connects with Pelham Parkway to the east. South of the road is the Bronx Zoo, and to the north is the New York Botanical Garden. These highly regarded institutions take advantage of the Bronx River landscape, home to the last remnant of hemlock forest that covered most of New York City's footprint. (To the north is Van Cortlandt Park, almost twice as large as Bronx Park and the site of the first municipal golf course in the United States.) To the west of Bronx Park on Fordham Road is Fordham University (the main campus is here; its law school is adjacent to Lincoln Center on the Upper West Side) and a popular shopping district closer to the Grand Concourse. At quite a remove from the park and Fordham are Fieldston and Riverdale, the neighborhoods west of Van Cortlandt Park, making up the northwest corner of the Bronx and therefore of all of New York City. In the nineteenth century, many wealthy businesspeople built mansions on large landscaped grounds here, and that character prevails to this day, with few commercial streets, a physical remove from its neighbors, lots and lots of trees, and a couple of historic districts.

18

172 WCS CENTER FOR GLOBAL CONSERVATION
FXFOWLE ARCHITECTS, 2009

2300 Southern Boulevard
❷ ❺ to Pelham Parkway; 🚌 Express Bus from Midtown

Founded in 1895 as the New York Zoological Society, the Wildlife Conservation Society (WCS) has as its mission to save wildlife and wild lands around the world. Locally it operates five zoos: the Bronx Zoo, Central Park Zoo, New York Aquarium, Prospect Park Zoo, and Queens Zoo. The first is the oldest and biggest (265 acres), and the site of the Zoological Society's new 40,000-square-foot headquarters for international operations. Following WCS's conservation ethic, FXFOWLE's design for the building respects its location in the zoo by bending in plan to preserve trees and integrating its three floors with the rocky outcroppings and natural topography of the site. As in the Administration and Visitor Center at the Queens Botanical Garden (**190**), the admirable sustainable strategies—these also include daylighting, natural ventilation, green roofs, and native landscaping—stem from the need for a headquarters aligned with the practices of the client. Previously FXFOWLE renovated and expanded the historic Lion House with relevant sustainable strategies.

The building is located on the northern edge of the zoo, in the C. V. Starr Science Campus near the Fordham Road Gate, but entry to the zoo via the Bronx River Gate is recommended. Not only is this most convenient to public transportation, but also it is immediately adjacent to the Eco Restroom. Designed by Edelman Sultan Knox Wood, these facilities feature composting toilets, a graywater garden, daylighting, and automatic faucets that are charged by the water that flows through them, among other green features. Costing close to $1,500 per square foot, it won't be replicated anytime soon, but the accompanying exhibits that explain its inner workings make it as much an educational display as a restroom.

172 The long and low building hunkers down in its setting (above). The sloping green roof creates a distinctive profile for the building (left).

200th Street and Kazimiroff
Boulevard, NYBG
Conservatory Gate Entrance
④ ⑧ ⑩ to Bedford Park
Boulevard; Metro North to
Botanical Garden

The New York Botanical Garden
(NYBG) and the Bronx Zoo
share the Bronx Park, close to
seven hundred acres split by
East Fordham Road; only the
Bronx River is able to cross this
busy thoroughfare to link these
two entities physically. Visitors
to NYBG enter to the north of
Fordham Road, off Dr. Theodore Kazimiroff Boulevard, through the perimeter
stone pylons, and under the flattened wood arches of the Leon Levy Visitor Center.
Architect Hugh Hardy envisions the different pavilions—ticketing, café, bookstore,
restrooms—as an "elegant transition from urban surroundings to the pastoral
expanse."¹ The recipe for this elegance is a low scale and a careful juxtaposition
of natural materials; the latter is found in the curved wood beams, rough stone
walls, and smooth stone walking surface. Additionally the selective use of steel—
wood beam connections, mullions, and lattice-like column covers and trellises—
integrates well with the natural surfaces. All of the materials work together to
create a particularly tactile and understandable construction, traits missing from
buildings situated in the city instead of the garden.

173 The Visitor Center's buildings sit on either side of the covered walkway's axis. Curved wood beams define the shape of the roofs. Photos by Robert Benson.

18

174 NYBG PFIZER PLANT RESEARCH LABORATORY
ENNEAD ARCHITECTS, 2006

200th Street and Kazimiroff Boulevard, Mosholu Parkway Entrance
④ ⑧ ⑩ to Bedford Park Boulevard; Metro North to Botanical Garden

The New York Botanical Garden offers visitors 250 acres of gardens, forest, walkways, greenhouses, conservatories, and other treats. Behind the scenes is NYBG's International Plant Science Center, a research institution targeted toward understanding and managing plant diversity. Its facilities are located at the northern tip of the Botanical Garden, just outside the entrance at Mosholu Parkway. These include the stately Beaux-Arts Mertz Library, the adjoining Steere Herbarium, and the Pfizer Plant Research Laboratory; the last two were designed by partner Susan Rodriguez of Ennead Architects (formerly Polshek Partnership). The Herbarium, completed in 2002, stores over 7 million preserved plant specimens from all over the world. Needless to say, the exterior walls supporting the massive vault are primarily solid, layered with a framework for plants to crawl up the façade.

Four years later the Pfizer Laboratory opened on a site just across from the Herbarium and perched above the Botanical Garden's Twin Lakes. The 28,000-square-foot building provides research laboratories, educational facilities, offices, meeting rooms, and conference facilities on two floors. The long, low building reiterates the light earth tones and some of the details of the Herbarium; but the fact that the building houses scientists as well as science calls for windows, which are found behind the projecting cast-stone wall. In combination with the Herbarium and the Science Center's other facilities, the laboratory building aims to yield great discoveries that will benefit not only its namesake corporation but also the landscapes where the plants these facilities focus on flourish.

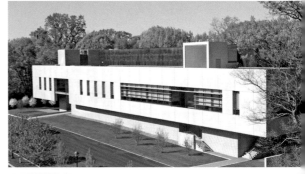

174 The south façade of the Pfizer Plant Research Laboratory **(right).** Photo by Meg Mingione. **The west façade of the Steere Herbarium (below).** Photo by Robert Benson.

Edgar Allen Poe Park, Grand Concourse at East Kingsbridge Road
B **D** to Kingsbridge Road

It's not uncommon for an old house with important architectural or historical character to be moved from its original location to a context free of encroaching development, with room to breathe. Recently Alexander Hamilton's house was lifted from Convent Avenue to Saint Nicholas Park, and about a hundred years ago, facing the threat of demolition, Edgar Allan Poe's nineteenth-century cottage was moved less than five hundred feet to a park that now bears his name. This setting enables the house to be seen as a historical object, an approximation of the rural conditions Poe encountered when he moved to the village of Fordham in the 1840s aiming to cure his wife's tuberculosis. Run by the Bronx County Historical Society, the cottage is tucked into the north end of the park, with a bandstand on the south and a playground occupying the center; the 2,400-square-foot Visitor Center is sited next to the playground.

Toshiko Mori's design was inspired by Poe's stories and poems, most notably "The Raven," as we can see in the flattened V shape of the roof ("a form suspended between ascent and descent," according to Mori) and the featherlike dark gray slate shingles covering the walls ("an element of the uncanny").[1] The bar-shaped building bends in plan to point toward the two buildings at either end of the park. A large window frames a view from the exhibition and assembly space to the cottage, elevating it in importance over the bandstand. Contemporary with the construction of the Visitor Center is the restoration of Poe Cottage, ongoing at the time of writing.

175 Ascent, descent, and the uncanny on the Grand Concourse.

176 BRONX LIBRARY CENTER
DATTNER ARCHITECTS, 2005

**310 East Kingsbridge Road,
at Briggs Avenue
Ⓑ Ⓓ to Fordham Road**

Of the five boroughs, three are served by the New York Public Library: Manhattan, the Bronx, and Staten Island; both Brooklyn and Queens have their own library systems. In this regard the Bronx Library Center is actually a branch, though its 75,000 square feet, 300,000 volumes, and Fordham location make it the borough's main library. Its presence on Kingsbridge and visibility from East Fordham Road reiterate this importance, as does the swooping roof floating above a four-story curtain wall.

Inside, the floor plan is compact, with open spaces on each of the four above-grade floors taking advantage of the generous east-facing glazing. The west side is given over to the communicating stair wrapping around the elevators; the stairway's channel glass walls offer diffuse natural light and an invitation to walk rather than ride between floors. Most impressive is the top floor below the curving roof, a light-filled space—like most of the library—with wood ceilings. A reading terrace on the third floor is a rarity for this type of building, particularly in a branch library.

The library's Percent for Art installation, Iñigo Manglano-Ovalle's *Portrait of a Young Reader*, can be glimpsed from the entry vestibule, through a small window that seems to exist just to give a view of it. Colored disks are fused into the dark walls of the stair leading from the lobby to the concourse level, representing the DNA sequence of an anonymous patron. While this feature appears at odds with the library's orthodox modern spaces, it is quite memorable and successful at celebrating movement to the library's below-grade spaces.

176 A strong presence seen from Fordham Road (left). Photo © Jeff Goldberg/Esto. **Inigo Manglano-Ovalle's** Percent for Art contribution (above). Photo © Francis Dzikowski/Esto.

BRONX PARK EAST **177**
JONATHAN KIRSCHENFELD ARCHITECT, 2010

2330 Bronx Park East, at Waring Avenue
② **⑤** to Pelham Parkway

177 The building layers separate volumes onto an irregular site.

Jonathan Kirschenfeld's Web page groups a handful of SRO (single-room occupancy) residences in the Bronx and Brooklyn under the label "Projects on Irregular Sites." In these, the architect of the Marcy Avenue Residence (**142**) has discovered the hidden potential in urban "remnants" deemed too difficult for conventional housing solutions. Uniquely, he proactively scouts the sites, develops feasibility studies, and then approaches nonprofit developers, with the hope of ending up with a project. Holding the street wall on this tapering trapezoidal lot is a five-story volume containing a gym, a laundry room, offices, and a community room, all overlooking Bronx Park and the New York Botanical Garden. Immediately behind is a courtyard, and beyond it a seven-story volume containing the sixty-nine studio residences; the latter building is visible through and above the notch in the upper floor of the first building's street façade. Side-yard setbacks give the project an object-like presence, even as it joins in the urban assemblage with its neighbors.

DERFNER JUDAICA MUSEUM **178**
LOUISE BRAVERMAN ARCHITECT, 2009

5901 Palisades Avenue
❶ to 231st Street and **Bx7** Bus; Metro North to Riverdale

Riverdale, in the northwest corner of the Bronx, is a park-like setting with lots of trees, winding roads, and detached houses. Two cultural institutions call Riverdale home: WaveHill, a public garden and cultural center, and the Derfner Judaica Museum, part of the nineteen-acre Hebrew Home at Riverdale. The museum was founded in 1982, when neighborhood residents Ralph and Leuba Baum donated about eight hundred objects from their Judaica collection to the Hebrew Home.

178 A circular wall of channel glass defines the gallery's center. Photo © Michael Moran.

Its 5,000-square-foot exhibition space can be found on the ground floor of the Jacob Reingold Pavilion, adjacent to an activity-filled winter garden (residents were being entertained by a piano performance on my visit). Louise Braverman's design animates the space with translucent channel glass walls—straight and curved—that incorporate display cases housing Jewish ceremonial art while also framing views toward the Hudson River. A walk outside to the sculpture garden and its expansive views up and down the river is highly recommended.

18

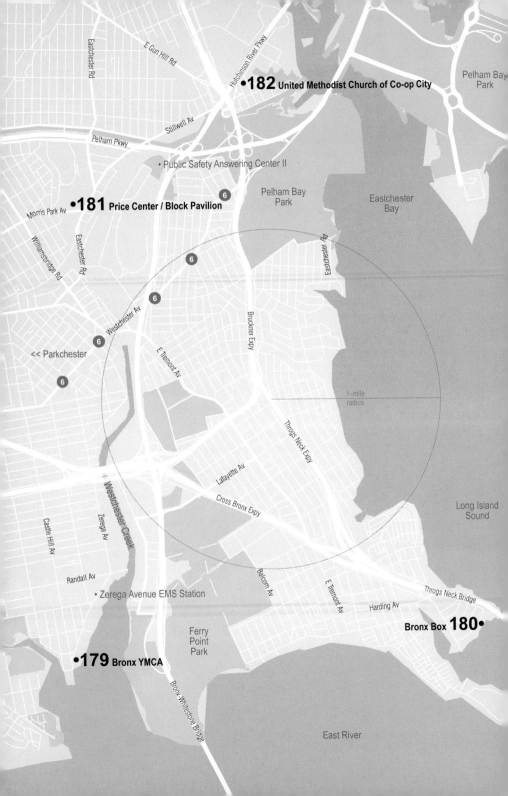

CASTLE HILL, THROGS NECK, MORRIS PARK, BAYCHESTER

As noted in the introduction to the last chapter, the land east of the Bronx River slopes downhill toward Long Island Sound, in contrast to the hills and valleys that make up the areas west of the river. As in the rest of the Bronx, expressways and parkways further define the square miles, including Pelham Parkway, Bruckner Expressway, Cross Bronx Expressway, and Hutchinson River Parkway; the last two carry drivers into Queens across the Throgs Neck and Bronx-Whitestone Bridges, respectively. Although this combination of topography and high-speed roadways may make the eastern section of the Bronx little more than something to glance at through the windshield of a moving car, the area nevertheless contains some buildings worth highlighting, in places as far removed from Lower Manhattan as any in this book.

This large area is the land of "chesters," with Eastchester, Baychester, and Parkchester marching southward from the border with Westchester County. Parkchester is home to a fifty-one-building housing development that, like the well-known Stuyvesant Town–Peter Cooper Village complex on Manhattan's East Side, was undertaken by Metropolitan Life Insurance Company, in this case just before World War II. Not to be outdone, in Baychester the massive Co-op City was constructed on the ashes of Freedomland, an amusement park built in 1960 by C. V. Wood on over two hundred acres in the V created by the New England Thruway and Hutchinson River Parkway. It was envisioned as the city's answer to Disneyland, but it closed only four years later, the same year as the World's Fair in Flushing, Queens.

Some of the buildings in this chapter can be found in the neighborhoods of Castle Hill, an area of single-family houses, apartment buildings, and public housing that tapers to a peninsula between Westchester Creek and Pugsley Creek; Morris Park, where a racetrack was the site of the Belmont Stakes until 1905, now an Italian American community; and Throgs Neck, a remote peninsula at the base of the bridge of the same name (derived from the name of a seventeenth-century English settler, John Throckmorton) and home to the nineteenth-century Fort Schuyler.

19

179 BRONX YMCA
DONALD BLAIR & PARTNERS ARCHITECTS, 2003

2 Castle Hill Avenue, at Zerega Avenue
⑥ to Pelham Bay Park and 🚌 Bus

In the first decade of the twenty-first century the YMCA of Greater New York undertook a $150 million capital redevelopment program targeting each of its nineteen branches, including expansion or renovation of sixteen of the facilities and three new construction projects. One of the latter is the Howard and Minerva Munch Day Camp and Family Center (the full name for the Bronx YMCA) in the Castle Hill neighborhood. It is designed by Donald Blair, who is also responsible for the renovation and expansion of the Bedford-Stuyvesant branch in Brooklyn. Located just north of Castle Hill Park on a peninsula in the East River, the Bronx YMCA project consists of a new 21,000-square-foot building, renovation of the original building, and the reconfiguration of the surrounding waterfront site.

Blair's design contrasts with the original, a traditional-looking gable-roofed building to the south. The new building takes on an industrial appearance through its choice of materials in a grayscale palette: corrugated aluminum siding, concrete blocks, insulated translucent panels, and exposed structural steel. The last, on the building's north end, includes cross-bracing as well as columns and beams. It is the articulation of the different volumes that keeps the YMCA rooted in an industrial aesthetic and not actually looking like an industrial building. From the short entrance tucked into the corner of a two-story volume to the stair tower and pool beyond, the formal manipulation of these spaces melds into an inexpensive yet considered composition.

19

179 An interlocking of different volumes in metal and glass (above). The stair tower and pool with exposed cross-bracing (right).

3272 Tierney Place, between Chaffee and Longstreet Avenues

🚌9 Express Bus from Midtown;

⑥ to Westchester Square–East Tremont Avenue and 🚌22 Bus

180 The prefab construction lends the house a unique presence on its block (above). Lifting the second-floor module into place (below). Photos courtesy Resolution: 4.

Prefabricated houses certainly aren't a new phenomenon. MoMA's 2008 "Home Delivery" exhibition surveying prefab homes traced the method all the way back to 1833 and the Manning Cottage in Australia (or the balloon frame around the same time in Chicago, depending on how one defines prefab). In the subsequent 175-plus years, construction methods and styles have changed, but the basic idea is the same: the off-site assembly of components for the production of single-family houses. Today's crop of prefab houses share more than this methodology: they promote an affordable option for living with modern architecture; they embrace sustainability by reducing construction waste; and they offer a flexibility in aspects such as layout and finishes that has given rise to the new label "mass customization."

New York's Resolution: 4 has been a prolific designer of modern prefab, ever since the firm won *Dwell's* 2003 Home Design Invitational, in which the magazine championing the technique asked for designs that would clock in at under $200,000. Joseph Tanney and Robert Luntz's winning design called for stacking prefab modules on site after assembly in a factory; various configurations were possible, depending on the site and other conditions. The same "modern modular" technique applies to this 1,800-square-foot single-family house near the Throgs Neck Bridge, but the urban infill site necessitated a simple double-decker stacking, rather than the L-shaped, courtyard, or other options suited to suburban or rural sites. A small penthouse, a side "saddlebag," and front and rear stairs are the only additions to the two modular units built over the 900-square-foot footprint of the old house. Façades in cement board and ipe wood lend the house a distinctive presence in the secluded neighborhood, signaling the arrival of modern prefab in the big city.

19

181 Looking across Morris Park Avenue from the south campus (above). Photo by Rachellynn Schoen. Looking northwest at the blend of punched openings and curtain wall (right). Photo by Robert Benson.

181 PRICE CENTER/BLOCK PAVILION
PAYETTE, 2008

1301 Morris Park Avenue, at Eastchester Road
🚌 Express Bus from Midtown; ⑤ to East 180th Street and 🚌 Bus

The Albert Einstein College of Medicine of Yeshiva University is an institution focused on medical education and biomedical research, the latter of which is shaping its growth in the Morris Park neighborhood. Its 2008 addition to the forty-acre Jack and Pearl Resnick campus is officially called the Michael F. Price Center for Genetic and Translational Medicine/Harold and Muriel Block Research Pavilion, and the college boasts it is the largest research facility to be built in the Bronx since the medical school opened its first building in 1955. The 223,000-square-foot five-story building with a $220 million price tag is the first phase of a major expansion for the school. It acts as a gateway to the campus north of Morris Park Avenue, something Boston-based Payette was cognizant of in its design of the building.

The mix of wet labs, dry labs, and common spaces for research facilities focused on genetic medicine yielded an L-shaped plan. The wet labs are housed in the two wings, articulated with punched openings; the dry labs occupy the glass prow banded with stripes of green and blue; the common spaces sit behind a recessed clear glass curtain wall on an axis with the entrance to the south campus. These common areas are envisioned as sites for collaboration, something most institutions of graduate education aim to achieve with their new buildings, be it law (**14**), liberal arts (**122**), or other areas of research (**110**). Here that collaboration is aided by sculptural stairs visible above the entrance. Recalling DNA strands, they promote walking from floor to floor instead of riding the elevator, while from the outside they subtly announce the nature of the research taking place behind the glass walls.

19

UNITED METHODIST CHURCH OF CO-OP CITY
GLUCKMAN MAYNER ARCHITECTS, 2005
182

2350 Palmer Avenue, at Hutchinson River Parkway
🚌7 Express Bus from Midtown

Most visitors to New York City may see Co-op City only from the air, as their plane loops over Long Island Sound and buzzes the Bronx on descent into LaGuardia. Certainly the late 1960s housing development isn't a typical tourist attraction, but it is impressive in terms of sheer numbers: thirty-five towers of thirty-five stories each; 236 town houses; 15,500 residential units; 55,000 residents; eight parking garages; three shopping centers; six schools; all on 320 acres, with 80 percent of the land devoted to open space in one form or another. Co-op City is the single largest housing development not just in the city but purportedly in all of the United States. It also is home to a fairly diverse population, by age, ethnicity, and religion.

This diversity is evident in the United Methodist Church of Co-op City, "a multi-ethnic, multi-cultural, bilingual congregation"[1] formed in 1974. The church is located south of the Bay Plaza Shopping Center, which splits Co-op City into two sections, on a corner overlooking a small patch of green and Interstate 95. The elevated building includes a sanctuary, a children's chapel, a meeting and/or classroom space, a kitchen, and offices, all in a compact 9,400-square foot L-shaped plan. Parking spaces are tucked beneath the building, in response to the location's floodplain. The fairly utilitarian-looking building is enlivened by abundant glazing and a three-dimensional cross anchored to a triangular steel cage, a low-budget church steeple.

182 The Co-op City towers provide a backdrop to the church building (above). The building's walls touch the earth only where the stair is located (right). Photos by Lydia Gould Bessler.

FURNISHING THE PUBLIC REALM

Architecture's contribution to the public realm is not limited to the building façades that line the streets and the landscapes that shape the parks. It also consists of what's referred to as street furniture, the small-scale pieces of urban design that we interact with as we move through the city. These range from the benches we sit on and the lampposts that light our way to the kiosks where we buy our morning paper. The transformation of Broadway as it cuts through Times Square into a pedestrian mall illustrates the importance of street furniture: the temporary chairs and tables were criticized, but they were only a step toward the eventual elements designed especially for the space. Throughout the city, many of the furnishings are dated or express little beyond function, but this recent crop of street furniture illustrates the diversity of purposes the objects serve as well as the potential of design to influence our experience of the public realm.

NYSE/FINANCIAL DISTRICT STREETSCAPES
ROGERS MARVEL ARCHITECTS, 2004
Wall Street, between Broadway and William Street (Map 1)

One immediate effect of the September 11 attacks was the closing of Wall Street and other rights of way near the Stock Exchange to automobiles. The ubiquitous Jersey barriers—normally used along highways and other high-speed thoroughfares—steel fencing, and other temporary measures gave way to these gem-like bollards in bronze, the first phase of ongoing security streetscapes in the Financial District by Rob Rogers and Jonathan Marvel. The porous barrier on Wall Street just west of William Street also features lighted barriers atop a paved turntable that swivels to allow occasional access to cars or trucks.

UNION PARK NORTH END EXPANSION
ARCHITECTURE RESEARCH OFFICE (ARO), 2010
Union Square Park at 17th Street (Map 7)

Restrooms in public spaces have a strong stigma associated with them, stemming from concerns of safety and cleanliness, and their use as makeshift sleeping quarters by homeless individuals. But alternatives to Starbucks are increasing as the city's Bugaboo population continues to grow. These facilities at the northeast corner of Union Square Park directly serve the new playground to the south and the plaza that hosts the popular farmer's market three times a week. ARO's design for the restrooms provides a foil to the neighboring historic pavilion. It extends the ashlar wall as a base to walls of stainless steel fencing; behind is an eco-resin backing that glows in the evening. Photo by Chang Kim Kyun.

CEMUSA NEW YORK STREET FURNITURE
GRIMSHAW, 2006

In 2005 the Spanish street furniture company Cemusa was awarded the contract for the city's Coordinated Street Furniture franchise, including bus shelters, newsstands, automated toilets, and sheltered bike parking. The company provides and maintains the furnishings at no cost the city, in exchange for advertising rights, a now familiar strategy subtly transforming cityscapes around the world. In Nicholas Grimshaw's design the various pieces are tied together aesthetically by a sleek and simple enclosure and a floating glass canopy. The bus shelters are the most ubiquitous pieces, with a target of replacing all of the city's old shelters and adding hundreds more, 3,300 in total. Photo by Cemusa.

MTA FLOOD MITIGATION
ROGERS MARVEL ARCHITECTS, with di Domenico + Partners, 2009
Steinway Street (Map 20), Hillside Avenue (Map 21)

Ever waited for a train on a rainy day, only to encounter a wall of water drenching the edge of the subway platform from above? If that wait happened recently at a station on Hillside Avenue in Jamaica or Steinway Street in Astoria (pictured)—among other locations in Queens—then the answer is assuredly no. These undulating boxes of stainless steel in effect raise the grates at sidewalk level at least six inches, keeping floodwaters from infiltrating. Some incorporate benches. The wavelike tops express the unique function they serve while performing as sculptural additions to their streetscapes.

CITYRACKS BY BETTLELAB
BIKE RACKS BY DAVID BYRNE, 2008

The New York City Department of Transportation held the CityRacks design competition in 2008 for a new standard bike rack in place of those bulky—and in many cases rusty—horseshoe-shaped racks that litter the city. Not surprisingly, winners Ian Mahaffy and Maarten De Greeve (Bettlelab) hail from Copenhagen, which is arguably the Western capital of commuter and recreational biking. Their design is a slender circle with a horizontal brace that tangentially, and almost magically, sits atop the sidewalk. In addition, musician, CityRacks juror, and avid bicyclist (he penned the 2009 *Bicycle Diaries*) David Byrne contributed nine original designs that respond to their locations in Brooklyn and Manhattan, such as this provocative shape on 44th Street just west of Seventh Avenue (Map 9). The playful silhouettes should stand out against the rest of the city's racks, old and new.
City Racks by Bettlelab (left). Byrne's "Olde Times Square" (right). Photo by Michael Surtees.

QUEENS

LONG ISLAND CITY, ASTORIA   **20**

FLUSHING, BAYSIDE, JAMAICA, OZONE PARK   **21**

The greenest building in Queens **(190)**
is also the greenest building in New York City.
Photo © Jeff Goldberg/Esto.

Astoria Park •

N **Q**

Socrates Sculpture Park •

• The Noguchi Museum

N **Q**

Broadway Av

• Westview/Eastview

N **Q**

Roosevelt
Island

F

M **R**

MTA Flood Mitigation •

N **Q** **185•** **•186** Museum of
Frank Sinatra School of the Arts High School the Moving Image

Ironworkers Local 40 & 361 •

1-mile
radius **Ironworkers Local 580** **184•**

East
River

F

N **Q**

M **R**

• La Escuela New York Presbyterian Church •

7 **N** **Q**

• FDR Four Freedoms Park • Queens Plaza

E **M** **R**

LIRR to Woodside Sunnyside Gardens

E **M** • CitiGroup Skillman Av

7 **G**

• Sculpture Center

46th Av **•183** MoMA PS1

• Gantry Plaza State Park **G** Thomson Av **Young Architects Program**

Van Dam St Queens Blvd

• Queens West

7 Jackson Av

39th St

Murano • **7** Greenpoint Av

• Hunters Point South 49th Av

Long Island Expy

Queens
Brooklyn

LIRR to Jamaica

G

Along with Brooklyn, Queens is one of two New York City

boroughs on Long Island. This fact is apparent in the name of the area with the closest proximity to Manhattan: Long Island City. Its location across the East River from Midtown and the Upper East Side, coupled with the decline in the industry that once thrived along most of the city's waterfronts (evident in the 120-foot-long neon Pepsi sign overlooking Manhattan), has led to developments on the waterfront and near the Queensboro Bridge. Largest in scale are the numerous towers of Queens West and its park along the East River, complete with repurposed gantry cranes announcing the neighborhood's name to the skyscrapers in Midtown. More housing and riverfront parks are planned for the peninsula south of Queens West, on the land above Newtown Creek that was the proposed site for the Olympic Village in the city's bid for the 2012 games. Farther north the new developments turn commercial, clustered around the Queensboro Bridge and nearby Citigroup Building, the tallest building on Long Island.

Long Island City is also home to a number of well-regarded art institutions—MoMA PS1, Sculpture Center, Isamu Noguchi Museum, and Socrates Sculpture Park, the last two of which are found north of the bridge. This area is a mix of low-scale residential, public housing, and light-industrial uses; hotels started to pop up around the last, taking advantage of zoning allowance for transient hotels in manufacturing districts, spurring the Department of City Planning to rezone areas just north of the bridge to prevent further "pencil buildings."

North of Broadway and east of the elevated train that runs up and down 31st Street (in Queens, streets run north-south and avenues east-west, rotated 90-degrees from Manhattan, and to add to the confusion, avenues *decrease* in number as one moves north, and streets increase to the east) is Astoria, home to the largest Greek population outside the Mediterranean, as well as a growing number of Muslims. To the south of Astoria, across Northern Boulevard and the expansive rail yards, is Sunnyside, worth a mention here for Sunnyside Gardens, a seventy-seven-acre planned community from the 1920s that was home to Lewis Mumford, and to its north the New York Presbyterian Church, a striking renovation of the old Knickerbocker Laundry factory by Doug Garofalo, Greg Lynn, and Michael McInturf.

20

183 MOMA PS1 YOUNG ARCHITECTS PROGRAM
VARIOUS ARCHITECTS ANNUALLY

22–25 Jackson Avenue, at 46th Avenue
7 to 45th Road–Court House Square;
G to 21st Street; **E** **M** to 23rd Street–Ely Avenue

In 1971 Alanna Heiss founded the Institute for Art and Urban Resources, an organization focused on exhibitions in the city's abandoned and underutilized spaces. Five years later, as PS1, it moved into its namesake, a former public school in Long Island City, a location befitting its unique mission. In 1997 architect Frederick Fisher renovated the building and, more significantly, added concrete walls to frame courtyard spaces for site-specific installations. This front door to the institution (affiliated with MoMA since 2000) is the site of a yearly competition inviting young architects to envision an urban refuge for cooling off in the steamy New York summer; it also acts as a backdrop for the museum's "Warm Up" concerts. The four most recent winners at the time of writing are presented here, but other recipients include SHoP Architects (2000), Roy Design (2001), and nARCHITECTS (2004), each of which went on to design buildings featured in this guidebook.

Los Angeles–based designers Benjamin Ball and Gaston Nogues, a duo who almost exclusively produce site-specific installations, assembled tinted Mylar petals in tent-like forms to create *Liquid Sky* (2007). Sunlight filtered through the pinks, purples, and oranges cast kaleidoscopic patterns on the ground and on the revelers relaxing in hammocks stretched below the installation.

The following year New York architects Amale Andraos and Dan Wood of WORKac used the competition as a way to explore urban farming in *PF1* (Public Farm 1). An inclined plane of cardboard tubes (thick ones typically used as formwork for concrete columns) held aloft lightweight soil and a variety of edible plants and herbs. A wading pool was placed where the tubes touched the ground, complete with a periscope giving the curious a close-up view of a locavore's delight.

In 2009 Michael Meredith and Hilary Sample of MOS draped an inexpensive lightweight structure with a geo-textile skin that drew allusions to a woolly mammoth or Snuffleupagus. *Afterparty*'s cluster of chimneys poked above the courtyard's concrete walls, but they served to cool the spaces underneath, not just call attention to themselves. And cool they did; the dark spaces and subtle breezes combined to create one of the most successful installations in this regard.

One year later the means of cooling moved from "relax in the shade" to "play in the sun," in *Pole Dance* by Florian Idenburg and Jing Liu of SO – IL. The highly interactive design broke up the courtyard spaces with a grid of 30-foot-tall poles draping an elevated field of netting that held large inflatable balls. Bungee cords and holes in the netting, combined with the swaying poles, created opportunities for games that made one forget about the heat.

20

183 *Liquid Sky* by Ball-Nogues, 2007 (top, left). Photo courtesy Ball-Nogues Studio. *PF1* by WORKac, 2008 (top, right). Photo by Elizabeth Felicella. *Afterparty* by MOS, 2009 (right). *Pole Dance* by Solid Objectives–Idenburg Liu, 2010 (above).

20

184 IRONWORKERS LOCAL 580
DANIEL GOLDNER ARCHITECTS, 2004

37–31 30th Street, between 37th and 38th Avenues
Ⓝ Ⓠ to 39th Av

New York City has two local unions for ironworkers: Local 40 for structural steel and Local 580 for ornamental steel, which includes curtain walls, storefronts, stairs, and the like. Architect Daniel Goldner has designed training facilities for both Local 40 and Local 580, situated just over a half mile from each other. The 33,000-square-foot building for the first is located on 36th Street in Astoria, across the street from the Frank Sinatra School of the Arts (**185**); the latter is housed in an 18,000-square-foot conversion of a warehouse and auto body shop in the Dutch Kills section of Long Island City. Ironworkers Local 580 is discussed here because it strongly illustrates how architecture can act as the expression of the client's occupation.

Fourteen different metals are used throughout the project, many on the façade, making the project also a learning tool for apprentices during construction. The sidewalk level features panels of bead-blasted stainless steel and oxidized blackened steel, as well as a canopy of gloss black steel. Narrow openings with the occasional colored glass insert interrupt the panels, culminating in a large window under the canopy that provides a glimpse of the lobby stairway, which uses no fewer then ten of the fourteen metals. Running most of the length of the building above the ground-floor panels is a stainless steel mesh that allows the old brick façade to be recognized, but just barely. The articulation of the mesh gives the impression that it could be raised like blinds to reveal the masonry it veils.

184 A low wall screens the parking and shop building beyond (left). The different metals comes together at the entrance (below). Photos by David Joseph.

185 The whitish appearance of the curtain wall is created by names of artists etched into the glass.
Photo © Jeff Goldberg/Esto.

FRANK SINATRA SCHOOL OF THE ARTS HIGH SCHOOL **185**
ENNEAD ARCHITECTS, 2009

35–12 35th Avenue, at 36th Street
N Q to 36th Avenue; M R to 36th Street

In 2001 Tony Bennett and his wife, Susan Benedetto (the singer's non-stage name), founded the Frank Sinatra School of the Arts, named for Ol' Blue Eyes three years after his death. The school followed on the heels of the duo's founding of Exploring the Arts, a nonprofit organization aimed at returning "arts-enriched programming" to public schools. Like the Bronx Charter School for the Arts (**170**), the high school stresses academic excellence built around a core arts curriculum. It offers six majors: fine art, dance, drama, film, instrumental music, and vocal music. In 2009 the seven hundred–student school moved into its permanent home in what can be considered Astoria's arts and entertainment district; it sits across the street from the Kaufman Astoria Studios (where *Sesame Street* is produced) and cater-corner to the Museum of the Moving Image (**186**).

The focus of attention of this five-story, 150,000-square-foot building, designed by partner Susan Rodriguez, is the north-facing 35th Avenue façade. Here the school's main entrance can be found, recessed below a three-story transparent curtain wall with integral signage projecting toward the intersection. The school displays itself along this frontage, be it in the artwork on the glass walls, the dancing bodies behind the same, or, visible from the sidewalk, the bright yellow wall that highlights the Tony Bennett Concert Hall in the center of the building. While it remains out of sight and reach, it should be noted that this yellow wall culminates in a rooftop courtyard for performances and other uses. The elevations on the north-south streets and rear alley are fairly utilitarian, with ribbon windows, gray brick, buff terracotta, translucent insulated panels, and corrugated metal siding.

20

186 MUSEUM OF THE MOVING IMAGE
LEESER ARCHITECTURE, 2011

35th Avenue at 37th Street
N Q to 36th Avenue; M R to 36th Street

In 1988 the Museum of the Moving Image—formerly the Astoria Motion Picture and Television Center Foundation—opened its doors in a three-story landmarked loft building in Astoria, in an old film production studio renovated by Charles Gwathmey. The museum broadly encompasses the different media of the moving image: Its offerings include a collection of historical artifacts, permanent and temporary exhibitions, and screenings, frequently accompanied by discussions or other related programming. Over time the museum's popularity, particularly with school groups, necessitated an expansion that would double its size to about 100,000 square feet.

Thomas Leeser's design accomplishes this enlargement by appending a volume to the rear of the building and reconfiguring portions of the interior. From its main entrance on 35th Avenue, one would be hard-pressed to realize that such an undertaking had occurred; only minimal changes to the storefront windows and a small canopy diverge from the landmarked exterior. But inside, the presence of the new is dramatically apparent: walls canted 83 degrees and a 50-foot-long video installation lead to the lobby. On one side of this space a sloped ceiling and floor hint at the new 264-seat theater lined in Yves Klein blue panel, entered through a portal lined with the same color; opposite a stairway leads to a video screening amphitheater and upward to the exhibition spaces. Surprisingly, one can visit the museum without even noticing its most striking element, the light blue addition clad in over one thousand pieces of triangular aluminum panels. It is worth walking through the lobby to the new courtyard to take in this skin, which sometimes disappears into the sky.

186 The video screening ampitheater and stair to the top floor exhibition spaces (opposite). The ramp and portal to the theater (top, left). The rear addition extending from the old building (top, right). Inside the dramatic theater punctuated by a Cindy Sirko-designed curtain (above).

20

East River

Throgs Neck Bridge

Whitestone Bridge

• Fort Totten Park

Cross Island Expy

Little Neck Bay

Utopia Pkwy

New York Times Printing Plant •

• LaGuardia Airport
New York Police Academy •

28th Av

College Point Blvd

Ulmer St

Union St

Parsons Blvd

Willets Point Blvd

154th St

Bayside Av

•192 Bayside Residence

Flushing Bay

• Latimer Gardens Community Center

Northern Blvd

7

Sanford Av

•191 Tenrikyo Mission New York Center

Northern Blvd

• Citi Field

Roosevelt Av

• Queens Library Flushing Branch

Kupferberg Holocaust Research Center and Archives **193** •

Northern Blvd

• Louis Armstrong House Museum

189•

Francis Lewis Blvd

Clearview Expy

56th Av

Flushing Meadows Corona Park Pool & Rink

•187

•190 QBG Administration & Visitor Center

Bell Blvd

Queens Museum of Art Expansion

New York Hall of Science

Kissena Park

•188 Queens Theatre in the Park

Booth Memorial Av

Grand Central Pkwy

Van Wyck Expy

Main St

Kissena Blvd

1-mile radius

164th St

Long Island Expy

Junction Blvd

Long Island Expy

• Rego Park II

98th St

108th St

Jewel Av

Harry Van Arsdale Jr Av

Parsons Blvd

73rd Av

Union Tpke

Cunningham Park

LIRR from Woodside

• Kew Gardens Hill Library

Grand Central Pkwy

Yellowstone Blvd

E **F** **M** **R**

• Queens Hospital EMS

F Hillside Av

Jamaica Av

Metropolitan Av

LIRR from Long Island City

MTA Flood Mitigation •

LIRR Hempstead Branch

•194 Children's Library Discovery Center

Jackie Robinson Pkwy

Myrtle Av

Jamaica Av

119th St

E **J** **Z**

Forest Park

•195 LIRR Jamaica Station

Farmers Blvd

Sutphin Blvd

Guy Brewer Rd

Merrick Blvd

Queens Brooklyn

Atlantic Av

•196 High School for Construction Trades, Engineering and Architecture

104th St

LIRR from Atlantic Terminal

A

Lefferts Blvd

Linden Blvd

AirTrain to JFK

LIRR Far Rockaway Branch

LIRR West Hempstead Branch

Liberty Av

Rockaway Blvd

Although Queens is New York City's largest

borough in terms of area (110 square miles), it is distinguished more by the large number of nationalities and ethnicities that call it home. With nearly half of the borough's population foreign-born, Queens is considered the most heterogeneous place in the world; the 7 train that runs west from Flushing is even referred to as the "international express." The borough is also home to two of three international airports that serve New York City: LaGuardia and JFK. On a map, the Grand Central Parkway and Van Wyck Expressway running from airport to airport basically draw a vertical line down the middle of Queens.

This chapter features projects in neighborhoods mostly east of this divide: Flushing, a large area south of Flushing Bay that extends east from Flushing Meadows Corona Park (site of two World's Fairs and now of the New York Mets' stadium and the U.S. Open tennis tournament) to encompass the largest Chinatown in New York City; Bayside, a former waterfront community (cut off from access to Little Neck Bay by none other than Robert Moses and his Cross Island Parkway) with a white, Asian, Hispanic, and Indian population, and one of CUNY's six community colleges; Jamaica, the county seat, dating back to 1683, home to the borough's largest African American community and the central location of the nation's highest-circulating library system; and one neighborhood west of the Van Wyck, Ozone Park, a residential area near Jamaica Bay with African American residents, immigrants from Latin America, the Philippines, India, and the Caribbean, and the only racetrack in Queens. In this fairly expansive portion of Queens (the map comprises about twenty neighborhoods), the fabric varies from dense urban development in downtown Flushing and Jamaica to Bayside's suburbia.

21

187 NEW YORK HALL OF SCIENCE
ENNEAD ARCHITECTS, 2004

47-01 111th Street, at 49th Avenue
⑦ to 111th Street

Atop the "valley of ashes" memorialized in F. Scott Fitzgerald's *The Great Gatsby*, two World's Fairs rose: "The World of Tomorrow" (1939) and "Peace Through Understanding" (1964–65). While the only substantial remnant of the first is the Queens Museum of Art (formerly the New York City Building and temporarily the United Nations General Assembly), a number of structures from the latter fair still survive: the Unisphere, the New York State Pavilion, the Port Authority Building, the Hall of Science, and of course the grounds themselves, now Flushing Meadows Corona Park. On the west side of Grand Central Parkway, which cuts the park in two, sits the New York Hall of Science. Its original 80-foot-tall undulating walls of concrete and cobalt blue glass were designed by Wallace Harrison, best known for the UN's permanent home on the banks of the East River in Manhattan.

Since 1964 the museum has been renovated and reconfigured numerous times, including a new entrance, auditorium, and dining area in the late 1990s by Beyer Blinder Belle, but the largest additions are the North Wing's exhibition space and the adjacent office and gallery volume, designed by Ennead Architects' (formerly Polshek Partnership) partner Todd Schliemann. The North Wing juts out horizontally from the extruded walls of Harrison's design, a counterpoint to the translucent walls and roof that appear to float above the first floor. At the tip of the wing is James Carpenter's *Inclined Light Wall*, his Percent for Art installation, which channels daylight into ever-changing compositions of colors and patterns on an adjacent wall. One subsequent addition to the museum is also its hardest to find: nestled among the trees south of its building is a preschool park designed by BKSK Architects. It adds 30,000 square feet to the Science Playground and provides another reason to visit this part of Queens.

187 The dynamic bar juts from the Harrison's undulating walls in the background (left). South of the museum is the Science Playground (right). Photo © Jeff Goldberg/Esto.

QUEENS THEATRE IN THE PARK **188**
CAPLES JEFFERSON ARCHITECTS, 2008

Flushing Meadows Corona Park, just east of
Grand Central Parkway
7 to Mets–Willets Point

Of the structures from the 1964–65 World's Fair still standing in Flushing Meadows Corona Park, the New York State Pavilion designed by Philip Johnson and Richard Foster Architects is the most striking, owing no doubt to its now ruined state. The pavilion actually comprises three separate structures: a plaza ringed by sixteen columns and once covered in a colorful canopy, a grouping of three observation towers, and a circular theater, the last of which was renovated by Queens Theatre in the Park in 1993 to house 464-seat and 99-seat theaters. Fifteen years later a 3,000-square-foot lobby/party room was added to the east of the theater. Appropriately Sara Caples and Everardo Jefferson's design picks up on the pavilion's circular motif, but its glass walls also give the impression of ascent by angling the normally horizontal mullions. This movement is accentuated by a ceiling plane that rises as it travels 360 degrees from the entrance, culminating in an elliptical opening in the yellow ceiling that frames a view of the observation towers.

188 The New York State Pavilion's observation towers loom over the Queens Theatre.

FLUSHING MEADOWS CORONA PARK POOL & RINK **189**
HANDEL ARCHITECTS with Kevin Hom + Andrew Goldman Architects, 2008

Flushing Meadows Corona Park, just west of Van Wyck Expressway
7 to Mets–Willets Point

Plans began in 1999 for the construction of a facility with a competition-level pool and an NHL regulation ice rink in the northeastern corner of Flushing Meadows Corona Park. But the project was quashed by high costs, only to be resurrected five years later by Mayor Bloomberg as part of the city's 2012 Olympics bid. We all know how that turned out, but the $66 million, 110,000-square-foot pool and rink were realized after nearly a decade in the making. To accommodate these two large open spaces and room for spectators—what's called the largest recreational facility ever built in a New York City park—Handel Architects suspended the roof from two cable-stayed masts. These tall structural elements recall bridges, but the designers contend that the inspiration came from the 1939 and 1964–65 World's Fair pavilions that temporarily occupied the site. Random strips of yellow, green, and blue enliven the otherwise gray perimeter of precast concrete walls below the curling roof. This is a public building, but use of the facilities requires a yearly membership for all but children.

189 The east-side entrance is detached from the long span section.

190 QBG ADMINISTRATION & VISITOR CENTER
BKSK ARCHITECTS, 2007

43–50 Main Street, between Dahlia and Peck Avenues
⑦ to Flushing–Main Street

At only thirty-nine acres, the Queens Botanical Garden (QBG) may have long been overshadowed by the New York Botanical Garden's 250-acre home in the Bronx and the Brooklyn Botanic Garden in Prospect Park. But the popularity and recognition of QBG since 2007 mark a paradigm shift of sorts: sustainable architecture successfully raising the profile of an institution. Let's call it the QBG effect, a variation on the Bilbao effect. Coincidentally, the 15,000-square-foot Administration & Visitor Center opened shortly after Mayor Bloomberg unveiled the ambitious sustainability agenda, PlaNYC. The mayor cited the LEED Platinum Certified building as a major asset in his plan, certainly boosting the garden's exposure throughout the city. Yet the building is actually part of a larger master plan, QBG's 2001 Sustainable Landscapes and Buildings Project, which considers how all parts of its facilities and grounds contribute to the well-being of the garden and the surrounding neighborhood.

Located directly east of the Van Wyck Expressway and Flushing Meadows Corona Park, QBG traces its origins to a 1939 World's Fair exhibition held in the latter. The garden was moved by Robert Moses from the park to its current location in 1963 to make way for the World's Fair the following year. Much later, in 1999, QBG started to develop its master plan, and scrapping its administration building to construct a sustainable replacement became a priority. As realized, the design by BKSK Architects is, as QBG's publicity describes it, "a veritable encyclopedia of building techniques that conserve water, tap renewable energy, and work with nature to mitigate global warming." In fact, listing all the green features and their benefits would take up pages in this book, but the visible elements include an accessible sloping green roof that insulates the auditorium below; a dramatic canopy over the forecourt that collects rainwater and shades the administration bar from the summer sun; a wood brise-soleil further shading the offices; and a cleansing biotope that filters the captured rainwater through soil and native wetland plants. A touch screen inside the Visitor Center presents information on these and other green features, both visible and invisible.

As is apparent, much of what is green about the building relates to water, and this reflects a coordinated effort on the part of QBG and the design team to respond to cultural concerns, not just to the goal of keeping water out of the city's storm sewer system. The garden is about a half mile south of downtown Flushing, a Chinatown that tops Manhattan's in population, and it was determined through resident workshops that many of the area's diverse populations place a high importance on water in gatherings and celebrations. The presence of water in the landscape design by Conservation Design Forum and Atelier Dreiseitl is apparent just steps inside the pedestrian gate on Main Street, in a fountain with water that courses to the cleansing biotope. Those arriving by car are greeted by the porous paving of the "parking garden." From this access on the north edge of QBG, a walk to the Visitor Center yields a view of another BKSK addition to the garden, the Horticulture & Maintenance Building, clad in corrugated metal siding, cedar, and translucent panels.

21

190 The dynamic and playful canopy steals the show (top, left). Between the canopy and office bar, water moves to the cleansing biotope (top, right). The sloping green roof rises from the gardens on the east (above). Looking down on the terrace from the roof of the auditorium (left). Photos © Jeff Goldberg/Esto.

21

191 TENRIKYO MISSION NEW YORK CENTER

MARBLE FAIRBANKS, 2009

**42-19 147th Street, between
Ash and Sanford Avenues
⑦ to Flushing–Main Street and ⑫ Bus**

Tenrikyo is a religion founded in Tenri, Japan, in 1838 that promotes living "the joyous life." While most of its followers reside in Japan, over 2 million people practice the religion worldwide; in the United States the majority are on the West Coast. The New York branch was founded in 1976, and fifteen years later it was augmented by the Tenri Cultural Institute in Manhattan. The institute runs a School of Japanese Language and hosts art shows and concerts in a space designed by Scott Marble and Karen Fairbanks. With this prior experience, Tenrikyo asked the architects to design a 7,000-square-foot building for religious ceremonies next door to two houses owned by the church on a residential block in Flushing. The resulting design addresses the scale and visual characteristics of the neighborhood by respectively burying half of the two-story building below grade and wrapping the façades in a cement board rain screen. This two-tone siding varies in width and height, an unfolding gradient on all four sides that roots the building in its place.

While the building's skin relates to things immediate, the interior looks to Japan. First, the stage (Jodan) of the worship hall needed to be oriented to Jobi, the main sanctuary in Japan. This was achieved by making the space parallel to the street and putting the entrance to the building on the side, but the orientation is accentuated by a complex folding of the roof and clerestories that bring in sunlight and frame views. Second, the spaces exhibit Japanese styles, both traditional (the offering shrine on the Jodan) and contemporary (the Tadao Ando–esque courtyard adjacent to the cellar dining hall). Additionally, the moss, trees, and rock garden in the rear also exhibit a Japanese aesthetic. Given Tenrikyo's origins in Japan and its spread around the world, it is fitting that the design incorporates and bridges the local and the distant. The church is welcoming to visitors, but checking its Web page for service times and contact information is recommended.

191 The worship hall opens to the rear yard (above). The complex roof section is hinted at from the street (below). Photos by Marble Fairbanks.

BAYSIDE RESIDENCE **192**
GRZYWINSKI + PONS, 2007

33-23 161st Street, between 33rd
and 35th Avenues
7 to Flushing-Main Street and **13** Bus

In the heated debates over contemporary versus traditional architecture, who would have thought that a quiet street in Murray Hill, a small section of Flushing east of downtown, would be picketed by neighbors over a Modernist addition to the block's neocolonial houses? But in the middle of 2007, as contractor-developer John Hsu worked to build his 3,000-square-foot dream house, designed by Matthew Grzywinski and Amador Pons, his neighbors, preservationists, and even the Department of Buildings tried to derail the project, though they were able only to slow him down. As realized, the house is a split-level (two stories in the front, three in the back), flat-roofed box covered in reddish-brown siding. Asymmetrical openings further depart from the predominantly neo-traditional neighbors, but the overall effect is of restraint, not a bombastic design worthy of picketing.

192 A modern addition to the neighborhood. Photo by Floto + Warner.

KUPFERBERG HOLOCAUST RESEARCH CENTER AND ARCHIVES **193**
TEK | ARCHITECTS, 2009

222-05 56th Avenue, between Cloverfield and Springfield Boulevards
7 to Main Street-Flushing and **27** Bus

193 A wall of limestone from near Jerusalem fronts the small plaza.

Neither a museum nor a memorial, the Harriet and Kenneth Kupferberg Holocaust Research Center and Archives (KHRCA) is considered a laboratory for the fifteen thousand students at Queensborough Community College in Bayside, where the building is located. Housed in the library's basement for a couple of decades, KHRCA is now appended to the Administration Building, a prominent location overlooking one of the school's largest parking lots and along a major walking path into the middle of campus. The center uses interviews with Holocaust survivors, an interactive timeline, photographs, and other artifacts to help students and other visitors "grasp the hatred, greed, fear, and indifference that resulted in this unparalleled tragedy."[1] The architectural representation of this goal is found in the translucent glazing and its erratic diagonal grid of mullions, a reference to Kristallnacht, the "Night of Broken Glass," in 1938, when Jewish shops and synagogues were ransacked and set on fire in Germany and Austria. At night this corner glows like a lantern, an optimistic beacon of lessons learned.

21

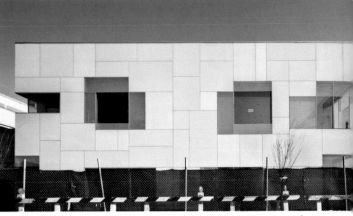

194 Translucent glass panes frame the window openings (left). Four types of glass cover the Merrick Boulevard elevation (right). Photos by Jackie Caradonio.

194 CHILDREN'S LIBRARY DISCOVERY CENTER
1100: ARCHITECT, 2011

89-11 Merrick Boulevard, at 90th Avenue
🄵 to 169th Street

Queens is one of two boroughs, along with Brooklyn, that operate their own library system, as opposed to being part of the New York Public Library (NYPL). Over sixty branches and learning centers serve the borough's 2.2 million residents, housed in some buildings dating to the nineteenth century and others built with the help of Andrew Carnegie between 1904 and 1924. The Central Library in Jamaica houses one fifth of the library's 6 million items, and it also the site of the two-story, 14,000-square-foot Children's Library Discovery Center (CLDC). Billing itself as "a totally new concept in children's libraries," the CLDC incorporates "learning labs," interactive exhibits, "information plazas," and other resources to teach kids the skills for finding information and to spark in them an interest in books and reading. Queens Library partnered with the San Francisco Exploratorium, the New York Hall of Science (**187**), and Brooklyn's Children's Museum (**140**) to realize its hybrid program.

The CLDC is located on the southwest corner of the block it shares with the Central Library. Its two street elevations are covered in four types of glass, the panes composed like a child's stacking blocks. In the design by David Piscuskas and Juergen Riehm opaque white glass and textured opaque glass predominate, while clear openings of various sizes and orientations are fitted into the block pattern, highlighted by translucent borders. The white palette extends inside, much as in the same architects' NYPL Battery Park City Branch (see page 138), here allowing the books, exhibits, furniture, and other elements to come to the fore.

21

195 Looking north up Sutphin with the Control Center in the foreground (left). Under the canopy are the LIRR platforms and tracks (right).
Photos by John Bartelstone.

LIRR JAMAICA STATION **195**
PANYNJ, 2006

Sutphin Boulevard, between 94th and Archer Avenues
E **J** **Z** to Sutphin Boulevard

Downtown Jamaica has long been a transfer point between the MTA's Long Island Rail Road (LIRR) and its subway system, but the 2003 completion of the AirTrain station linking JFK to these railways greatly expanded the complexity of this node. In conjunction with the construction of the AirTrain platform south of the LIRR tracks, the Port Authority of New York and New Jersey (PANYNJ) undertook a $316 million development consisting of a seven-story office building (Jamaica Control Center) and an interconnecting terminal (Vertical Circulation Building). The first is a mirrored glass box hinged between the AirTrain platform to its west and the LIRR and subway to the north. Its clear glass atrium contains the stairs, escalators, and elevators that link the various modes of transportation, but it is obviously the canopy reaching over Sutphin Boulevard that receives all the architectural attention, and deservedly so. Like an airport terminal transported to the city, it makes a grand gesture, celebrating travel, in this case by rail. The impressive canopy covers a mezzanine that runs from the Control Center to the old Jamaica station on the north, but it also covers a portion of the LIRR platforms one level below the mezzanine.

One year after completion of Jamaica Station, the Department of City Planning approved the Jamaica Plan, a rezoning of 368 blocks that responds to the area's role as a transportation hub by creating a special district "to strengthen and revitalize Downtown and foster a new gateway at the AirTrain area."[2] Plans for redeveloping the blocks around the station have not materialized, raising the question whether the AirTrain's presence brings people to the area or merely gives them a stopover on the way to somewhere else.

21

196 HIGH SCHOOL FOR CONSTRUCTION TRADES, ENGINEERING AND ARCHITECTURE

ARQUITECTONICA with STV, Inc., 2006

94–06 104th Street, at 95th Avenue
J Z to 104th Street

Will the next Frank Gehry come from Ozone Park, Queens? Before 2006 it might have seemed unlikely that the land of John Gotti and horseracing would produce a great architect, but with the completion of the city's first and only school focused on the building trades and crafts, engineering, and architectural design, the chances have improved. The school for Construction Trades, Engineering and Architecture aims to prepare students for post-secondary education or apprenticeships in these fields, while still providing the core curriculum required for a well-rounded education.

In an institution housing students who will someday design and build other institutions, the role of its architecture as a learning tool is readily apparent. Beyond the provision of teaching spaces for CAD drafting instruction and project reviews, and labs for hands-on work with construction technology, the building expresses what architecture is capable of and how it is built. In this regard Miami's Bernardo Fort-Brescia and Laurinda Spear see volume, materiality, and color as means of arranging and expressing function, the three fields constituting the school's curriculum. North- and west-facing elevations of unadorned red brick, with matching mortar and punched openings, make up most of the exterior. Each of the smaller volumes cradled by this L-shaped mass is articulated with different materials: corrugated metal siding with ribbon windows, battered precast concrete walls, glass block. A window projecting over the entrance is wrapped in yellow porcelain panels, a splash of color among the grays. With only one tree in the corner plaza, a focus on form over sustainability points to what is missing from the school and the architecture.

196 From the main intersection to the east, all of the school's volumes are visible (opposite). Unadorned red brick walls frame the corner volumes (above). Photos by Norman McGrath.

21

Looking across New York Harbor to Lower Manhattan, from the Staten Island September 11 Memorial. Photo © Francis Dzikowski/Esto.

STATEN ISLAND

ST. GEORGE, SNUG HARBOR,
CLOVE HILL, GRYMES HILL

Staten Island is distinguished by being the borough

farthest removed from Manhattan and the rest of New York City as a whole. It is located closer to New Jersey (only five hundred feet away along Arthur Kill, the heavily trafficked waterway on Staten Island's west edge) than to the nearest borough, Brooklyn (approximately one mile). Connection to the last is accommodated by the Verrazano-Narrows Bridge, completed in 1964 and named for Giovanni da Verrazano, who anchored on the island in 1524 and thereafter sailed through the narrows into the Upper Bay. Before the completion of the bridge, most of the development was concentrated around St. George, in the northeast corner of the island. Here boat service in one form or another has existed since the early 1700s, making the five-mile trip to the southern tip of Manhattan. Now the free Staten Island Ferry shuttles seventy thousand passengers a day and is a popular tourist attraction in its own right for the views it offers of the Statue of Liberty and Lower Manhattan. While construction of the bridge spurred development toward the middle and southern portions of the island, St. George remains the most densely populated area in the least populous and least densely developed borough.

Occupying much of the west-central portion of Staten Island is the old Fresh Kills Landfill, created in 1948 as a three-year project to fill in marshland for future parks and highways. The landfill ended up being used until the spring of 2001, reopening for ten months in the aftermath of the September 11 terrorist attacks as a staging area for the recovery effort. The 2,200-acre site (just under three Central Parks in area) is being transformed into Fresh Kills Park (see **New York City 2020**), which will become the city's second-largest park (behind Pelham Bay Park in the Bronx) and will contribute to the 30 percent of open space that covers the island. This landfill is notable not only for being New York City's dumping ground (it was once the largest landfill in the world) for fifty years beyond the original estimates, but also for spurring interest in the island; a 1993 attempt at secession from the city was obviously unsuccessful, but it helped bring about the eventual closure of the landfill. Recently the city has actively revitalized the St. George waterfront and civic center, which included a new baseball stadium next to the ferry terminal for the borough's minor league team. Efforts to the south focused on rezoning much of the island to preserve its low-density residential character and the rehabilitation of the extensive beaches along the Lower Bay.

22

197 ST. GEORGE INTERMODAL AND CULTURAL CENTER
HOK, 2005

1 Richmond Terrace, at Bay Street
Staten Island Ferry

This guidebook begins with the Whitehall Ferry Terminal (**1**), the Manhattan dock for the Staten Island Ferry, so it's fitting that the last chapter should start with the ferry's eponymous destination. Like the terminal in Lower Manhattan, the St. George Intermodal moves people from one mode of transportation to another; in this case ferry riders can connect with the Staten Island Railway or one of more than twenty bus lines, and vice versa. An estimated seventy thousand passengers per day move back and forth between these three modes of public transportation, for many years through a generic 1950s building hardly befitting its role as a frequently traveled gateway.

The two-phase project, designed by HOK's New York office, included the renovation of the old terminal—opening up the space and the walls to provide harbor views—and the addition of 20,000 square feet of retail, bumping the terminal's area to over 200,000 square feet. Other features include a pedestrian connection to the neighboring ballpark and September 11 Memorial (see page 265), an 18,000-square-foot green roof visible from the new walkway, and a 350-foot arch that reaches toward the water. The last especially beckons tourists riding the ferry for a quick glimpse of New York Harbor and Lower Manhattan to get off the ferry and explore Staten Island.

197 The 350-foot arch identifies the ferry terminal from all sides. Photo by Ben Rahn.

STATEN ISLAND CHILDREN'S MUSEUM 198
PRENDERGAST LAUREL ARCHITECTS, 2003

1000 Richmond Terrace, between Tysen Street and Kissel Avenue
Staten Island Ferry and 🚌 40 Bus

Snug Harbor Cultural Center and Botanical Garden, on Staten Island's north shore, dates back to the early 1800s, when Robert Richard Randall built three buildings for retired sailors. Its eighty-three acres evolved into a community nine hundred residents strong, with a farm, dairy, sanatorium, hospital, and music hall, among other institutions. Its eventual decline led to the demolition of many of its Greek Revival, Beaux-Arts, and other structures, but the Landmarks Preservation Commission designated the remaining buildings as landmarks in 1965, the first in the city. The most impressive of these are the five grand edifices facing the water, what is considered "temple row."

Toward the south end of the property is the Staten Island Children's Museum, which moved into a renovated Italianate-style building in 1985. Two expansions followed: the 2001 incorporation of a nineteenth-century barn and the Connector Building two years later. The latter, which links the barn with the original building, is the only overt piece of contemporary architecture to be found at Snug Harbor. Sloped glass walls on both sides of the Connector face an exhibition plaza on the east and a patio on the west; a curving lead-coated copper roof joins the two exterior walls. The same metal covers a new silo-like structure housing an elevator, a dose of Postmodernism for this nineteenth-century campus.

198 From the east, the assemblage is eclectic (above). The sloped wall embraces the playground (left). Photos by Wing Peng.

22

199 The new entrance in the center of the zoo; a "snake" slithers in and out of the brick wall. Photo © Albert Vecerka/Esto.

199 STATEN ISLAND ZOO REPTILE WING

GRUZEN SAMTON with Curtis + Ginsberg Architects, 2007

614 Broadway, at Glenwood Place
Staten Island Ferry and 48 Bus

Compared to the five zoos in the other four boroughs, the seventy-five-year-old Staten Island Zoo is tiny at only eight acres. But the Staten Island Zoological Society uses the location in Clarence T. Barrett Park to its advantage, focusing on education and the display of small mammals, birds, tropical fish, reptiles, and amphibians. The last two (known as the "herps") constitute the most renowned aspect of the zoo, its extensive collection of rattlesnakes, thanks in great part to the four decades Carl Frederic Kauffeld served as curator of reptiles and director of the zoo.

Since the zoo's opening, the Reptile Wing, officially the Carl F. Kauffeld House of Reptiles, has been housed in a T-shaped neo-Georgian building near the Broadway entrance. The renovation and expansion of the WPA exhibit hall by Gruzen Samton—responsible for a similar task at El Museo del Barrio on the Museum Mile—bring the total area for its collection of two hundred species and specimens to 16,000 square feet. It also adds a new entrance at the end of the wing, smack in the middle of the zoo grounds. Inside, a path through the exhibition space curves like a slithering snake, capped by an oversized model of reptile vertebrae. Most original in the exhibit design by Curtis + Ginsberg is the Fear Zone adjacent to the venomous snakes, designed to help people overcome their fear of snakes through education and even interaction.

DASILVA ACADEMIC CENTER **200**
PERKINS EASTMAN, 2004

300 Howard Avenue, at Greta Place
Staten Island Ferry and 🚌 74 Bus

St. John's University, in the Grymes Hill section of Staten Island, is one of three New York City locations for the 140-year-old Catholic institution. Whereas its Manhattan campus is vertical and its main campus in Queens is spread across over one hundred acres, this sixteen-acre campus is basically suburban: isolated, surrounded by a neighborhood of large single-family houses, and ringed almost entirely by a sea of cars. This situation arose from the fact the campus started as the estate of the Gans family in the early twentieth century, later incorporated into Notre Dame College, which consolidated with St. John's in 1971. Needless to say, the intimate campus is a hodgepodge of old buildings and additions that seem to spring up at the rate of one per decade.

The three-story 40,000-square-foot DaSilva Academic Center (like other facilities at St. John's, this building is named in honor of John DaSilva, a member of the university's hockey team who was killed in a car crash in 1980, only one year after graduation) houses classrooms as well as computer labs, faculty offices, and informal gathering areas. Its exterior balances brick, curtain wall, and white metal panel, a contemporary addition to campus that tries to make peace with its predecessors. But the building's greatest benefit is its siting, which strongly defines the northern edge of an open space at the heart of campus.

200 At one end of the open space the building displays its occupants (below). At the other end the building displays the sky (above). Photos by Chuck Choi.

REMEMBERING

Memorials and monuments to the dead obviously aren't limited to cemeteries. Their integration into the urban fabric promises a better chance of affecting the living, conveying an understanding of loss as well as some hope of moving forward. It is no surprise that discussions of a memorial to the nearly three thousand lives lost on September 11, 2001, followed soon after the attacks, a testament to the desire to remember through some physical expression. The recent memorials gathered below are reminders of loss and markers of events both contemporary and historic, embodying the generally accepted abstraction that follows Maya Lin's powerful Vietnam Veterans Memorial (1982) in Washington, D.C.

NATIONAL SEPTEMBER 11 MEMORIAL
MICHAEL ARAD and PETER WALKER PARTNERS
with Davis Brody Bond Aedas, 2011
West Street, between Liberty and Vesey Streets (Map 1)

Four jurors (including Maya Lin) sifted through over 5,200 entries submitted to the Lower Manhattan Development Corporation's World Trade Center Site Memorial Competition. Michael Arad and Peter Walker's winning design, *Reflecting Absence*, drowns out the noises of the city with walls of water descending into pools standing in the footprints of the Twin Towers. A grid of four hundred white swamp oak trees covers the plaza around the square openings, and years down the road promise to give the area an impressive canopy. Commemorating both the September 11 attacks and the February 26, 1993, bombing of the North Tower, this memorial, like the WTC itself, dwarfs all others in size but also gravitas. Visualization by Squared Design Lab

AFRICAN BURIAL GROUND NATIONAL MONUMENT
RODNEY LÉON ARCHITECTS with AARRIS Architects, 2007
Duane and Elk Streets (Map 1)

Unbeknownst to workers excavating for a foundation in Lower Manhattan in 1991, approximately fifteen to twenty thousand free and enslaved Africans were buried in a 6.6-acre area below the site of the proposed federal building. An extensive archaeological dig reoriented plans for the new building to incorporate space for a memorial. Rodney Léon's design, *The Door of No Return*—a reference to the West African ports to which most slaves never returned—features an Ancestral Chamber that descends to a map of the Atlantic. From the stairs the movement of the visitor is eastward across the Atlantic, toward Africa. A visitor center for the monument can be found in the Ted Weiss Federal Building around the corner on Broadway. Photo by Jackie Caradonio.

IRISH HUNGER MEMORIAL
BRIAN TOLLE with Gail Wittwer-Laird and 1100: Architect, 2002
Vesey Street at North End Avenue (Map 1)

Between Battery Park City's World Financial Center and north residential neighborhood sits an oddity, a transported bit of Ireland on an inclined landscape. This is the impression one gets approaching along Vesey Street, as only the native grasses and a rebuilt stone hut are visible. But entry is on the west, along banded walls of dark granite and backlit glass blocks, the latter etched with quotations that refer to the nineteenth-century Irish famine as well as the hunger that still plagues many around the world. Movement through the portal brings one to raised landscape, a quarter acre (the most a family could own in Ireland and still receive famine relief). Photo © Aaron Dougherty.

FLIGHT 587 MEMORIAL
FREDDY RODRIGUEZ with Situ Studio
and Kaitsen Woo Architect, 2006
Beach 116th Street, south of Rockaway Beach Boulevard

Two months after the attacks of September 11, 2001, American Airlines Flight 587 crashed shortly after takeoff from JFK, killing all 260 on board and five on the ground in the Belle Harbor neighborhood of Queens. One of the largest tragedies in U.S. aviation history—ruled as human error by the TSA—is commemorated with an arching granite wall punctured by openings that frame views and receive flowers and mementos. Every November 12 at 9:12 a.m., sunlight streaks through the portal, aligning with the plaza's paving pattern, an ephemeral marker of the time of the crash. Photo by Jason Walz.

STATEN ISLAND SEPTEMBER 11 MEMORIAL
MASAYUKI SONO, 2004

Bank Street, near Hamilton Avenue (Map 22)

Staten Island's memorial to the more than 270 victims of the September 11 attacks who lived in that borough sits on the edge of New York Harbor, looking toward the void in the skyline where the Twin Towers once stood. The inside faces of two curving concrete planes display granite silhouettes of each victim at eye level. Nameplates are angled in plan to allow the placement of flowers and mementos and to admit sunlight through the slots cut in the concrete. The wing-like forms are reminiscent of both the tool of destruction, the airplane, and a symbol of hope and peace, the dove.
Photo © Francis Dzikowski/Esto.

While the bulk of this guidebook surveys structures and spaces built in New York City from 2000 until roughly the end of 2010, as in any city the plans and construction just keep going. So what will be coming up in the second decade of this century? This chapter looks forward to projects under construction and in planning at the time of writing, categorized by type. Beyond the buildings and spaces illustrated and/or described below, some major developments that will unfold in the current decade include Atlantic Yards in Brooklyn, Hudson Yards on Manhattan's West Side, the nearby 7 Line Extension, Willets Point in Queens, and the Second Avenue Subway on Manhattan's East Side, the last under construction (off and on) since 1972!

Keep in mind that change is inevitable in the early stages of any project: some of these may never come to fruition, and some may change dramatically from the renderings envisioned here, while others may even be done by the time this book is released. Unless noted otherwise after the address, projects are located in Manhattan.

The World Trade Center site's redevelopment will take center stage for the second decade of the twenty-first century. SOM | © dbox.

NEW YORK CITY 2020

WORLD TRADE CENTER REDEVELOPMENT 268

PUBLIC SAFETY 270

COMMERCIAL 272

EDUCATIONAL 274

INSTITUTIONAL 277

LIBRARIES 280

MEDICAL 281

PARKS AND RECREATION 283

WATERFRONTS 286

RESIDENTIAL 288

WORLD TRADE CENTER REDEVELOPMENT

In February 2003 Daniel Libeskind was selected as the winner of a competition for the master plan of the World Trade Center (WTC) site. "Memory Foundations" featured towers circling the memorial's Twin Towers footprints and rising to culminate in the 1,776-foot-tall Freedom Tower. Libeskind's drawings depicted a cohesive assemblage of skyscrapers defined by diagonal stripes and angled tops gesturing to the memorial, but as is the case with most master plans, the design of individual buildings is handled by other architects. This divergence from the preliminary master plan is apparent in the eclectic design of the four towers and the other components, all designed by architects of international acclaim. Realization of all pieces, including as of this writing an off-again, on-again Performing Arts Center designed by Frank Gehry, is (optimistically) anticipated for 2015.

1 WORLD TRADE CENTER
SKIDMORE, OWINGS & MERRILL
Vesey Street at West Street

The name Freedom Tower may have been dropped and the design transformed by SOM's David Childs (now symmetrical, the square tower turns 90 degrees as it ascends), but the symbolic height of 1,776 feet remains.

The three towers developed by Silverstein Properties are positioned on the east side of Greenwich Street. This trio increases in height from north to south, from 4 WTC to 3 WTC and 2 WTC, the last of which is across the street from 1 WTC. At the time of writing, of these three towers, only at 4 WTC was construction under way. SOM | © dbox

1, 2, 3, and 4 WTC step down the skyline.

2 WORLD TRADE CENTER
FOSTER + PARTNERS
200 Greenwich Street, at Vesey Street
A diamond-shaped sloped roof marks this tower "turning the corner" between the low towers and 1 WTC. The seventy-nine-story tower will be 1,270 feet tall.

3 WORLD TRADE CENTER
ROGERS STIRK HARBOUR + PARTNERS
175 Greenwich Street, between Liberty and Vesey Streets
A simple glass box is articulated with a cross-bracing structure facing the memorial. The seventy-one-story tower will be 1,140 feet tall.

4 WORLD TRADE CENTER
MAKI AND ASSOCIATES
150 Greenwich Street, at Liberty Street
Another simple glass box; the upper floors are cut at an angle, a subtle gesture toward 3 WTC. The sixty-four-story tower will be 975 feet tall.

NATIONAL SEPTEMBER 11 MEMORIAL & MUSEUM
SNØHETTA with Davis Brody Bond Aedas
Greenwich Street, between Liberty and Vesey Streets
Wedged between the footprints of the Twin Towers is a tapering pavilion with access to underground spaces containing relics of the original World Trade Center: the "Last Column" from one of the façades of the Twin Towers, the "Survivors' Stair," and the slurry wall built to keep the Hudson River at bay. Courtesy 9/11 Memorial, Visualization by Squared Design Lab

WORLD TRADE CENTER TRANSPORTATION HUB
SANTIAGO CALATRAVA
Greenwich Street at Fulton Street
Between 3 WTC and 2 WTC the new PATH station is a birdlike building by Spanish architect-engineer Santiago Calatrava, with a soaring space similar in scale to Grand Central Terminal. Underground it is connected to the MTA Fulton Street Transit Center by Grimshaw to the east. The Port Authority of New York and New Jersey

PUBLIC SAFETY

The types of buildings commissioned by government agencies serve varied needs, from learning and recreation to courts and transportation. As always, but increasingly since the attacks of September 11, 2001, buildings devoted to public safety are being built. An important piece in the realization of these project is the Design and Construction Excellence (D+CE) program of the city's Department of Design and Construction (DDC), which emphasizes design innovation and creativity for public projects of various types.

121ST POLICE PRECINCT STATIONHOUSE
RAFAEL VIÑOLY ARCHITECTS
974 Richmond Avenue, Staten Island

Staten Island's first new police precinct in decades will be housed in an L-shaped building on the island's west side. A linear bar clad in stainless steel cantilevers prominently toward Richmond Avenue. Courtesy Rafael Viñoly Architects / © Rafael Viñoly Architects

NEW YORK POLICE ACADEMY
PERKINS + WILL with Michael Fieldman Architects
College Point, Queens (Map 21)

The city's largest auto pound is being transformed into a thirty-acre campus for New York's Finest, consolidating training grounds dispersed across the boroughs into a single facility; the nearly $750 million first phase (scheduled for completion in 2013) includes an eight-story academic building, facilities for physical training, and a central utility plant. The City of New York Department of Design and Construction. Contribution by Perkins + Will with Michael Fieldman Architects.

QUEENS HOSPITAL EMS
DEAN / WOLF ARCHITECTS
Jamaica, Queens (Map 21)
Like the police station in Staten Island, a cantilever characterizes this 12,000-square-foot building on the Queens General Hospital Campus, the division's home for Emergency Medical Services and offices. From the street the design looks like two tapered volumes sliding past each other.
© Dean/Wolf Architects

PUBLIC SAFETY ANSWERING CENTER II
SKIDMORE, OWINGS & MERRILL
Pelham Parkway, Bronx (Map 19)
A backup facility to the city's 911 emergency call system center is anticipated to be completed by 2013 on a site near Pelham Bay Park in the Bronx. The fortress-like cube, articulated with metal panels undulating to reveal windows, rises from the flat landscape.
SOM | © dbox

ZEREGA AVENUE EMS STATION
SMITH-MILLER + HAWKINSON ARCHITECTS
Zerega Avenue, between Lacombe and Randall Avenues, Bronx (Map 19)
Another Emergency Medical Service station, this one near the Bronx YMCA (**179**) in Castle Hill, continues the apparently popular cantilever theme. Trapezoidal in plan, the building is adjacent to one of the area's New York City Housing Authority towers, so the architects designed a green roof for this "fifth façade." Copyright Smith-Miller + Hawkinson Architects (SMH+)

COMMERCIAL

Historically, commercial developments have driven New York City, defining its skyline, erecting its landmarks, and creating nodes of commerce. Developments by and for business and profit encompass various types: hotels, offices, malls, sports venues, even industry, each found in the projects illustrated below. One building is in the Brooklyn Navy Yards, where warships were built and docked for over 150 years. Its current incarnation as a three hundred–acre industrial park includes tenants as diverse as movie studios, furniture makers, ship repairers, and even architects.

15 PENN PLAZA
PELLI CLARKE PELLI ARCHITECTS
Seventh Avenue and 33rd Street (Map 9)

In August 2010 the City Council approved Vornado Realty Trust's proposed sixty-seven-story tower across from Madison Square Garden, against opposition to the Rafael Pelli–designed project arising from its proximity to the Empire State Building, and from the plan to demolish the McKim, Mead & White–designed Hotel Pennsylvania to accommodate it. The tall, tapering glass skyscraper is set for completion in 2014. Pelli Clarke Pelli Architects

22 BOND STREET
SMITH-MILLER + HAWKINSON ARCHITECTS
25 Great Jones Street, at Lafayette Street (Map 4)

This narrow fourteen-story building occupies a through-block lot from Great Jones Street to Bond Street, the same block as the three residential projects featured in the NoHo chapter of this book (see pages 52–53). Smith-Miller + Hawkinson is responsible for the exterior design, veiling the building in a stainless steel fabric with what the firm describes as "a decorative botanical overlay" inspired by Louis Sullivan's nearby Bayard-Condit Building. Copyright Smith-Miller + Hawkinson Architects (SMH+)

860 WASHINGTON STREET

JAMES CARPENTER DESIGN ASSOCIATES
with Gerner, Kronick + Valcarcel

**Northwest corner of Washington and
West 13th Streets (Map 5)**

Immediately adjacent to the Gansevoort Market Historic District, this ten-story glass office tower developed by Romanoff Equities responds to the High Line in an angled form that maximizes daylight both in the public realm and within the building itself. A two-story retail base reinforces the street edge, abutting the DVF Studio Headquarters (**52**) to the north; a one-story portion slips below the High Line itself. Anticipated completion date is 2013. James Carpenter Design Associates Inc.

BARCLAYS CENTER

SHOP ARCHITECTS (DESIGN ARCHITECT) with Ellerbe Becket Architects and Engineers (Architect of Record)

Atlantic and Flatbush Avenues, Brooklyn (Map 13)

The NBA Nets will return to New York, moving into this new arena anchoring the west end of Atlantic Yards, Forest City Ratner's $4.9 billion development over the MTA-LIRR Vanderbilt Rail Yards. A 30-foot-high canopy reaches toward the intersection, framing a view of the arena through a large oculus. Anticipated completion is in 2012. Brooklyn Events Center, LLC c/o Forest City Ratner Companies, LLC

BATTERY MARITIME BUILDING

ROGERS MARVEL ARCHITECTS

South Street, at Whitehall Street (Map 1)

Located next to Whitehall Ferry Terminal (**1**)—at one time a twin of that building's predecessor—the Battery Maritime Building is currently used to ferry people to Governors Island, but long-term plans envision a glass addition on top housing a boutique hotel, with the grand ferry waiting room used as a lobby and restaurant-bar. Rogers Marvel Architects

CITY POINT

COOK + FOX ARCHITECTS

Albee Square and Dekalb Avenue, Brooklyn (Map 13)

City Point is a 1.5-million-square-foot project on the site of the old Albee Square Mall, adjacent to the Fulton Street Mall. Set for completion in 2012, Phase 1, a four-story retail piece dubbed "One Dekalb," will face Fulton Street and the landmark Dime Savings Bank to the east. Cook + Fox Architects LLP

DUGGAL GREENHOUSE
THREAD COLLECTIVE
Front Avenue at Pier C, Brooklyn (Map 13)

Duggal Visual Solutions, a company that has understandably shifted its focus from (in its words) "photo solutions to energy-saving solutions," is planning to transform a former boat repair facility in the Brooklyn Navy Yard into a "greenhouse," a highly sustainable facility for the company. Duggal is responsible for installing solar- and wind-powered streetlamps in the Navy Yard. thread collective

PIER 57
LOT-EK
Hudson River, at West 15th Street (Map 6)

In 2009 the Hudson River Park Trust selected the RFP submission of developer YoungWoo & Associates with design architect LOT-EK to transform the historic Pier 57 into a "an innovative hub of cultural, recreational and public market activities."[1] Reused shipping containers will line a sloping pedestrian street leading to a public park on the roof. LOT-EK

EDUCATIONAL

A recession may be a bust for most, but for universities it means a boom, as people head back to school to pursue alternate career paths or just wait out the economic lull in the bastions of academia. Illustrated below are some of the many higher-education projects—and one primary school—in the works. Yet none comes close in scale, ambition, and controversy to Columbia University's Manhattanville Expansion, northwest of its Morningside Heights campus, designed by Renzo Piano Building Workshop with Skidmore, Owings & Merrill; look for it in twenty to thirty years.

CAMPBELL SPORTS CENTER
STEVEN HOLL ARCHITECTS
Broadway and 218th Street

Columbia University isn't building just in Manhattanville; it is also constructing a new sports center at its Baker Athletic Complex in Inwood, at the northern tip of Manhattan. When complete in 2012, the five-story building will house facilities for the school's outdoor sports programs, including workout spaces, offices, and an auditorium. © Steven Holl Architects

CUNY ADVANCED SCIENCE RESEARCH CENTER

KOHN PEDERSEN FOX ASSOCIATES
with Flad

St. Nicholas Terrace, between West 130th and West 135th Streets (Map 12)

Under construction at the time of writing, two 200,000-square-foot buildings will provide research facilities for nanotechnology, neuroscience, photonics, and other specialties. It is located on the City College campus just south of the School of Architecture (**124**). Luxigon, Courtesy KPF

EDIBLE SCHOOLYARD

WORK ARCHITECTURE COMPANY

350 Avenue X, Brooklyn (Map 16)

In 2010 the garden at P.S. 216 Arturo Toscanini School north of Coney Island opened, the first phase of a project undertaken with Edible Schoolyard NY and Alice Waters's Chez Panisse Foundation. Next is the Kitchen Classroom and "Mobile Greenhouse," the latter sliding over part of the garden to extend the growing season into the winter. Courtesy of WORKac

F.I.T. – C2

SHoP ARCHITECTS

West 28th Street, between Seventh and Eighth Avenues (Map 9)

This proposed addition to the Fashion Institute of Technology's C Building squeezes itself into a narrow, almost unbuildable sliver of land. A highly transparent and expressive façade allows daylight to penetrate to the existing building behind. SHoP Architects

FITERMAN HALL
PEI COBB FREED & PARTNERS
30 West Broadway, at Barclay Street (Map 1)
The Borough of Manhattan Community College's Fiterman Hall was damaged on September 11, 2001, by the collapse of 7 WTC; dust and mold necessitated the destruction of the 1950s building. Its replacement is a fifteen-story "vertical campus" covered in brick-faced precast concrete and generous glazing overlooking the WTC site. Pei Cobb Freed & Partners

FORDHAM UNIVERSITY LAW SCHOOL
PEI COBB FREED & PARTNERS
West 62nd Street, between Columbus and Amsterdam Avenues (Map 10)
Fordham University was part of the original 1955 Lincoln Center development, eventually moving its law school to a campus south of 62nd Street. Housing classrooms, lounges, and a huge library, the new building features a low curving slab of stone and glass bisected at an angle by a tall glass tower, all facing Lincoln Center to the north. Pei Cobb Freed & Partners

THE NEW SCHOOL UNIVERSITY CENTER
SKIDMORE, OWINGS & MERRILL
Fifth Avenue, at 14th Street (Map 4)
A new heart for The New School's Greenwich Village campus will contain an auditorium, classrooms, a library, lecture halls, a cafeteria, and even a six hundred–bed dormitory. Transparent cuts in the base express the circulation route through the building. © SOM

NYU CENTER FOR ACADEMIC AND SPIRITUAL LIFE
MACHADO AND SILVETTI ASSOCIATES
Washington Square South, at Thompson Street (Map 4)
Across from Washington Square Park, New York University, in conjunction with the Archdiocese of New York, is building a six-story center for religious observance, with classrooms, rehearsal space, conference rooms, and offices, replacing the petite Holy Trinity Chapel from 1964. The design's stone façade dissolves into a lattice-like screen facing the park. © Machado and Silvetti Associates / dbox, Inc.

INSTITUTIONAL

The number of cultural institutions expanding their facilities belies any indication of an economic slump. Spread across the different boroughs, these projects range from spaces for art and performance to places of worship and communing with nature.

ASTIN JACOBO CENTER
ROGERS MARVEL ARCHITECTS
Prospect Avenue and East 181st Street, Bronx (Map 17)

Billed as an "interactive green facility," this initiative of the Mary Mitchell Family and Youth Center combines a diversity of programming (education, community, fitness) in the Crotona neighborhood. One of the goals is to "showcase and nurture arts in the Bronx"[2] through an auditorium and gallery space in the new facility. Rogers Marvel Architects

BROOKLYN BOTANIC GARDEN VISITOR CENTER
WEISS/MANFREDI
Washington Avenue, at President Street, Brooklyn (Map 14)

The one hundred-year-old Brooklyn Botanic Garden occupies a triangular patch of land northeast of Prospect Park. Its new Visitor Center takes advantage of the site's natural topography to become an extension of the landscape, a sinuous path from city to garden. Weiss/Manfredi

BROOKLYN NAVY YARD CENTER AT BUILDING 92
BEYER BLINDER BELLE with workshop/apd
South Street and Seventh Avenue (near Flushing and Carlton Avenues), Brooklyn (Map 13)

BNYC92 will be the first public building in the Navy Yard's current incarnation as an industrial park, housing a historical exhibition of the place in the renovated 1857 Marine Commandant's Mansion and extension; combined, they create a new outdoor plaza. Scheduled completion date is 2011. workshop/apd

LCT3

H3 HARDY COLLABORATION
ARCHITECTURE

**West 65th Street, between Broadway
and Amsterdam Avenue (Map 10)**

Lincoln Center Theater is expanding in one
of the few places left in Lincoln Center: its roof. A 23,000-square-foot two-story
addition atop the Eero Saarinen–designed Vivian Beaumont Theater will house
the Claire Tow Theater and other spaces for LCT3, its initiative devoted to a new
generation of theater. H3 Hardy Collaboration Architecture

LINCOLN SQUARE SYNAGOGUE

CETRA/RUDDY

**Amsterdam Avenue, between 68th and
69th Streets (Map 10)**

A series of undulating ribbons define the new home of
the Lincoln Square Synagogue, near Lincoln Center.
A sanctuary and prayer spaces are accompanied by
classrooms and a banquet space for catered events.
Seventh Art Group, Courtesy Cetra Ruddy

LOUIS ARMSTRONG HOUSE MUSEUM VISITOR CENTER

CAPLES JEFFERSON ARCHITECTS

107th Street, between 34th and 37th Avenues, Queens (Map 21)

Exhibition and performance areas will be located in a new building
across the street from the Louis Armstrong House Museum,
Satchmo's home in the Corona neighborhood from 1943 until his
death in 1971. A glass street façade means that his home, visible to
the west, will remain the center of attention. Rendering by Cicada Design
for Caples Jefferson Architects

PARK51

SOMA ARCHITECTS

**51 Park Avenue, between Church Street
and West Broadway (Map 1)**

The most controversial project in New York City in 2010
(along with 15 Penn Plaza), this cultural and recreation
center two blocks from the WTC site infuriated people
for its incorporation of a room for Muslim prayer in the
building's lower floors. Diagonal lines crisscross the
façade in varying widths, subtly expressing the various
spaces behind. SOMA

QUEENS MUSEUM OF ART
GRIMSHAW
Flushing Meadows Corona Park, Queens (Map 21)
Located in the original New York City Building from the 1939 World's Fair, QMA is doubling its size to approximately 100,000 square feet. Modifications to the museum's landmark building include new entrances on the east and west sides, the latter with etched glass fins visible from the Grand Central Parkway. Grimshaw

STRAND THEATER
LEESER ARCHITECTS
Fulton Street, at Rockwell Place, Brooklyn (Map 13)
The not-for-profits UrbanGlass and BRIC make their home at the old Strand Theater, which is undergoing a transformation and expansion. The theater is located adjacent to the Brooklyn Academy of Music (BAM) in Fort Greene. A new façade layered over the old one will signal the presence of these arts and cultural groups. Leeser Architecture

WEEKSVILLE HERITAGE CENTER
CAPLES JEFFERSON ARCHITECTS
158 Buffalo Avenue, at St. Marks Avenue, Brooklyn (Map 15)
The Hunterfly Road Houses are all that remains of the African American community of Weeksville, initially settled in the 1830s by freed slaves, now encompassed by Bedford-Stuyvesant. The new Education Building and Interpretive Campus will provide space for exhibitions and research centered on the site's "living museum." Rendering by Cicada Design for Caples Jefferson Architects

WHITNEY DOWNTOWN
RENZO PIANO BUILDING WORKSHOP
Gansevoort Street, between Washington Street and Tenth Avenue (Map 5)
On a site next to the High Line's southernmost entrance originally eyed by the arts institution Dia as a new home, the Whitney Museum of American Art will expand into a 50,000-square-foot building by the Italian architect responsible for the New York Times Building (**93**) and Morgan Library Expansion (**76**). Renzo Piano Building Workshop, architects in collaboration with Cooper Robertson & Partners (New York)

LIBRARIES

The supposedly imminent demise of books, combined with the increasing reliance on the Internet and other digital resources, would lead one to believe that libraries should be closing. But libraries continue to grow, mainly because they are reshaping themselves as places for finding information, not just as storehouses for books. And in New York City, libraries continue to embody explorations of creativity and innovation through the efforts of DDC and its D+CE program. Below are a few planned ground-up libraries in New York City, most in the highest-circulating library system in the country, Queens, which will also see a new branch in Hunters Point (Long Island City) designed by Steven Holl. In Staten Island, the Stapleton Library will expand into a new home designed by Andrew Berman. And not to be outdone by the outer boroughs, the New York Public Library has tapped Norman Foster to transform its landmark building on Fifth Avenue, with work expected to be complete by 2013.

ELMHURST BRANCH LIBRARY
MARPILLERO POLLAK ARCHITECTS
86-01 Broadway, Queens
Elmhurst is one of the most popular branches of the Queens Public Library, currently occupying one of the early-1900s libraries built with money from Andrew Carnegie. Its popularity signals its replacement with a three-story terracotta-clad building that will double the library's space. A children's reading room in a glass volume would face the street.
Courtesy of Marpillero Pollak Architects

GLEN OAKS LIBRARY
MARBLE FAIRBANKS
256-04 Union Turnpike, at 256th Street, Queens
In the easternmost section of Queens, the cityscape is more suburban than urban, down to the existing library's undistinguished brick building across from a strip mall. Its replacement—half above grade, half underground—opens the library visually to the busy thoroughfare, incorporates a small plaza, and lets the building glow through a wall of translucent channel glass. Marble Fairbanks

KEW GARDENS HILLS LIBRARY EXPANSION
WORK ARCHITECTURE COMPANY
72–33 Vleigh Place, Queens (Map 21)

This design adds a sliver of space to the corner of an existing one-story library, reworking the new, combined interior in the process. The new wrapper lifts at the corner to reveal the library behind a glass wall. The entrance is marked by a curling up of the façade, like a dog-eared corner in a book. Courtesy of WORKac

MARINERS HARBOR PUBLIC LIBRARY
ATELIER PAGNAMENTA TORRIANI
South Avenue, between Arlington Place and Brabant Street, Staten Island

This one-story NYPL branch library, envisioned as a "cracked open shell, rough on the outside, smooth on the inside,"[3] is located in the former oystering community of Mariners Harbor in the northwest corner of Staten Island. A skylight runs the length of the 10,000-square-foot building, bringing plenty of natural light to the space.
Atelier Pagnamenta Torriani

MEDICAL

The 2008 economic collapse affected just about every sector of design and construction, slowing down many projects and halting some entirely. This is true even of hospitals and other medical institutions, which also had to contend with potential changes brought about by President Obama's health care reform. Now we can see that a number of fairly large projects are moving forward.

HOSPITAL FOR SPECIAL SURGERY
SMITH-MILLER + HAWKINSON ARCHITECTS
with Cannon Design
East River Drive, at East 70th Street (Map 11)

HSS, the oldest orthopedic hospital in the country, is located off the York Avenue corridor alongside other medical institutions that likewise are growing and expanding. Recently HSS added three floors to its existing building and will next expand into the 90,000-square-foot River Building one block north. The glass building housing offices and patient rooms straddles FDR Drive. Copyright Smith-Miller + Hawkinson Architects (SMH+)

MOUNT SINAI CENTER FOR SCIENCE AND MEDICINE
SKIDMORE, OWINGS & MERRILL

Madison Avenue, at East 101st Street (Map 11)

Mount Sinai Medical Center occupies a three-block campus in the midst of Museum Mile, easily identified by its Cor-Ten-clad tower. The hospital and teaching facility is expanding into a large new building to the north, a cube-ish volume with two-story openings framed in masonry. Anticipated completion is in 2013. SOM | © SWIM by THE 7th ART

WEILL CORNELL MEDICAL RESEARCH BUILDING
ENNEAD ARCHITECTS

East 69th Street, between York and First Avenues (Map 11)

Ennead Architects' first building for Weill Cornell (**109**) included a fairly flat milky white curtain wall pleated across the north-facing façade. Around the corner, this even larger project for the medical college will repeat similar folds, but with a double wall that screens windows which must now contend with direct sunlight. When completed, the new building will link to its predecessor by a second-floor garden. © Ennead Architects LLP

WORLD PRODUCT CENTRE
KOHN PEDERSEN FOX ASSOCIATES

555 West 33rd Street, at Eleventh Avenue (Map 9)

This sixty-story, 1.5-million-square-foot tower planned for a site adjacent to Hudson Yards bills itself as "healthcare marketplace and education center catering exclusively to the needs of healthcare providers and medical suppliers." The future of this showroom for medical professionals is not certain, but WPC's optimistic literature anticipates completion in 2013. Courtesy of Kohn Pederson Fox Associates

PARKS AND RECREATION

In a city with an extreme density of buildings, not to mention tall buildings, any bit of open space is valued, especially if it is well designed and responsive to the needs of residents. The shaping of public space seems to be riding a high, as industrial land is reclaimed for parks (High Line [**54**], Hudson River Park [**60**], Brooklyn Bridge Park [**127**]), and busy streets are being taken over for pedestrian use (Times Square, Herald Square). A variety of shapes, sizes, scales, and uses of public space are found in the public spaces below, touching every borough as well as an island in the East River and one in Upper New York Bay.

BATTERY PARK CITY COMMUNITY CENTER
HANRAHAN MEYERS ARCHITECTS
West Street, between Murray and Warren Streets (Map 1)

Referred to by the architects as the Digital Water Pavilion, one of the last pieces in the Battery Park City puzzle is this low arcing building below the north neighborhood's last two residential towers. The digital water is in the etched frit pattern (inspired by the composition *Water* by Michael Schumacher) on the 550-foot-long glass wall overlooking the existing playing fields. Under construction at the time of writing, the building was set for completion in 2011. hanrahan Meyers architects LLP

CROTON WATER FILTRATION PLANT
GRIMSHAW with Ken Smith
Landscape Architect
3701 Jerome Avenue, Van Cortlandt Park, Bronx (Map 18)

New York City's tap water is fed by watersheds upstate into three systems, the Croton System being the oldest and now the smallest. To meet increased demand and bring the system up to EPA standards, a plant is being built in the southeast corner of Van Cortlandt Park. But it's the aboveground buildings and landscapes that are of concern here. Influenced by lily pads, the designers create a circular area that filters and reuses water, while also providing recreational amenities such as a driving range and clubhouse. Grimshaw

FDR FOUR FREEDOMS PARK

LOUIS I. KAHN with Mitchell/Giurgola Architects

Southern tip of Roosevelt Island (Map 20)

In 1973 Welfare Island in the East River was renamed Roosevelt Island, in honor of President Franklin Delano Roosevelt. At that time four acres at the island's southern tip were set aside as a memorial to FDR, designed by Louis I. Kahn. The architect died the following year, but it was New York City's fiscal crisis one year later that put the project on hold. After a 2007 pledge from the governor to help realize the park, it is finally moving forward and will soon commemorate FDR's "Four Freedoms" speech, as well as the great architect who designed it. Computer Rendering: Christopher Shelley. Base photograph: Amiaga Photographers, Inc. Image courtesy of Franklin D. Roosevelt Four Freedoms Park, LLC.

FRESH KILLS PARK

JAMES CORNER FIELD OPERATIONS

Staten Island

Shortly after Fresh Kills Landfill closed in 2001, the city started a five-year master planning process to turn the infamous dumping ground into a "world class park." At 2,200 acres (less than half actually landfill; the rest is wetlands, open waterways, and unfilled lowland areas), it will be three times as large as Central Park. Recreational areas will be interspersed with habitat restoration areas, limited park drives, and of course the four landfill mounds. Image by James Corner Field Operations, courtesy of The City of New York

GOVERNORS ISLAND, PARK & PUBLIC SPACE

WEST 8 with Rogers Marvel Architects, Diller Scofidio + Renfro, Mathews Nielsen Landscape Architects, Urban Design+

Governors Island, Upper New York Bay

Now only a short ferry ride from Lower Manhattan or Brooklyn Bridge Park, Governors Island was used for two centuries as a military facility, most recently by the Coast Guard, until 1995. Subsequently 22 acres of the island were designated as a national monument (managed by the National Park Service), and the remaining 150 acres were transferred to the people of New York. Plans for turning part of the latter into a park stem from a 2007 design competition won by a team led by West 8, which envisioned the transformation of asphalt parking lots into spaces for relaxation, recreation, bicycling, and cultural events. West 8/Rogers Marvel Architects/Diller Scofidio + Renfro/Matthews Nielson/Urban Design +, Courtesy The Trust for Governors Island

JANE'S CAROUSEL
ATELIERS JEAN NOUVEL
Empire–Fulton Ferry Park,
Brooklyn (Map 13)

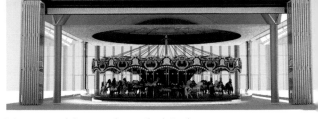

David and Jane Walentas purchased the carousel that now bears the latter's name at an auction in 1984 in Youngstown, Ohio. After a two-decade-long restoration, the couple put it on display in a ground-floor DUMBO gallery, but the confined space unfortunately would not allow for safe riding by children. Thankfully, for children and wooden horses alike, the carousel is moving to Brooklyn Bridge Park, into an enclosure by French architect Jean Nouvel. Ateliers Jean Nouvel, Courtesy Jane Walentas

LAKESIDE CENTER
TOD WILLIAMS BILLIE TSIEN ARCHITECTS
Prospect Park, Brooklyn (Map 16)

In 1961 the oversized Wollman Rink brought ice skating to Prospect Park, but it also defaced Olmsted and Vaux's design. Its replacement will take over the adjacent parking lot and opt for two smaller rinks, one for hockey and one for recreational skating; the former will be covered and bordered by a new building with ancillary facilities. The rinks will function as shallow pools in the summer, and the old Wollman Rink footprint will be returned to its pre-1961 lakeside glory. Tod Williams Billie Tsien Architects

MCCARREN PARK POOL
ROGERS MARVEL ARCHITECTS
McCarren Park, Brooklyn (Map 15)

Originally built by Robert Moses along with other outdoor pools in the 1930s, this massive pool with an impressive brick building was used as a concert venue in recent years after sitting unused for decades. Its renovation will bring the pool back into active use, with a gym, community rooms, and café in and atop the restored bathhouse building. Rogers Marvel Architects

QUEENS PLAZA
WALLACE ROBERTS & TODD with Margie Ruddick,
Marpillero Pollak Architects, and Michael Singer
Queens Plaza North, Queens (Map 20)

Queens Plaza is a confusing tangle of fourteen lanes of traffic, the elevated 7 and N/Q trains, and two bridges in Long Island City. This project for the improvement of a one-mile area for bicycles and pedestrians imagines a "lush, navigable landscape."[4] Courtesy of Marpillero Pollak Architects

WATERFRONTS

As mentioned elsewhere in this guidebook, the reclamation of industrial land for public parks is transforming New York City, like many other U.S. cities. Perhaps the most dramatic transformation is occurring on the waterfronts, where designs such as Hudson River Park (**60**) and Brooklyn Bridge Park (**127**) stand where working piers once did. With approximately 560 miles of waterfront in the city, those parks are just the tip of the iceberg.

EAST RIVER WATERFRONT
SHoP ARCHITECTS and KEN SMITH LANDSCAPE ARCHITECT

East River, from Battery Maritime Building to Montgomery Street (Map 1)

Extending from the Battery Maritime Building on the south to the East River Park north of the Manhattan Bridge, the two-mile East River Waterfront Esplanade and Piers Project will add bike paths, seating, and pavilions for various uses. Pictured is Pier 15, near South Street Seaport, which will house a maritime education center and café. Construction started in late 2009 on a pilot project at the southern end of the park. SHoP Architects

HUNTERS POINT SOUTH
ARUP, THOMAS BALSLEY
ASSOCIATES, WEISS/MANFREDI
East River, from 2nd Street to 49th Avenue, Queens (Map 20)

Hunters Point South is a mixed-use, middle-income housing development proposed for Long Island City, on the peninsula formed by the East River and Newtown Creek. (The site was designed to be the Olympic Village in New York City's unsuccessful 2012 Olympic bid.) An important part of the development, predating building designs by SHoP Architects, is the waterfront park, which will face midtown Manhattan. The park will provide a variety of space along its meandering path, connecting on the north to Queens West and a park also designed previously by landscape architect Thomas Balsley. Arup / Thomas Balsley Associates / Weiss/ Manfredi

THE NEW DOMINO
RAFAEL VIÑOLY ARCHITECTS
East River, from South 5th Street to Grand Street, Brooklyn (Map 15)

In the redevelopment of the eleven-acre former Domino Sugar site in Williamsburg, the waterfront park is as important as the 2,200 apartments and the commercial and retail space proposed. The iconic smokestack-topped brick factory building, a highly visible landmark from the Williamsburg Bridge, will be flanked by residential towers, all fronting the four-acre park with esplanade, lawn, and playgrounds. Courtesy Rafael Viñoly Architects / © Rafael Viñoly Architects

RIVERSIDE PARK SOUTH
THOMAS BALSLEY ASSOCIATES
Hudson River, from 59th to 72nd Streets (Map 9)

To date, the first few phases of Riverside Park South have been realized, stretching along the water from 72nd Street (the tip of Olmsted and Vaux's original Riverside Park) to 59th Street, in front of Trump's wall of residential towers and the elevated West Side Highway. The last phase, currently under way, will bury this roadway under a sloping landscape to give the residents of Riverside Drive a beautiful front yard and direct access to the waterfront.
Thomas Balsley Associates

RESIDENTIAL

Residential developments were easily the market hardest hit by, and the slowest to recover from, the 2008 economic crash. Depending on pre-2008 progress in design or construction, projects were either shelved or stalled; the former have created some holes in the city where buildings were demolished, and the latter have left structural frames waiting to be covered. High-profile victims include 56 Leonard Street, designed by Herzog & de Meuron; Rem Koolhaas's 23 East 22nd Street; and Five Franklin Place, designed by UNStudio. But for each project that proved unsuccessful, one or two rose to the forefront somewhere else. Besides the projects below, these include three large developments by French architect Christian de Portzamparc—Riverside Center, near Riverside Park South; 400 Park Avenue South, north of Madison Square Park; and Carnegie 57, two blocks south of Central Park—the nearby MoMA Tower by Jean Nouvel, and the pyramid-like W57 on, appropriately, West 57th Street by Danish architect Bjarke Ingels.

980 MADISON AVENUE
FOSTER + PARTNERS
980 Madison Avenue, at East 77th Street (Map 11)

Norman Foster may have been able to add a forty-story tower atop a six-story Art Deco building for Hearst Corporation (**99**), but he had to return to the drawing board twice after he proposed a twenty-two-story tower above the landmark Parke-Bernet Building. The version finally approved by the Landmarks Preservation Commission adds four stories wrapped in a bronze-colored aluminum scrim that adds texture to the glass walls. Foster + Partners

BROOKLYN ARTS TOWER
BEHNISCH ARCHITECTS/STUDIOMDA
Flatbush Avenue and Hanson Place, Brooklyn (Map 13)

As part of the BAM Cultural District, this residential tower places 187 apartments (about half affordable) above a podium containing cultural amenities. Most original are clearly the five "sky communities" that ascend what is essentially two towers attached to the central core. Through the articulation of the façades, the design further attempts to distinguish itself from the norm. studioMDA & Behnisch Architekten

MERCEDES HOUSE
TEN ARQUITECTOS

Eleventh Avenue, at West 54th Street (Map 9)

Enrique Norten was very busy at the beginning of the twenty-first century, with a spate of hotels and residential projects in Manhattan and Brooklyn. This is the largest, a multiphase, nearly full-block development overlooking Clinton Park. In addition to condos, it houses a car dealership and a horse stable for the NYPD. Rendering courtesy of Enrique Norten |TEN Arquitectos

CONEY ISLAND COMMONS
DATTNER ARCHITECTS

West 29th Street and Surf Avenue, Brooklyn (Map 16)

New York City's Coney Island Strategic Plan from 2005 didn't limit itself to the amusement area that most people associate with the place. The planners looked at the larger neighborhood and the incorporation of affordable housing. This project includes one hundred affordable apartments and a 40,000-square-foot community center, to be operated by the YMCA. Dattner Architects

MELROSE COMMONS NORTH
ROGERS MARVEL ARCHITECTS

Elton Avenue and East 163rd Street, Bronx (Map 17)

This large four-building mixed-use project across from the new Boricua College campus includes apartments, retail space, a performance venue, a greenhouse, and a K–8 school. The first are housed in the three buildings that wrap around the site toward the last, a low volume that brings sunlight into the generous courtyard space. Rogers Marvel Architects

VIA VERDE
GRIMSHAW AND DATTNER ARCHITECTS

Brook Avenue and 156th Street, Bronx (Map 17)

The 2006 New York New Housing Legacy Project competition asked architects to team with developers toward realizing an affordable, sustainable two hundred–unit development in the South Bronx. The winning scheme—translated as "the Green Way"—terraced up the perimeter of the site; a series of roof gardens start at the courtyard and culminate in the sky terrace and distant views. Dattner Architects

Chapter 1

1. From architect's Web site, Preston Scott Cohen, Inc., www.pscohen.com

Chapter 2

1. From architect's Web site, SmithGroup, www.smithgroup.com
2. Rossi, Aldo. *The Architecture of the City.* Cambridge: The MIT Press, 1984: 130.
3. From architect's Web site, Gluckman Mayner Architects, www.gluckmanmayner.com

Chapter 3

1. From New York Department of City Planning Web site, www.nyc.gov/dcp
2. Ibid.
3. From architect's Web site, Bernard Tschumi Architects, www.tschumi.com
4. From The New Museum Web site, www.newmuseum.org

Chapter 4

1. From architect's Web site, Deborah Berke & Partners Architects, LLP, www.dberke.com
2. Goldberger, Paul. "Green Monster." *The New Yorker* (May 2, 2005): 106–107.
3. From architects's Web site, Thom Mayne, Morphosis Architects, www.morphosis.com

Chapter 5

1. From architect's Web site, Hani Rashid and Lise Anne Couture, Asymptote Architecture, www.asymptote.net
2. From Building of the Week feature at www.american-architects.com.
3. From architect's Web site, James Corner Field Operations, www.fieldoperations.net

Chapter 6

1. From New York Department of City Planning press release, September 24, 2003 www.nyc.gov/dcp
2. From architect's Web site, Jared Della Valle and Andrew Bernheimer, Della Valle + Bernheimer, www.d-bc.com

Chapter 7

1. From architect's Web site, Audrey Matlock Architect, www.audreymatlock.com
2. From LearningSpring School Web site, www.learningspring.org
3. From architect's Webs site, SHoP Architects, www.shoparc.com

Chapter 9

1. Muschamp, Herbert. "A Latin Jolt to the Skyline." *New York Times* (October 22, 2002).
2. Goldberger, Paul. "Miami Vice." *The New Yorker* (October 7, 2002).

Chapter 10

1. Huxtable, Ada Louise. "Columbus Circle Gallery Will Open in Mid-March." *New York Times* (February 25, 1964).

2. Ouroussoff, Nicolai. "New York City, Tear Down These Walls." *New York Times* (September 26, 2008).
3. Gray, Christopher. "The 'Hybrid Pseudo-Modern' on Columbus Circle." *New York Times* (April 26, 1987).
4. From Lincoln Center for the Performing Arts Web site, www.lincolncenter.org
5. From architect's Web site, Diller Scofidio + Renfro, www.dsrny.com
6. Ibid.
7. From American Museum of Natural History Web site, www.amnh.org
8. From Stephen Gaynor School Web site, www.stephengaynor.org
9. From Ballet Hispanico Web site, www.ballethispanico.org

Chapter 12

1. From architect's Web site, W Architecture & Landscape Architecture, w-architecture.com

Chapter 13

1. Platt, Charles A., Dovell, Ray H., White, Samuel G., Byard, Paul Spencer. *Architecture on Architecture.* New York: Monacelli Press, 2007.

Chapter 16

1. From architect's Web site, BKSK Architects, www.bkskarch.com

Chapter 17

1. Hammet, Jerilou, and Hammett, Kingsley, Eds. *The Suburbanization of New York.* New York: Princeton Architectural Press, 2007.

Chapter 18

1. From architect's Web page, H3 Hardy Collaboration Architecture, www.h3hc.com
2. Mori, Toshiko. *Toshiko Mori Architect.* New York: Monacelli Press, 2008: 73.

Chapter 19

1. From United Methodist Church of Co-op City Web site, www.co-opcityumchurch.org

Chapter 21

1. From Queensborough Community College, Kupferberg Holocaust Research Center and Archives Web site, www.qcc.cuny.edu/khrca
2. New York Department of City Planning Web site, www.nyc.gov/dcp

Chapter 23

1. From Hudson River Park Web site, www.hudsonriverpark.org
2. From Mary Mitchell Family and Youth Center Web site, www.themarymitchellfyc.org
3. From architect's Web site, Atelier Pagnamenta Torriani, www.atelier-pt.com
4. From UrbanOmnibus blog, www.urbanomnibus.net

GLOSSARY

ADA The 1990 Americans with Disabilities Act is a federal law that requires accessibility to buildings and spaces, with some exceptions; the most overt expression of the requirements are ramps at building entries.

air rights Unused development rights to the area above a building, transferred from one property to another, not necessarily contiguous property; for example, MoMA used the air rights above the museum to build its adjacent residential tower taller than the property's zoning allowed.

avant-garde A term applied to artists and architects working outside conventions; ultimately their output is assimilated into the mainstream, like twentieth-century Modernism.

basement A precise term in New York City: a building's below-grade level with at least 50 percent of the floor's height above grade. Basements can be used as residences and other habitable functions, as long as they meet light and air requirements (see also **cellar**).

BID (Business Improvement District) Officially, in New York City a BID is "a formal organization made up of property owners and commercial tenants who are dedicated to promoting business development and improving an area's quality of life." Unofficially, BIDs use special assessments paid by property owners to perk up neighborhood streets; they do the things the city can't afford to do and are a mirror of the economic circumstances of the BID's area.

Bilbao effect Coined in relation to the success of Frank Gehry's design for the Guggenheim Museum in Bilbao, Spain, in which the architecture of a major cultural institution revitalizes a city in its transition from industrial to postindustrial.

BIM Building information modeling is a recent advance in computer software being utilized by architects; it treats the design as an assemblage of systems in a three-dimensional virtual model, carrying with it a database of embedded information. It is slowly supplanting traditional computer drafting (**CAD**).

brise-soleil French term meaning "sun break," used in architecture to describe the assembly of elements on a façade that shade the interior and add texture to the exterior.

Brutalism The late style of influential architect Le Corbusier, marked by rough concrete walls and the impression of weight or heft; derivative architecture briefly popular in the 1960s bears this name.

building code A legal document setting the minimum requirements for construction, focused on public health, safety, and welfare.

butt-glazing An inelegant term for glass wall assemblies without exterior mullions; interior mullions combine with structural silicon on the outside to hold the glass in place and give the wall an extremely flat appearance.

CAD The first iteration of computer-aided drafting (sometimes design), utilizing vector-based software that locates points and lines in space, like traditional hand drafting on a computer screen; slowly being supplanted by "smart" building information modeling (**BIM**).

cast iron An alloy of iron and iron carbide, easy to shape in molds; its decorative use can be found in the SoHo's Cast Iron Historic District.

cellar A precise term in New York City, referring to a building's below-grade level(s) with at least 50 percent of the floor's height below grade; cellars cannot be used as residences or for other habitable functions (see also **basement**).

channel glass U-shaped self-supporting glass system, translucent in appearance; it is increasingly popular for the diffuse light it permits and the reduced need for intermediate structural members.

cladding Protective and aesthetic cover over a structural frame; typically water- and airtight, cladding is increasingly ventilated, as in **rain screens**.

CNC Computer numerical control allows, among other applications, complex patterns and shapes to be cut from (typically) metal sheets with a router; used for interiors and installations, but also building façades.

curtain wall A non-load-bearing wall hung in front of a structural frame; it is usually made of glass and steel or aluminum (see also **window wall**).

drywall Wallboard made from gypsum plaster pressed between paper, also known as gypsum board and by the brand name Sheetrock.

façadectomy The preservation of the façades of historical buildings in front of new buildings; the phenomenon is best seen during construction, when the old front is literally freestanding (with the help of structural bracing), awaiting the new building behind it.

fiber cement A concrete that is reinforced by fibers instead of steel rebar, making it lightweight and rust resistant; suitable for thin, prefabricated elements (façade panels, copings).

frit Ceramic pattern baked onto glass, often used to filter sunlight entering a building while adding a distinctive appearance on the exterior.

geothermal Literally the "heat of the earth"; geothermal technology is used increasingly to maintain water at a constant temperature by circulating it in deep wells in order to take advantage of the earth's natural heat and reduce the energy required to heat and cool a building.

GFRC Glass fiber reinforced concrete (see **fiber cement**).

green roof Usually a flat roof bearing vegetation either intensively (at least six inches of soil, often in planters, to support plants) or extensively (a thin layer of soil with sedum or similar plants). Green roofs help reduce the greenhouse effect in cities; they absorb and release water at a slower rate than hard roofs; and they provide neighbors with an aesthetically pleasing "fifth façade."

heliostat Mirror devices that track the sun and direct its rays to places where the sun doesn't shine.

historic district An area designated by the city's Landmarks Preservation Commission "because it has a special character or special historic or aesthetic interest or value"; restrictions are placed on new construction in these areas, subject to LPC (see **landmark**) review.

insulated glass A glass unit made up of two pieces of glass with an air space in between; also referred to as IGU (insulated glazing unit). Many times used in combination with a **low-E** coating.

landmark The legal designation of a building, interior, landscape, or district by the Landmarks Preservation Commission (LPC) toward "safeguarding the city's historic, aesthetic, and cultural heritage"; potential changes to landmarks must be minimal and require LPC approval.

LED Light-emitting diode, a semiconductor device used in everything from small electronics to billboards in Times Square.

LEED Leadership in Energy and Environmental Design, a green building certification system developed by the U.S. Green Building Council (USGBC) in 1993. Projects earn credits based on building performance and other factors to gain certification in one of four categories, from least to most credits: Certified, Silver, Gold, and Platinum.

low-E A low-emissivity coating applied to glass—in many cases **insulated glass**—that reflects infrared energy, keeping heat out in summer and keeping it indoors in winter, thereby reducing the need for air conditioning and mechanical heating.

Modernism A twentieth-century movement or style that broke with tradition in the arts (architecture, painting, sculpture, literature, music) and continues to dominate Western culture.

mullions The typically horizontal and vertical members that hold glass panes and metal panels in **curtain wall** and **window wall** assemblies.

parametric modeling A form of **CAD** modeling in which changes made to one part of the virtual 3-D model affect change throughout the rest of the model; a blob-like building is one such expression of this technique.

parapet A short wall that extends past a (usually flat) roof; the New York City building code requires at least three-and-a-half-foot-tall parapets on most buildings over two stories.

party wall The shared wall between buildings, usually solid, or with few openings, and perpendicular to the street.

patina A tarnish that forms on copper and similar metals from oxidation, giving copper, for example, its distinctive green color.

Percent for Art A program started in 1982 that requires 1 percent of the budget for a new or reconstructed city-owned building to be set aside for commissioned artwork.

photovoltaics (PVs) Solar cells that absorb sunlight to produce electricity; its thin cross-section enables the cell to be integrated into glass walls and roofs.

pilotis Slender columns; one of French architect Le Corbusier's "five points of architecture" (also including roof gardens, free design of the ground plan, horizontal windows, and free design of the façade), predating his **Brutalist** phase.

pixelations Digital pixels formalized onto building façades; sometimes kinetic, in most cases they take the form of static arrangements of windows, multicolored metal panels, or other materials or assemblies.

podium The base of a set-back high-rise, an attempt to relate to low-scale neighbors by making the building look smaller from the sidewalk.

Postmodernism Alternately seen as both a reaction to and an extension of **Modernism**, in architecture it was a style borrowing historical elements for use in hybrid and ironic compositions, popular in the 1970s and 1980s.

precast concrete Concrete poured into forms, usually off site, to create panels hung on building frames as **cladding** or used as structural elements, such as floors and walls.

Pritzker Architecture Prize Considered the Nobel Prize for architects, the annual prize is awarded by Chicago's Pritzker family, who founded it in 1979; its purpose is to honor "a living architect whose built work demonstrates a combination of those qualities of talent, vision and commitment, which has produced consistent and significant contributions to humanity and the built environment through the art of architecture."

Privately Owned Public Space (POPS) Plazas, arcades, and other usually outdoor spaces that are open to the public and incorporated into private developments in exchange for additional floor area, a means of incentive zoning passed in 1961.

rain screen An exterior wall **cladding** system that controls water penetration into buildings differently than traditional construction. Rain screens are built of two layers: the outer—a panelized system made from a material such as terracotta—is open yet keeps out the majority of the water; the inner is an airtight layer that sheds moisture; in between is an air space that depressurizes the air outside the building, keeping water from being sucked into the building.

sliver building A tall building on a narrow lot, defined by the city's **zoning** as less than 45 feet wide.

spandrel A cover, usually glass or metal, mounted in front of the edge of a floor slab in a **curtain wall** or **window wall** assembly.

starchitect An architect with celebrity status (star + architect) in the profession as well as a degree of fame among the general public; many of these architects create iconic buildings around the world. Frank Gehry is the preeminent starchitect.

sustainability By definition, the ability to sustain something over time. Sustainable architecture aims to meet current needs without compromising the needs of future generations; also known as "green building" (see also **LEED**).

tectonic Pertaining to the way a building in constructed; a work of architecture is said to be tectonic when it expresses this process, whether literally or symbolically.

tenement Apartment buildings from the 1800s with unsatisfactory living conditions, followed by "new-law" versions in the early twentieth century that are found predominantly in the Lower East Side; the former are often associated with Jacob Riis's muckraking depiction in his book, *How the Other Half Lives.*

tripartite The traditional three-part base-middle-top composition of high-rise architecture, first articulated by Louis Sullivan in the nineteenth century with his groundbreaking (now short) tall buildings, based on the orders of ancient Greece, the Doric, Ionic, and Corinthian.

value engineering Part of the design/construction process where alternative solutions are developed to reduce construction costs; in many cases design features are reduced or eliminated, often to the detriment of the initial vision.

vernacular Sometimes called "architecture without architects" (after Bernard Rudofsky's 1964 MoMA exhibit of the same name), it refers to buildings made from local materials and created without reference to style or theory; with a beauty that arises from "untainted" responses to functional needs, these buildings are increasingly mined for inspiration by contemporary architects.

window wall Similar to a **curtain wall**, yet with the glass and metal spanning from floor to ceiling, between structural slabs.

zoning Legal restrictions that determine "the size and use of buildings, where they are located," and neighborhood densities by the designation of different districts (R for residential, C for commercial, M for manufacturing). New York City's first Zoning Resolution in 1916 gave the skyline its distinctive stepped skyscrapers, while the 1961 resolution allowed the modern glass office slabs which mark that era; today's zoning is basically a hybrid of these two resolutions.

It's impossible, and really unnecessary with a guidebook, to list every source that contributed to the text. So what follows is a bibliography of selected recommended books, magazines, and Web pages for people interested in gaining further information on the buildings and places mentioned in this book. It should be noted that architects' Web pages are a very good, if partial, source for learning about individual buildings.

Books

Ascher, Kate. *The Works: Anatomy of a City*. New York: Penguin, 2005.

Ballon, Hilary, and Kenneth T. Jackson, eds. *Robert Moses and the Modern City: The Transformation of New York*. New York: W. W. Norton, 2008.

Berner, Nancy, and Susan Lowry. *Garden Guide: New York City*. Rev. ed. New York: W. W. Norton, 2010.

Byles, Jeff, and Olympia Kazi, eds. *The New York 2030 Notebook*. New York: Institute for Urban Design, 2008.

Caro, Robert A. *The Power Broker: Robert Moses and the Fall of New York*. New York: Vintage, 1975.

City of New York. *PlaNYC: A Greener, Greater New York*. 2007. nyc.gov.

Copquin, Claudia Gryvatz. *The Neighborhoods of Queens*. New Haven: Yale University Press, 2009.

Goldberger, Paul. *Building Up and Tearing Down: Reflections on the Age of Architecture*. New York: Monacelli Press, 2009.

Jackson, Kenneth T., ed. *The Encyclopedia of New York City*. 2nd ed. New Haven: Yale University Press, 2010.

—. *The Neighborhoods of Brooklyn*. New Haven: Yale University Press, 2004.

Jacobs, Jane. *The Death and Life of Great American Cities*. New York: Random House, 1961.

Kayden, Jerold S., New York City Department of Planning, and Municipal Art Society of New York. *Privately Owned Public Space: The New York City Experience*. Hoboken, N.J.: Wiley, 2000.

Koolhaas, Rem. *Delirious New York: A Retroactive Manifesto for Manhattan*. Reprinted. New York: Monacelli Press, 1997.

Luna, Ian, ed. *New New York: Architecture of a City*. New York: Rizzoli, 2003.

Miller, Kristine F. *Designs on the Public: The Private Lives of New York's Public Spaces*. Minneapolis: University of Minnesota Press, 2007.

Morrone, Francis, and Matthew A. Postal. *The Municipal Art Society of New York: Ten Architectural Walks in Manhattan*. New York: W. W. Norton, 2009.

Muschamp, Herbert. *Hearts of the City: The Selected Writings of Herbert Muschamp*. New York: Knopf, 2009.

New York City Department of City Planning. *Zoning Handbook*. 2006. nyc.gov.

New York City Department of Transportation. *Street Design Manual*. 2009. nyc.gov.

New York Landmarks Preservation Commission. *Guide to New York City Landmarks*. 4th ed. Hoboken, N.J.: Wiley, 2008.

Phifer, Jean Parker. *Public Art New York*. New York: W.W. Norton, 2009.

Plunz, Richard. *A History of Housing in New York City*. New York: Columbia University Press, 1990.

Sanders, James. *Celluloid Skyline: New York and the Movies*. New York: Knopf, 2003.

Sorkin, Michael. *Twenty Minutes in Manhattan*. London: Reaktion, 2009.

Stern, Robert A. M., David Fishman, and Jacob Tilove. *New York 2000: Architecture and Urbanism from the Bicentennial to the Millennium*. New York: Monacelli Press, 2006.

White, Norval, Elliot Willensky, and Fran Leadon. *AIA Guide to New York City*. 5th ed. New York: Oxford University Press, 2010.

Willis, Carol. *Form Follows Finance: Skyscrapers and Skylines in New York and Chicago*. New York: Princeton Architectural Press, 1995.

Zukin, Sharon. *Naked City: The Death and Life of Authentic Urban Places*. New York: Oxford University Press, 2009.

On-line & Print Resources

ArchDaily (www.archdaily.com) • Architizer (www.architizer.com) • The Architect's Newspaper (www.archpaper.com) • Architectural Record (archrecord.construction.com) • The City Review (www.thecityreview.com) • Curbed (www.curbed.com) • Galinsky (www.galinsky.com) • *Metropolis Magazine* (www.metropolismag.com) • newyork-architects (www.newyork-architects.com) • *New York Construction* (newyork.construction.com) • *The New Yorker*, articles by Paul Goldberger (www.newyorker.com) • *New York Magazine*, articles by Justin Davidson (nymag.com) • *New York Times*, articles by Nicolai Ouroussoff and David W. Dunlap (www.nytimes.com) • NYCityMap (www.nyc.gov.nycitymap) • Places: Design Observer (places.designobserver.com) • Urban Omnibus (urbanomnibus.net) • Wired New York (wirednewyork.com)

Local NYC Resources

These institutions and organizations host architecture-related lectures, exhibitions, tours, and other events. Checking their Web pages for schedules and location of events is recommended. Addresses are in Manhattan unless otherwise noted.

AIANY/Center for Architecture, 536 LaGuardia Place (Map 4), cfa.aiany.org

The Architectural League of New York, 594 Broadway, Suite 607 (office address; events are held in other locations), www.archleague.org

City College of New York, 160 Convent Avenue (Map 12), www.ccny.cuny.edu/ssa

Columbia University GSAPP, 1172 Amsterdam Avenue (Map 12), www.arch.columbia.edu

Cooper-Hewitt National Design Museum, 2 East 91st Street (Map 11), www.cooperhewitt.org

Cooper Union, 30 Cooper Square (Map 4), archweb.cooper.edu

Municipal Art Society, 111 W. 57th Street (office address; tours and events are held in other locations), www.mas.org

Museum of Modern Art, 11 West 53 Street (Map 8), www.moma.org

Open House New York, 115 West 27th Street, 9th Floor (office address; tours and events are held in other locations, focused on October "open house"), www.ohny.org

Parsons The New School for Design, 66 Fifth Avenue (Map 4), www.newschool.edu/parsons

Pratt Institute, 200 Willoughby Avenue, Brooklyn (Map 14), www.pratt.edu

SkyscraperMuseum, 39 Battery Place (Map 1), www.skyscraper.org

Storefront for Art and Architecture, 97 Kenmare Street (Map 3), www.storefrontnews.org

Studio-X, 180 Varick Street (Map 2), www.arch.columbia.edu/studiox

Van Alen Institute, 30 W. 22nd Street, 2nd Floor (Map 7), www.vanalen.org

CREDITS

cover, pp. 4–5, 108: Photos by David Plakke, davidplakke.com, NYC, courtesy Austrian Cultural Forum New York

p. 10: SOM/© Ruggero Vanni

pp. 16, 37 (bottom), 42 (right), 43 (top), 44, 45 (bottom, right), 57 (right), 59 (bottom), 64 (top), 74, 75 (top), 77 (top, middle), 82 (right), 83, 102, 105 (bottom), 107 (top-left, top-right, bottom, right), 109 (top), 111, 123 (top-middle, top-right, middle), 127 (top, bottom-right), 135 (top-right, bottom-left), 136 (bottom): Scott Norsworthy

p. 21: SOM/© Robert Polidori

pp. 24 (right), 27 (right), 123 (bottom), 136 (top), 161 (bottom): © 2009 Francis Dzikowski/Esto, from *Public Art New York* (W.W. Norton, 2009)

pp. 23 (left), 127 (bottom-left), 224 (top), 256, 265 (bottom): © 2009 Francis Dzikowski/Esto

p. 23 (right): Photography: Richard Bryant/arcaidimages.com, courtesy Tsao & McKown Architects

p. 23 (left): Nathan Sayers Photography, courtesy Rogers Marvel Architects

p. 25 (right): © Seong Kwon for Cook+Fox Architects LLP

pp. 26 (left), 28, 41 (top), 43 (bottom), 61 (bottom), 174, 252, 264 (bottom): Jackie Caradonio

pp. 26 (right), 29 (bottom), 33 (bottom), 41 (bottom), 47 (bottom), 53 (bottom), 54, 57 (left, middle), 103, 113 (top), 125 (bottom), 162, 168 (bottom), 178, 265 (top): © Aaron Dougherty

pp. 27 (left), 142: SOM/© David Sundberg/Esto

p. 33 (top): Photo by Eduard Hueber/Archphoto, courtesy TEN Arquitectos

p. 36 (left): Photo: Stephen Murray

p. 42 (left): © Peter Mauss/Esto, courtesy Bernard Tschumi Architects

p. 45 (left, top-right): Dean Kaufman, courtesy New Museum of Contemporary Art

pp. 46 (top-left, right), 139 (middle), 186 (middle, bottom), 191–193: © barkowphoto.com

p. 48 (top): Leeser Architecture

p.48 (bottom): Courtesy workshop/apd

p. 49 (top): H.G. Esch, courtesy Kohn Pederson Fox Associates PC

p. 49 (middle): © Paul Warchol, courtesy Rogers Marvel Architects

p. 53 (top): © Paul Warchol, courtesy BKSK Architects

pp. 55, 56, 110, 130 (top), 143 (bottom), 190 (bottom), 202 (bottom): Photo: Adam Friedberg

p. 76 (bottom): Derek Lam International LLC

pp. 58 (top), 137 (bottom), 169 (bottom), 206 (top): © David Sundberg/Esto

pp. 59 (top), 61 (top), 94, 117 (top), 124 (bottom), 138 (top), 171, 207 (middle), 212 (left), 225 (bottom): Photos © Michael Moran

p. 60 (left): © Sam Lahoz, courtesy AIANY

p. 60 (right): © Björn Wallander, courtesy AIANY

pp. 65 (top), 240: Photos by David Joseph, courtesy Daniel Goldner Architects

p. 65 (bottom): Photographer: Jan Staller, courtesy Christoff:Finio architecture

p. 67 (bottom): Nikolas Koenig

p. 69: Paúl Rivera/Archphoto, courtesy Kohn Pederson Fox Associates PC

pp. 71, 239 (top-right): Elizabeth Felicella, courtesy Work Architecture Company

p. 72 (top): Richard Anderson

pp. 81, 84–85, 86 (top), 89 (top), 92, 152, 154, 155 (top), 156, 159 (bottom), 208, 212 (right), 262: © Albert Vecerka/Esto

p. 87 (right): Courtesy NMDA

p. 88 (top, middle): Photography Frank Ouseman 2010, courtesy Della Valle Bernheimer

p. 93 (bottom): Frederick Charles, courtesy Platt Byard Dovell White

p. 99 (bottom): Photography by Michael Denancé, courtesy The Morgan Library and Museum

pp. 104, 148: Erik Freeland, courtesy Peter Gluck and Partners

p. 109: Photo © Michael Moran, courtesy American Folk Art Museum, New York

p. 112: Photo © Paul Warchol, courtesy WXY Architecture + Urban Design

p.113 (bottom): © Paul Warchol, courtesy Davis Brody Bond Aedas

p. 115: Cook+Fox Architects

p. 116 (bottom): © Peter Aaron/Esto, courtesy H3 Hardy Collaboration Architecture

p. 117 (bottom): © Peter Aaron/ Esto, courtesy Andre Kikoski/Susan Grant Lewin Associates

p. 120: copyright Paúl Rivera/Archphoto, courtesy Perkins Eastman

p. 121: Elliott Kaufman, courtesy Platt Byard Dovell White

pp. 124 (top), 216, 254–255: © Norman McGrath, courtesy Arquitectonica

p. 126: Photo by Thomas Balsley Associates

p. 130 (bottom): Hélène Binet, courtesy Museum of Arts and Design

p. 131: SOM/© Michael Amechi Photography

p. 137 (top): Photo by Jonathan Calderon Flores

pp. 139 (bottom), 143 (top), 241, 246: © Jeff Goldberg/Esto

pp. 144, 161 (middle), 179: © Aislinn Weidele/Ennead Architects LLP

p. 145 (top): Michele Curel, courtesy Kohn Pederson Fox Associates PC

p. 145 (bottom): John Chu, courtesy Kohn Pederson Fox Associates PC

p. 146 (top): © Peter Aaron/Esto

p. 146 (bottom): © Paul Warchol, courtesy Peter Gluck and Partners

pp. 147, 175, 205: Jonathon Wallen, courtesy Platt Byard Dovell White

p. 153, 250: Courtesy Marble Fairbanks

p. 155 (bottom-left, bottom-right): © Paul Warchol, courtesy Weiss/Manfredi

p. 157: Alison Cartwright, courtesy W Architecture and Landscape Architecture

p. 125: Photo by Cody Upton, AAAL, courtesy James Vincent Czajka, Architect

p. 172 (top): Photo by Russell Gera, courtesy Tina Manis Associates

p. 183: Photos: marclins.com

p. 185: © Paul Warchol, courtesy hanrahanMeyers architects

p. 186 (top): Ty Cole, courtesy Hangar Design Group

p. 195: © Paul Warchol, courtesy George Ranalli, Architect

p. 201: Photos by Jonathan Wallen, courtesy BKSK Architects

p. 202 (top): Photo by Jonathon Wallen, courtesy Acconci Studio

p. 203: Photos by Elliott Kaufman, courtesy H3 Hardy Collaboration Architecture

p. 206 (top): © Michael Anton, courtesy Caples Jefferson Architects

p. 206 (bottom): © Frank Oudeman 2010, courtesy Stephen Yablon Architect

p. 207 (bottom): Beckhard Richlan Szerbaty Associates Architects

p. 215: © Paul Warchol, courtesy Rafael Viñoly Architects

p. 221: Photos by Robert Benson, courtesy H3 Hardy Collaboration Architecture

p. 222 (top): Photo by Meg Mingione, courtesy New York Botanical Garden

p. 222 (bottom): Photo by Robert Benson, courtesy New York Botanical Garden

p. 224 (bottom): © Jeff Goldberg/ESTO, courtesy Dattner Architects

p. 229: Resolution: 4 Architecture

p. 230 (top): © Payette, photograph by Rachellynn Schoen

p. 230 (bottom): © Robert Benson Photography, courtesy Payette

p. 231: Photos: Lydia Gould Bessler, courtesy Gluckman Mayner Architects

p. 232 (bottom): Chang Kim Kyun Photography, courtesy Architecture Research Office

p. 233 (top): CEMUSA, courtesy Grimshaw Architects

p. 233 (bottom-right): Michael Surtees

p. 234, 249: © Jeff Goldberg/Esto, courtesy BKSK Architects and Queens Botanical Garden

p. 239 (top-right): Courtesy of Ball-Nogues Studio

p. 251: Photo by Floto + Warner, courtesy Grzywinski + Pons

p. 253: John Bartelstone Photography

p. 260: Ben Rahn, courtesy HOK

p. 261: Photos by Wing Peng

p. 263: © Chuck Choi, courtesy Perkins Eastman

p. 264 (top): Courtesy 9/11 Memorial, Visualization by Squared Design Lab

p. 265 (middle): Photograph © Jason Walz, courtesy Kaitsen Woo Architect, P.C., Project Architect

Architect/Building Index

Note: Only the main building entries and buildings noted in the sidebars and NYC 2020 section are indexed (by page number), followed by the date of their construction. Architectural works and the page(s) of their entries appear in bold. Architects and designers are only indexed in conjunction with their work on these projects.

1 World Trade Center, 268
2 World Trade Center, 269
3 World Trade Center, 269
3LD Art & Technology Center (2003), **48**
4 World Trade Center, 269
7 WTC (2006), 10, **27**, 29
8 Spruce Street (2011), **26**, 76, 122, 132
14 Townhouses (2006), 169, **170**, 172
15 Central Park West (2008), 131, **132**
15 Penn Plaza, **272**
15 Union Square West (2010), **92**
22 Bond Street, **272**
25 Bond Street (2007), **53**
30 Orchard Street (2010), **41**, 68, 89
39 East 13th Street Building (2008), **58**
40 Bond (2007), **52**, 53
40 Mercer Residences (2006), **36**, 37, 184
41 Cooper Square (2009), 48, 54, **56–57**
48 Bond Street (2008), **53**
100 Eleventh Avenue (2010), 10, 30, 66, **82**
101 Warren Street (2009), **29**, 132
115 Norfolk Residences (2011), **43**
121st Police Precinct Stationhouse, **270**
163 Charles Street (2008), **65**
165 Charles Street (2006), **64**, 65, 178
166 Perry Street (2010), 65, **66**, 80
173–176 Perry Street (2002), **64**, 65, 66, 178
200 Eleventh Avenue (2011), 61, **86**
200 West Street (2010), **28**
245 Tenth (2009), 80, 87, **88**
290 Mulberry (2009), **47**, 96
322 Hicks Street (2006), **171**
351 Keap Street (2011), **192**
385 West 12th Street (2010), **67**
441 East 57th Street (2009), **104**, 145
459 West 18th (2009), **80**, 196
497 Greenwich Street (2004), **34**, 37, 70
505 Fifth Avenue (2005), **49**
580 Carroll Street (2009), 80, **174**
860 Washington Street, **273**
980 Madison Avenue, **288**
1055 Park Avenue (2010), **145**
1100: Architect, 29, 61, 89, 138, 252, 265

A

AARRIS Architects, 264
Abraham, Raimund, 108
Acconci Studio, 190, 202
Adamson Associates Architects, 28, 46, 83, 105, 114–15, 127

Adjaye Associates, 187
African Burial Ground National Monument (2007), **264**
Agrest and Gandelsonas Architects, 207
Alexander Gorlin Architects, 146, 197, 212
Allied Works Architecture, 130
American Academy of Arts and Letters (2009), **159**
American Folk Art Museum (2001), **109**
Andre Kikoski Architect, 117
Andrew Berman Architect, 60
Aoki, Jun, 105
Apple Store Fifth Avenue (2006), **106–7**
Arad, Michael, 264
Archi-Tectonics, 34
Architecture Research Office (ARO), 196, 232
Armani Fifth Avenue (2009), **77**
Arquitectonica, 124, 216, 254–55
Arup, 156, 287
Astin Jacobo Center, **277**
Asymptote Architecture, 66
Atelier Pagnamenta Torriani, 281
Atelier Raimund Abraham, 108
Ateliers Jean Nouvel, 30, 82, 285
Audrey Matlock Architect, 80, 93
Austrian Cultural Forum New York (2002), 4–5, **108**, 145
Avant Chelsea (2008), **89**

B

Ball-Nogues Studio, 238–39
Ballinger, 143
Balsley Park (2000), **126**
Bank of America Tower at One Bryant Park (2009), 48, **114–15**
Barclays Center, 273
Baruch College Vertical Campus (2001), **94**
Battery Maritime Building, 273
Battery Park City Community Center, **283**
Bayside Residence (2007), **251**
BBG-BBGM, 214
Beckhard Richlan Szerbaty Associates Architects, 139, 207
Behnisch Architects, 288
Bernard and Anne Spitzer School of Architecture (2009), 158, 195, 275
Bernard Tschumi Architects, 42
Bertomen, Michele, 192
Betances Community Center (2007), **206**
Bettlelab, 233
Beyer Blinder Belle, 82, 98–99, 134–35, 277
Bialosky + Partners, 40
Bike Racks, 233
Bill Peterson Architect, 58
BKSK Architects, 32, 53, 201, 246, 248–49
Bloomberg Tower (2005), **105**
Blue Condominium (2007), **42**, 43
Bohlin Cywinski Jackson, 106–7
Brasserie 8½ (2000), **116**
Brasserie (2000), **117**
BriggsKnowles, 196

Bronx Box (2008), 197, **229**
Bronx Charter School for the Arts (2003), **217**, 241
Bronx County Hall of Justice (2008), **215**
Bronx Library Center (2005), **224**
The Bronx Museum of the Arts (2006), **216**
Bronx Park East (2010), **225**
Bronx YMCA (2003), **228**, 271
The Brook (2010), **212**
Brooklyn Arts Tower, 288
Brooklyn Botanic Garden Visitor Center, 277
Brooklyn Bridge Park (2010), **166–67**, 192, 283,
  286
Brooklyn Children's Museum (2008), **180**
Brooklyn College West Quad Center (2009),
  200
Brooklyn Museum Entry Pavilion and Plaza
  (2004), **179**
Brooklyn Navy Yard Center at Building 92, 277
Butler Street Town House (2005), **172**
Byrne, David, 233

C
Calatrava, Santiago, 136, 269
Campbell Sports Center, 274
Cannon Design, 281
Caples Jefferson Architects, 206, 247, 278, 279
Carriage House (2006), **65**
Cassa NY (2010), **113**
Cemusa New York Street Furniture (2006), **233**
Center for Architecture (2003), **60**
Cetra/Ruddy, 95, 113, 278
Chelsea Enclave (2010), **88**
Chelsea Modern (2009), **80**
Children's Library Discovery Center (2011), **252**
Choi Ropiha, 120
Christoff:Finio Architecture, 65
Citterio, Antonio, 54
City Point, 273
Cityracks, 233
Community & Parents Day Care (2005), **139**
Concrete Plant Park (2009), 208, **217**
Coney Island Commons, 289
Cook + Fox Architects, 25, 114–15, 273
Cooper, Robertson & Partners, 23
Cooper Square Hotel (2009), 44, **54**, 55
CR Studio Architects, 85, 160
Croton Water Filtration Plant, 283
CUNY Advanced Science Research Center, 275
Curtis + Ginsberg Architects, 262
Czajka, James Vincent, 159

D
Daniel Goldner Architects, 65, 191, 240
Dasilva Academic Center (2004), **263**
daSilva Architects, 159
Dattner Architects, 22, 161, 224, 289
David Hotson Architect, 34, 187
David Rubenstein Atrium at Lincoln Center
  (2009), **133**
Davis Brody Bond Aedas, 102, 113, 152, 264, 269
Dean Maltz Architect, 81
Dean / Wolf Architects, 271
Deborah Berke & Partners, 53
Della Valle Bernheimer, 80, 88, 196

Derek Lam (2009), **76**
Derfner Judaica Museum (2009), **225**
DHS Prevention Assistance and Temporary
  Housing (2010), **213**
di Domenico + Partners, 233
Diana Center (2010), 57, 145, **154–55**, 156, 230
Diller Scofidio + Renfro, 73–75, 117, 134–35, 284
The Dillon (2010), 80, **124**
DMJM+Harris, 215
Donald Blair & Partners Architects, 228
Dream Downtown Hotel (2011), 55, **89**
Duggal Greenhouse, 274
DVF Studio Headquarters (2007), **71**, 273

E
The East Harlem School at Exodus House (2008),
  148
East River Waterfront, 286
East Village Brownstone (2004), **58**
Edible Schoolyard, 275
Ehrenkrantz Eckstut & Kuhn, 138
Elevated Acre at 55 Water Street (2005), **24**
Ellerbe Becket Architects and Engineers, 273
Elmhurst Branch Library, 280
Engine Company 75 (2000), **161**
Engine Company 277 (2004), **161**
Ennead Architects, 29, 72, 88, 97, 136, 143, 144,
  161, 169, 179, 181, 190, 213, 222, 241, 246, 282

F
FDR Four Freedoms Park, 284
F.I.T. - C2, 275
Fiterman Hall, 276
Flad, 275
FLANK Architecture, 67, 104
Flight 587 Memorial (2006), **265**
Flushing Meadows Corona Park Pool & Rink
  (2008), **247**
Fordham University Law School, 276
Foster + Partners, 46, 127, 269, 288
Frank Sinatra School of the Arts High School
  (2009), 240, **241**
Frederic Schwartz Architects, 20
Fresh Kills Park, 259, **284**
FXFOWLE Architects, 122–23, 125, 134–35, 220

G
G TECTS, 76
Gateway Center at Bronx Terminal Market
  (2009), **214**
Gehry Partners, 26, 76, 83
Gensler Associates, 35, 44–45, 122
George Ranalli Architect, 195
Gerner, Kronick + Valcarcel, 273
GF55 Partners, 53
Glen Oaks Library, 280
Glenmore Gardens (2006), **196**
Gluckman Mayner Architects, 37, 231
Governors Island, Park & Public Space, 284
Green-Wood Columbarium and Mausoleum
  (2006), **204–5**
GreenbergFarrow, 214
Grimshaw, 233, 279, 283, 289
Gruzen Samton, 56–57, 262

Grzywinski + Pons, 41, 43, 251
Gwathmey Siegel & Associates Architects, 55, 103

H
H. Thomas O'Hara Architect, 37, 145
H3 Hardy Collaboration Architecture, 116, 139,
    221, 278
Handel Architects, 20, 33, 52, 89, 247
Hangar Design Group, 186
hanrahan Meyers architects, 61, 185, 207, 283
Hardy Holzman Pfeiffer Associates, 203
Harlem Children's Zone Promise Academy
    (2005), **152**
Harvard Club of New York City (2003), **113**
Hearst Tower (2006), 71, **127**, 184
Heatherwick Studio, 77
Helfand Myerberg Guggenheimer Architects, 109
Helpern Architects, 93
Herzog & de Meuron, 52
Higgins Hall Insertion (2005), **184**
High Line 519 (2007), **86**, 87, 145
High Line (2009), 71, 72, **73–75**, 79, 80, 81, 82, 86,
    87, 88, 217, 283
High School for Construction Trades,
    Engineering and Architecture (2006), **254–55**
Historic Front Street (2005), **25**
HL23 (2011), 86, **87**, 88
HM White Site Architects, 122
HOK, 260
Hospital for Special Surgery, 143, **281**
Hudson Hill Condominium (2009), 67, **125**, 173
Hudson New York (2000), **49**
Hudson River Park Segment 5 (2010), **84–85**, 166,
    283, 286
Hunters Point South, **287**

I
IAC Building (2007), 16, 26, 54, 81, 82, **83**
Infinity Chapel (2010), **61**
io Architects, 58
Irish Hunger Memorial (2002), 28, **265**
Ironworkers Local 580 (2004), **240**
Irving Place (2011), **93**

J
Jambhekar/Strauss, 202
James Carpenter Design Associates, 27, 127, 131,
    246, 273
James Corner Field Operations, 73–75, 284
Jane's Carousel, 166, **285**
John Jay College of Criminal Justice (2011), **125**
Jonathan Kirschenfeld Architect, 181, 225
Judith Heintz Landscape Architecture, 179
Juliana Curran Terian Design Center (2007),
    185

K
Kahn, Louis I., 284
Kaitsen Woo Architect, 265
Ken Smith Landscape Architect, 24, 283, 286
Kevin Hom + Andrew Goldman Architects, 247
Kew Gardens Hills Library Expansion, **281**
Kiss + Cathcart Architects, 202
Kohn Pedersen Fox Associates (KPF), 49, 69, 94,
    110–11, 145, 275, 282

Kupferberg Holocaust Research Center and
    Archives (2009), **251**

L
Lakeside Center, **285**
Larsen Shein Ginsberg Snyder Architects, 171
Latimer Gardens Community Center (2007), **207**
LCT3, **278**
LearningSpring School (2010), **93**
Leeser Architecture, 48, 242–43, 279
Lincoln Center Redevelopment (104), **134–35**
Lincoln Square Synagogue, **278**
LIRR Jamaica Station (2006), **253**
Loadingdock5, 182–83
L'Observatoire International, 190
Local Projects, 112
Longchamp SoHo (2006), **77**
Loreley (2010), **193**
LOT-EK, 67, 274
Louis Armstrong House Museum Visitor Center,
    278
Louis Vuitton Store (2004), **105**
Louise Braverman Architect, 29, 225
LSA Family Health Service (2004), **146**
LTL Architects, 142, 196
Lycée Français de New York (2003), **144**, 169
Lyn Rice Architects, 59

M
M127 (2008), **96**
Machado and Silvetti Associates, 276
Maki and Associates, 269
Marble Fairbanks, 153, 250, 280
Marcus Garvey Houses Community Center
    (2010), **206**
Marcy Avenue Residence (2003), **181**, 225
Marine Company 1 (2011), 85, **160**
Mariners Harbor Public Library, **281**
Marpillero Pollak Architects, 280, 285
Massimiliano Fuksas Architetto, 77
Mathews Nielsen Landscape Architects, 284
Matthew Baird Architects, 68
Maya Lin Studio, 40
McCarren Park Pool, **285**
Medgar Evers College School of Science, Health,
    and Technology (2010), **181**
Melrose Commons North, **289**
Melrose Community Center (2001), **207**
Memorial Sloan-Kettering Mortimer B.
    Zuckerman Research Center (2006), **142**, 143
Mercedes House, **289**
Metal Shutter Houses (2010), **81**
Metropolitan Tower Public Passage (2007), **49**
Michael Fieldman Architects, 270
Michael Van Valkenburgh Associates, 29, 84–85,
    166–67
Mitchell Giurgola Architects, 143, 284
MoMA Expansion (2004), 109, **110–11**
MoMA PS1 Young Architects Program, **238–39**
Moed de Armas & Shannon, 106-7
Moneo Brock Studio, 156
Moneo, José Rafael, 156
Morgan Library Expansion (2006), **98–99**, 279
Morimoto NYC (2006), **116**

Morphosis Architects, 56–57
Morris Adjmi Architects, 35
MOS, 238–39
Mott Haven Educational Campus (2010), **212**
Mount Sinai Center for Science and Medicine,
    282
MTA Flood Mitigation (2009), **233**
Museum for African Art (2011), **149**
Museum of Arts and Design (2008), **130**
Museum of Chinese in America (2009), **40**
Museum of the Moving Image (2011), 241,
    242–43
Myrtle Hall (2010), **186**

N
nARCHITECTS, 43, 238
National September 11 Memorial (2011), **264**
National September 11 Memorial and Museum,
    269
Nehemiah Spring Creek (2008), 196, **197**, 214
Neil M. Denari Architects, 87
New 42nd Street Studios (2000), **121**
New Amsterdam Plein and Pavilion (2011), **20**
The New Domino, 287
New Museum of Contemporary Art (2007),
    44–45, 46, 51, 76
The New School University Center, 276
New York City OEM (2006), 27, **168**
New York Hall of Science (2004), **246**
New York Law School (2009), **32**, 57
New York Police Academy, 270
New York Times Building (2007), 48, **122–23**, 279
New York Town House (2003), **146**
Newtown Creek Wastewater Treatment Plant
    (2007), **190**
The Nolitan (2011), **41**
noroof architects, 187
Northwest Corner Building (2010), 154, 155, **156**
NYBG Leon Levy Visitor Center (2004), **221**
NYBG Pfizer Plant Research Laboratory (2006), 222
NYC Department of Parks & Recreation, 217
NYC Information Center (2009), **112**
NYPD Brooklyn Tow Pound (2009), **160**
NYPL Battery Park City Branch, 29, **138**
NYPL South Court (2002), **102**
NYSE/Financial District Streetscapes (2004), **232**
NYU Center for Academic and Spiritual Life, 276
NYU Department of Philosophy (2007), **59**

O
Office for Design & Architecture, 92
Office for Metropolitan Architecture, 77
Ogawa/Depardon Architects, 41
On Prospect Park (2009), 162, **178**
One Astor Place (2006), 37, **55**, 56, 89
One Jackson Square (2009), 37, **69**, 184
One Kenmore Square (2006), **37**
One Madison Park (2010), **95**, 96
One York (2008), **33**, 34
Oudolf, Piet, 74

P
Pacific Street Condominiums (2007–2008), 80,
    182–83

Packer Collegiate Institute (2004), **139**
Park51, 278
Payette, 230
Pei Cobb Freed & Partners, 28, 159, 276
Pelli Clarke Pelli Architects, 22, 105, 272
The Pencil Factory (2010), **191**
Pentagram, 57, 139
Perkins Eastman, 54, 92, 120, 212, 263
Perkins + Will, 270
Peter Gluck and Partners, 104, 146, 148
Peter Walker Partners, 264
Pier 57, 85, **274**
Pio Pio Restaurant (2009), **117**
PKSB Architects, 194
Platt Byard Dovell White, 93, 121, 147, 175, 204–5
Poe Park Visitor Center (2011), **223**
Polshek Partnership. *See* Ennead Architects
Poly Prep Lower School (2007), **175**
Port Authority of New York and New Jersey
    (PANYNJ), 253
Porter House Condo (2003), 34, **70**
Prada (2001), **77**
Pratt Institute Security Kiosk (2006), 185, **186**
Prendergast Laurel Architects, 261
Price Center/Block Pavilion (2008), **230**
Projected Image (2009), 48
P.S. 42 Robin Hood Foundation Library (2002),
    139
P.S. 59, The Beekman Hill International School
    (2008), **138**
P.S. 69 Vincent D. Grippo School (2002), **203**
Public Safety Answering Center II, 271

Q
QBG Administration & Visitor Center (2007), 220,
    234, **248–49**
Queens Hospital EMS, 271
Queens Museum of Art, 279
Queens Plaza, 285
Queens Theatre in the Park (2008), **247**
Quennell Rothschild and Partners, 190

R
Rafael Viñoly Architects, 158, 180, 200, 215, 270,
    287
The Reece School (2006), **147**
Renzo Piano Building Workshop, 98–99, 122–23,
    279
Rescue Company 3 (2009), **161**
Resolution: 4 Architecture, 229
Richard Meier & Partners Architects, 64, 178
Rickenbacker + Leung, 193
Riverhouse (2009), **29**, 138
Riverside Park South, 287
Robert A. M. Stern Architects, 132, 149
Roberta Washington Architects, 181
The Rockefeller University Collaborative
    Research Center (2010), **143**, 230
Rockwell Group, 33
Rodney Léon Architects, 264
Rodriguez, Freddy, 265
Rogers Marvel Architects, 24, 49, 137, 152, 170,
    172, 184, 232, 233, 273, 277, 284, 285, 289
Rogers Stirk Harbour + Partners, 269

Roman and Williams, 72
Rose Center for Earth and Space (2000), **136**
Rose + Guggenheimer Studio, 116
Rosenbaum, Marc I., 87
Rossi, Aldo, 35
Roy Design, 86, 238
Ruddick, Margie, 285

S
SANAA, 44–45, 76
Saratoga Avenue Community Center (2008),
   195, 206
Satori (2009), **173**
Scandinavia House (2000), **97**
Scarano Architects, 173
Schermerhorn House (2009), 69, **169**, 170, 212
Scholastic Building (2001), **35**, 36
Schwartz, Frederic, 20
Sebastian Mariscal Studio, 117
Selldorf Architects, 86
Sephardic Community Center (2010), **201**
Shake Shack (2004), **95**
Sheila C. Johnson Design Center (2008), 48, **59**
Shigeru Ban Architects, 81
SHoP Architects, 47, 70, 96, 238, 273, 275, 286
Singer, Michael, 285
SITE, 95
Situ Studio, 69, 265
Skidmore, Owings & Merrill (SOM), 10, 21, 27, 29,
   125, 131, 142, 168, 268, 271, 276, 282
Skyscraper Museum (2004), **21**, 29
SLCE Architects, 22, 23, 36, 42, 69, 105, 132, 149
Slot House (2005), 187
Smith-Miller + Hawkinson Architects, 124, 171,
   271, 272, 281
SmithGroup, 32
Snøhetta, 269
Solid Objectives-Idenburg Liu (SO-IL), 238–39
SOMA Architects, 278
Sono, Masayuki, 265
Spacesmith, 160
Sperone Westwater Gallery (2010), 44, **46**, 51
St. George Intermodal and Cultural Center
   (2005), **260**
Standard Hotel (2009), **72**
Starck, Philippe, 49
Staten Island Children's Museum (2003), **261**
Staten Island September 11 Memorial (2004),
   256, 260, **265**
Staten Island Zoo Reptile Wing (2007), **262**
Stephanie Goto Design Group, 116
Stephen Gaynor School and Ballet Hispanico
   (2006), **137**
Stephen Yablon Architect, 206
Steven Holl Architects, 59, 184, 274
Stilwell Avenue Terminal (2005), **202**
Strand Theater, 279
Studio Carlos Zapata, 54
The Studio Museum in Harlem (2001), **152**
studioMDA, 289
STUDIOS Architecture, 105
STV, Inc., 161, 254–55
Swaynke Hayden Connell Architects, 168
Switch Building (2007), **43**, 96

T
Tadao Ando Architect & Associates, 116
Taniguchi, Yoshio, 110–11
TEK | Architects, 251
TEN Arquitectos, 33, 113, 174, 289
Tenrikyo Mission New York Center (2009), **250**
Third + Bond (2010), **172**, 173
Thomas Balsley Associates, 126, 287
thread collective, 274
Time Warner Center (2004), **131**
Tina Manis Associates, 172
TKTS (2008), **120**, 133
Tod Williams Billie Tsien Architects, 109, 133, 285
Tolle, Brian, 265
Toni Stabile Student Center (2008), **153**
Toren (2010), **168**, 169
Toshiko Mori Architect, 223
Town House (2005), **68**
The Townhomes of Downing Street (2011), **61**
TRA Studio, 61
Tribeca Isseymiyake (2001), **76**
Trump SoHo Hotel (2010), **33**
Tsao & McKown Architects, 23
Turrell, James, 49

U
Union Park North End Expansion (2010), **232**
United Methodist Church of Co-op City (2005),
   231
United States Mission to the United Nations
   (2010), **103**
UNStudio, 20
Urban Design+, 284
Urban Town House (2009), **104**, 137
UWS Town House (2010), **137**

V
Vanderbilt Studio (2005), **187**
Vertical Gardens Technology, 133
Via Verde, 289
The Visionaire (2009), **22**, 28
Vivian and Seymour Milstein Family Heart
   Center (2010), **159**

W
W Architecture and Landscape Architecture, 157
Wallace Roberts & Todd, 285
WASA/Studio A, 186, 207
Wavewall (2005), **202**
WCS Center for Global Conservation (2009), **220**
Weeksville Heritage Center, 279
Weill Cornell Medical Research Building, 143,
   282
Weill Greenberg Center (2007), **143**, 282
Weiner Residence/Studio (2007), **67**
Weiss/Manfredi, 139, 154–55, 277, 287
West 8, 284
West Brighton Community Center (2006), **207**
West Harlem Piers Park (2009), **157**
Westin New York (2002), **124**
WET, 135
Whitehall Ferry Terminal (2005), **20**, 260, 273
Whitney Downtown, 279
William Beaver House (2009), **23**, 37

William Fellows Architects, 120
Williamsburg Community Center (2003), **194**, 195, 206
Wittwer-Laird, Gail, 265
Work Architecture Company (WORKac), 71, 238–39, 275, 281
workshop/apd, 48, 137, 277
World Product Centre, 282
World Trade Center Transportation Hub, 269
The Wright (2009), **117**
WXY Architecture + Urban Design, 20, 112, 217

Z
Zerega Avenue EMS Station, 271
Zimmer Gunsul Frasca, Architects, 142
Zuccotti Park (2006), **23**

Index by Building Type

Note: Letters following a page number indicate the location on the page: b=bottom, m=middle, t=top; page numbers without a letter indicate all entries on that page are the building type listed. Where applicable, some entries are listed under multiple building types.

civic, 160–61, 168t, 204–5, 213, 215, 270–71
community center, 146b, 194–95, 201, 206–7, 228
cultural, 20b, 60, 97, 108, 112, 159b, 221, 223, 248–49, 262, 274m, 277, 278b, 279m-b
dining, 95b, 116–17, 133, 193
education, primary, 93b, 137b, 138b, 139t, 139m, 144, 147–48, 152t, 175, 203, 212b, 217t, 241, 254–55, 275m
education, secondary and higher, 32, 56–57, 59, 94, 125t, 143b, 153–56, 158, 181t, 184–86, 200, 230, 240–41, 251b, 263, 275t, 275b, 276
hospital, 142, 143t, 159b, 281b, 282t, 282m
hotel, 33b, 41t, 49b, 54, 72, 89t, 113t, 124t, 131, 272b, 273m-b
infrastructure, 20t, 190, 202, 253, 260, 269b, 283b, 285b
library, 102, 138t, 139b, 224, 252, 280, 281t, 281m
monument, 264–65, 284t
museum, 21, 40, 44–46, 98–99, 109–11, 130, 136, 149, 152b, 179–180, 216, 225b, 238–39, 242–43, 246, 261, 269m, 278m-b, 279t, 279b
office, 27, 28, 35, 49t, 71, 83, 103, 105t, 114–15, 122–23, 127, 131, 220, 222, 268, 269t, 272t, 273t, 274t, 282b
park, 23t, 24, 73–75, 84–85, 126, 157, 166–67, 217b, 284, 286, 287t, 287b
performing arts, 48t, 120, 133, 134–35, 247t, 278t, 279m-t
recreation, 113b, 247b, 273m-t, 274m, 274b, 283, 285t, 285m-t, 285m-b
religious, 61t, 231, 250, 276b, 278m-t
residential, multi-family, 22, 23b, 25–26, 29, 33–34, 36–37, 41b, 42–43, 47, 48b, 49m, 52–53, 55, 58b, 61b, 64, 65t, 66, 67t, 69–70, 80–82, 86–88, 89b, 92, 93t, 95t, 96, 104b, 105t, 113t, 124b, 125b, 131–32, 145, 168b, 169–171, 173–74, 178, 181b, 182–83, 191, 196–97, 212t, 225t, 287m, 288–89
residential, single-family, 58t, 65b, 67b, 68, 104t, 137t, 146t, 172t, 187, 192, 229, 251t
retail, 76–77, 105b, 106–7, 131, 214, 273b, 274m
urban design, 120, 232–33